Michèle Velthuizen-de Vries was born in The Hague and brought up in Asia. She was educated in Japan and Korea, and graduated from Sophia University with a BA in Japanese language and culture. She studied Mandarin in Singapore for a year before returning to the Netherlands to read for an MA in Korean at Leiden University. She met her husband Nop while acting as an interpreter for Japanese participants in a kite festival and currently has her own business translating, writing and working as a programme co-ordinator for the Japanese television market.

PEDALLING UNKNOWN PATHS

Michèle Velthuizen-de Vries

The Book Guild Ltd
Sussex, England

973

The Book Guild Ltd,
25 High Street,
Lewes, Sussex

First published 1995
© Michèle Velthuizen-de Vries
Set in Times
Typesetting by Southern Reproductions (Sussex)
Crowborough, Sussex
Printed in Great Britain by
Antony Rowe Ltd.
Chippenham, Wiltshire.

A catalogue record for this book is
available from the British Library

ISBN 0 86332 958 6

CONTENTS

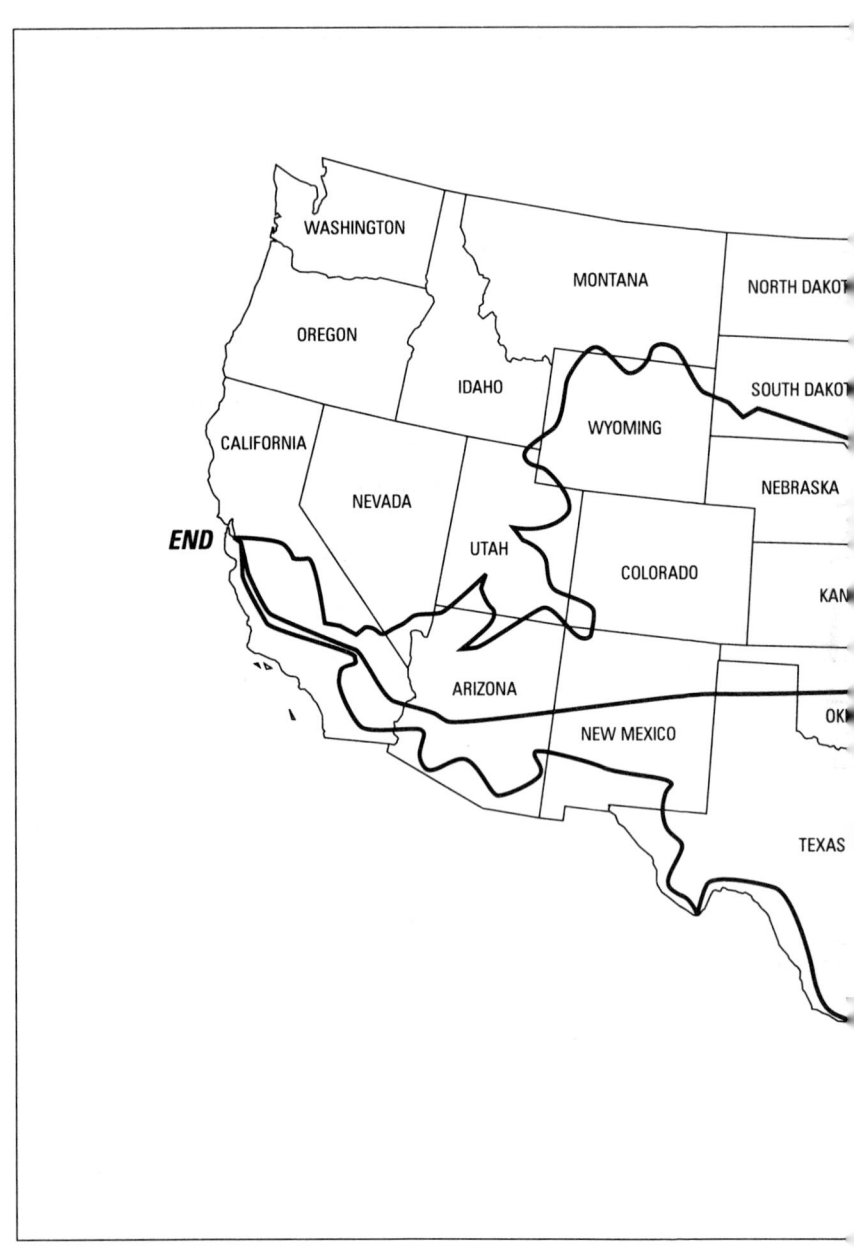

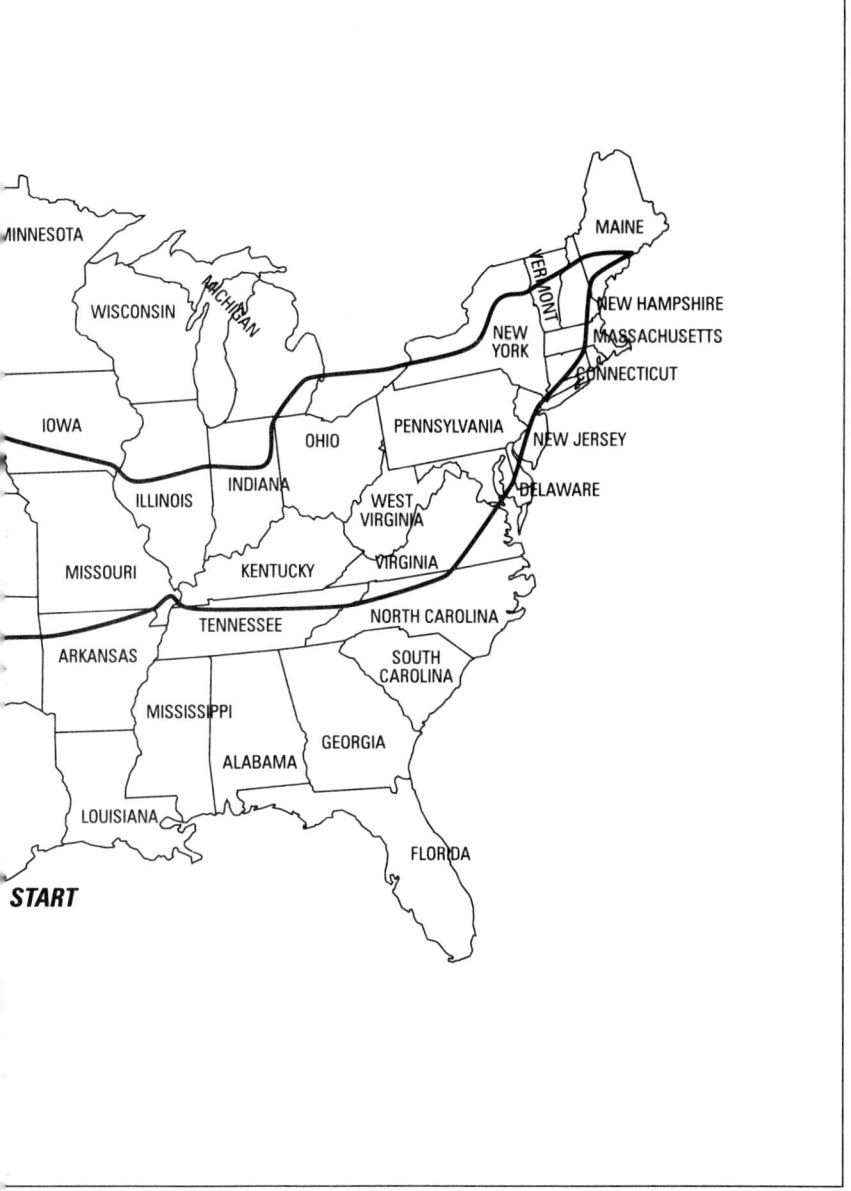

START

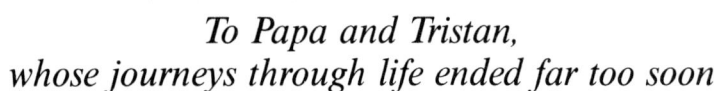

To Papa and Tristan,
whose journeys through life ended far too soon

PREFACE

Every traveller has his or her reasons for wanting to go on a long journey: to see the natural world, to meet new people, to experience other cultures or simply to get away from an all too monotonous life of work and play. For me it was certainly all these things, but also something more – it was the desire to travel indefinitely without having to worry about a return date, money or fear of losing a job.

The first thing we did when we decided to travel was to announce to all concerned that our proposed journey would not have a destination. We then solved the problem of money by living off Nop's salary and saving mine for the duration of two and a half years. And finally, the matter of jobs solved itself when Nop quit his job at Shell (let this be an example to all you job-security-minded-ambitious souls out there who are dreaming of travel) and when I, upon graduation, had to relinquish my job as student-assistant at the university.

Despite the nonchalant manner in which we decided to go on such an indefinite journey we have always considered ourselves fortunate in being able to do so. We were both healthy if not in too great a shape at the start of our trip, we had the opportunity to save money which lasted two entire years (true, we didn't travel like kings) and we were both gifted with a strong will and compatible stubbornness which sustained us through the harder times on the journey. And last but not least, we both had a very strong urge to travel.

*

Actually, my urge to travel was entirely the doing of my father. Because he was a diplomat by profession I spent my entire youth abroad. Not only was our growing up in Asia a cultural experience in itself, every four years we would go back to the Netherlands the 'long way' home during our 3-4 months' home leave. These months were mostly spent at sea because my father detested air travel and didn't want to be bothered by the Ministry during his leave. For us kids home leave meant two disastrous consequences: the horror of having to leave our dear friends and of having to miss school for months on end. For children who were never brilliant in the first place, missing school was more than a bit of a problem, but my father always insisted travel was a lot more educational than any school book could possibly be.

'Ach,' I can recall him saying as he would brush aside my concern as though it were a fly, 'don't worry about school – you'll be all right. By the way, did you know that our next port of call is Cape Town, Michèle? It's an *extremely* interesting country, South Africa. We should get up early because if it's good weather we may be lucky and see Table Mountain. Now, can you remember why it's called Table Mountain?'

ACKNOWLEDGEMENTS

Although it was never my intention to cycle around North America specifically in order to meet people, I must now admit that my faith in the human species has improved considerably as a result of the overwhelming hospitality we received in the US during our 14-month journey. I have yet to cycle through another country where the people are so spontaneously generous, so welcoming in their hospitality and so full of child-like curiosity about foreigners and cyclists alike. Many Americans are unaware they even possess such virtues which is what I find all the more commendable.

The list of people to whom I would like to extend my gratitude is, as you may guess, endless. But I would first of all like to thank those whose names we unfortunately never learnt – people who handed us food and drinks from their car windows or on the side of the road, people who left us alone although we were trespassing on their land, people who gave us tips and advice along the way, people who cheered us on as we climbed terrible passes, truck drivers who gave us wide berths, train conductors who greeted us by hooting their horns in the empty deserts, the pilot who circled above us and gave us the thumbs-up, roadside vegetable stand owners who refused payment, all the pastors, ministers and reverends of various churches whose names we never got and all the others who, in our brief encounter with them, gave some form of encouragement when the going was tough.

I would like to personally thank the following people

according to the name of the State they lived in at the time:

Arkansas: Reverend and Mrs Piercy. *Arizona:* Mr and Mrs Tung, Rob Jansen op de Haar and his sister Marion, Jim and Gloria Maender, Jean Williams, Joel and Anne Becheen, Clark Nelson, Steve Marcus and his gang of cyclists, Suzanne Couvrette, Blaine and Fern Heap, Layne and Beverlyne Hooper, Glenn and Judy Naylor. *California:* Fred and Ellen Weinberg, Greyland Bembry, June Cochrane, Simon Thorbill, Robert Gunn, Steve and Dell Etheridge, Roy and Pauline Pounds, Charles and Neva Wall, Fred Winters, Ron and Sue Herbig, Dan and Kim Carnahan, Mr and Mrs Keil, Joseph Fields, Angelica Meek, Matt Vining, Ellen Lagerwerff, Helen Colijn, Marc and Marcia Duisenberg and all the members of Good Sam's RV Club. *Colorado:* Marc and Barbara Fowler, Bob Mulcahy, Harry and Norman Ware. *Cincinnati:* Steve Taylor, Sabino Tamborra. *Florida:* Kent Vann. *Illinois:* Larry and Fonda Arvin, Philip Eureka, Francis, Pearl, Grace and Elaine of Saunemin's coffee shop. *Indiana:* Glenn and Virginia Sunderman and Mother Sunderman, Layne and Beverlene Hooper, Mr and Mrs Kiser. *Iowa:* Kyle and Margie Benson, Steve and Tina Berch, Pastor Degreef. *Louisiana:* Tim Leinbach. *Massachusetts:* Pam Brigham. *Maryland:* Mel and Valerie Govig, Jon Burckhardt and Sheila, David Cooper. *Maine:* Mr and Mrs Myers. *Minnesota:* Dean Almquist, Bill Domeier. *Mississippi:* Minister and Mrs Tootsie. *Montana:* Chamber of Commerce of Red Lodge. *North Carolina:* Yvonne Brown. *Nebraska:* Barret Hanson. *New Hampshire:* George and Rita Mayo. *New Jersey:* Martin Heydra, Professor and Mrs Mote, Marian Wilson. *New Mexico:* the Whitings family, Richard and Eleanor Watts, Chuck Matthews and Linda, Harry and Rosie Turner. *Nevada:* Carl and Misong Craven. *New York:* Richard Ennis, William and Bonnie Golden. *Ohio:* Bud and Maurie Hoekstra, Steve Roberts and Maggie Victor. *Oregon:* Harold and Marilyn Fullman. *South Dakota:* Art and Ben Niedan, Kathy and Lance Lynn. *Tennessee:* Mr and Mrs Hayes, Debbie Hayes.

Texas: Pink and Portia Brown, Snowbirds of Oleander Acres, Snowbirds of Condit Travel Park, Ben and Beverly Bowman, Betty and Bob Elmore, The Polos, Doctor and Mrs Lockhardt. *Utah:* Rim Tours Cyclery, Tod Campbell, Bessie Spencer, Reverend and Mrs Wilkie, Jan Burke and Cindy Schwandt, Allan and Jodie Mitchell, Minister and Mrs Ernst. *Virginia:* Per and Nancy Jenster and Sonya, Peter Anspatch and Brendan Shephard. *Washington:* Bud and Ardis Bartole, Allen Ray. *Wyoming:* Blaine and Fern Heap, 'Buckskin' Bader, Rudy Studbrook, Mr and Mrs Roberts. *Canada:* Wayne and Max Smith.

Special thanks go to David Beattie from Canada, Stefan Münzig from Germany and Randy Shannon from Arizona for being super cycling companions and Herbert and Anne Huizinga from Canada for being substitute parents to us throughout our trip. A very warm thank you goes to my sister Karen and her family (Mark, Tristan, Victor, Nina and Nicole) who put us up extensively twice on the trip and who made us feel secure in the thought that we could always count on them if we ever needed them regardless of where we were.

On the home front I would like to give a special hug to my mother who handled all our mail, administration, circulation letters and collect calls and to Nop's parents who also accepted countless collect calls without hesitation and kept the rest of his family informed of our whereabouts and to my aunt, Conny, who assembled and categorized in chronological order the hundreds of slides I sent home on a regular basis. A special thanks must also go to Petra and Leo, who stored all our belongings in their storeroom throughout our long journey. And it goes without saying that we are eternally grateful to *all* members of both our families for being so supportive and understanding throughout our long absence.

This being my first book, I would like to say that without the help of Marten Berkman, who edited the manuscript in its first dreadful stage and made countless useful comments I would have made a mess out of the whole thing and would never have had the courage to complete the project. A grizzly bear hug to you, Marten.

I must also thank my mother for proofreading the manuscript in great detail and the editors of The Book Guild, for their untiring help in turning my manuscript into a publishable book.

Last and definitely not least, I would like to thank Nop – the best companion I could have possibly had during the vicissitudes of such a journey – for being a good cycling companion, a stern but understanding coach, a patient listener, a wonderful mechanic and cook and, at the same time, an affectionate husband and friend. From the start it was Nop who believed I could overcome any obstacles and challenges during the journey. It was his unswerving belief in me which gave me the strength I at times desperately needed.

And finally a word to those of you out there who are considering a long journey: *Stop considering it and just go for it!*

LEAVING

Serious plans to travel came to us one day in 1983. We were chatting over coffee and the subject eventually drifted to 'When I finally *do* graduate from Leiden University . . . .'

We decided to set my graduation as a goal. I figured I could get my Masters by the summer of 1985, and that would give us a full two years to save money. Then came the question: how to travel?

Nop immediately suggested, 'By bicycle.'

'By bicycle?!' I gasped, 'I don't know if I can cycle long distances Nop . . . .' I added, as I thought of the backaches I got just by commuting to school every day on a ten-speed. Not to mention the regular rash on my behind and my numb neck!

'I don't know, Nop . . . .'

'But Michèle, I've got this brilliant idea about a totally different *kind* of bicycle,' Nop said excitedly.

'What kind of bicycle?' I asked suspiciously.

'Well . . . look, there's a bicycle show coming up in the RAI next month. Let's go and I'll show you what I mean.'

*

The 'Roeland' was the first recumbent I had ever seen in my life, and I wasn't convinced.

'How do you steer the thing?' I asked Nop.

'On the sides, here. Look, I'll show you,' he said and off he went as if it were the most natural mode of transport in the world.

1

'Here, you try it,' he said with a smile as he stopped, 'a couple of rounds and you'll get the hang of it.'

And indeed, once I ignored the small front wheel and relaxed in the seat I found myself actually cycling in *comfort*!

'I can't believe this thing. You want to buy it?' I asked Nop.

'No, I have a better design in mind,' he said. 'This one isn't strong enough and I don't like the plastic chair. I'm going to build one myself!'

So, in the following weeks, Nop isolated himself in his workshop for hours on end and when he finally emerged showed me the welded frame of the prototype. Nop then asked Ron, one of our housemates, to sit on it to see if it would hold. Ron sat on it and it collapsed. Unperturbed, back he went into his workshop and when he emerged again with a new frame and Ron again was asked to sit on it this time it held!

Within a few weeks the first prototype recumbent was ready. We decided to call it a 'Nopcycle'.

*

There is something very disturbing about seeing someone cycling in a reclining position – it just doesn't seem natural. At least that is what most people think when they see a recumbent for the first time. And it's true, it takes getting used to. But some of the discrimination we encountered was simply ridiculous.

On my first day of trying out the prototype by cycling all the way to university (about twelve miles), no sooner had I left our home than I was stopped by a police car.

'STOP' the sign on the hood glared and two policemen came out and slowly walked towards me with silly grins on their faces.

'*What* is that?' they said, pointing towards the bike as if it were a contagious disease.

'A bicycle, what else?'

2

'You can't ride *that*,' one of them said.

'And why not, may I ask?'

'Well . . . it doesn't have handlebars,' the other policeman said.

'Sure it does.'

'Where?'

'Here, on the sides,' I said.

'Well, you still can't ride it,' one of them insisted.

Nop and I had somehow anticipated this and, just the previous day, had the bike registered at the local police station. I showed the idiots the engraved registration number and it worked. They finally scratched their heads and let me go.

Nop had had a similar experience when he was stopped by a policeman in the town of Delft – likewise he was told he couldn't ride it.

Nop asked the same question: 'And why not, may I ask?'

He got the same answer: 'It doesn't have any handlebars!'

In Nop's case, a crowd had meanwhile gathered around them and was quite enjoying the argument.

'Well is that so?' Nop said incredulously as he looked around the crowd which was begining to take sides with him.

One man in the crowd even spoke up for Nop and said to the crowd, 'Ha! The man says there aren't any handlebars! What's this then?' he asked the policeman as he pointed to the obvious.

Having by then lost face in front of the ever-growing crowd the policeman finally left the 'scene of the crime', no doubt to find something better to do with the taxpayer's money.

*

During the first few months of riding around on the prototype Nopcycle we both defied and endured all sorts of criticism – an experience I can now recommend to anyone who is looking for a means to 'build character'. I certainly had my share of snowballs and firecrackers from local high school kids who always seemed to be waiting for me to ride by their school in the morning. Although most people were initially ignorant about the bike, by the following year attitudes in the neighbourhood did begin to change.

We started hearing kids say, 'Hey look man, that's the funny bike I've been telling you about,' or, a little boy pointing to our bikes and saying, 'Now *that's* called a recumbent daddy, isn't it cool?'!

Word seemed to have got round and we were never bothered by the police again.

*

In the summer of 1984 we decided to make a trial trip to Switzerland to see how the recumbents would fare upon mountains. Nop made an improved version of the first prototype – the difference was quite remarkable: a smaller front wheel which made balancing easier, a more comfortable seat and additional hub gears which improved take off after sudden stops, etc.

1,250 miles to and from Switzerland within two weeks was definitely something new to me. Nop had always travelled by bicycle to places like France, Germany and even Norway, but I was never a long-distance biker. So I was both surprised and pleased with myself when I did manage this trial trip. Nop, who had never had any doubts about *my* capabilities from the start, was extremely satisfied with the recumbent's performance. This was the decisive factor for us to use recumbents on the long journey to come.

*

I even surprised myself by managing to graduate from Leiden University in June 1985 – it was one of the happiest days of my life. I couldn't believe I would never have to take exams or have to write a thesis again. I was *free* at last and the world was waiting to be explored!

*

And then we heard the devastating news: my father was dying from *anaplastic carcinoma,* an incurable cancer. About a month before my graduation my father began to complain about a lump on his throat which he had had for the past twenty-five years but which was beginning to bother him. His house doctor had suggested he have it removed since it was beginning to push against his windpipe. So, while I was preoccupied with the last of my exams my father was hospitalised and operated upon. We all thought the operation was a standard, minor one – all tests prior to the operation indicated that my father was a very healthy man. But during the operation they discovered cancer cells and so, to be on the safe side, his entire thyroid gland was removed along with the lump. While my father was recuperating from the operation I graduated. But then my father began to suffocate terribly at home so more tests followed which finally revealed that somehow cancerous cells were spreading rapidly through his lungs. No doctor could explain the mystery of it all except that the type of cancer he had contracted was incurable and that it was too late to do anything. To this day I believe that the removal of his thyroid gland had been a terrible mistake – I can't help but think that it was the operation itself which activated whatever cancer cells were in his throat to start with.

For five agonising weeks we literally watched my father die. From the day he returned from the hospital he could no longer lie on his back and breathe properly, so we placed him in his favourite chair, surrounded him with cushions and did what we could to make him as comfortable as possible. Those unforgettable five weeks were the worst I have ever experienced in my life – my father was the core and most loved member of our family. To have to watch him die against his own will, without being able to help in any significant way was torture for all of us.

My father either knew he didn't have much time or he didn't want to prolong the agony for anyone; in any case, he was aware that time was running out. Having always been a systematic and meticulous individual who never procrastinated or left obligations undone, my father now felt the need to clear up his life and get everything straightened out in everyone's mind before he left this world. In the first few weeks while he could still breathe without too many oxygen bottles, he filled the hours with his personal history and the history of the family. Photographs were dug out so he could describe individuals he remembered one by one, and interesting episodes associated with them were carefully told. My father had a magnificent memory and could recall each incident and place almost to the exact date (a gift which made him an incredibly knowledgeable historian) and he didn't leave anything out, including family scandals. With nothing to lose, he was totally uninhibited as he related the most scandalous of scandals as well as his own personal episodes. As I watched him fighting against time, I decided to tape everything he said. He probably knew I was taping him but he didn't show it. To this day I've never once touched the series of tapes, afraid to hear his hoarse dying voice again, but I am glad I did it anyway – perhaps it will be a token for the next generation.

My father died on 24th August, 1985. Although we expected it, it was nevertheless a terrible blow to the whole family. We helped out as best we could at home, and in October, my mother, Nop and I went to Portugal for a month to calm down and start the long process of healing our wounds. It wasn't much of a vacation, but it did get us away from the house and by the time we got back to the Netherlands in November Nop and I knew we could no longer postpone our trip. We had both given up our jobs at the beginning of the summer when I graduated and were now living off our savings, so we had to either finally leave or forget the trip entirely. Hard as it was to leave my mother who was suffering most from the loss of my father, we decided to go. Had we not done so I somehow feel that my father's quick death would have, in a way, been for nothing. When my father had first heard he was dying he had actually apologised to us for keeping us from our trip.

*

On 10th November 1985, we got a phone call from Egon Oldendorff, our shipping agent in Lübeck, Germany (we were determined to start our trip by ship and *not* by aeroplane).

'Hello Mrs Velthuizen!' our contact said cheerfully. 'There's a ship leaving from Hamburg in three days – it's heading for the Gulf of Mexico – I don't know where in the Gulf – but are you interested?'

I ran to Nop and said breathlessly, 'Nop, there's a ship sailing from Hamburg to the Gulf of Mexico in three days!' He looked at me and we exchanged grins.

'Yes! We'll take it!' I blurted into the phone. Our trip was on!!!

*

We had anticipated the phone call already for a month so most of our gear was packed, yet when the time came – and two days' notice wasn't much time to say our last goodbyes to everyone – we got lumps in our throats at the thought of having to leave family, friends and our dog 'Happy' for an indefinite period. Yet the short notice was also a blessing in disguise: there was no time for tearful farewells.

My mother and my aunts Conny and Erny volunteered to accompany us to Hamburg in a rented van. Because of the distance we spent one night at an inn halfway and reached the harbour of Hamburg – a huge chaotic maze of piers with rows of ships berthed alongside – a few hours before departure time at 4.00 p.m. the following day. When we reached the *Seascout* coal was being unloaded and everything was covered in a fine layer of black dust, including the once-white overalls of the crew. Our bikes were lifted up onto the deck, wheeled into a room and tied to the walls.

We were shown to our cabin which looked more like a hotel suite, where we met our personal steward, a Portuguese called Napoleon, who was eager to please us, yet whose pidgin English was unfortunately quite unintelligible.

When the time came to say goodbye, we didn't know what to say to my mother and aunts. What *does* one say to loved ones when we couldn't even reassure them as to where we would be going and when we would be coming back, *if* we would ever come back? The best we could do was to give each of them a bear hug and promise to write.

The worst part was having to leave my mother who, from now on, would have to live alone; I felt very guilty about deserting her this way – to me it made no difference emotionally whether *I* stayed at home or left. For me the pain I felt at having lost my father would remain with me during the entire journey anyway, but she had to face an empty house with only memories to comfort her.

THE SEASCOUT

The *Seascout* was a 64,000 ton bulk carrier which sailed under the Liberian flag and was manned by a mixed crew of Germans (the Captain and Third Officer), Philippinos (First and Second Officers, 'Sparks' the Radio Officer, 'Blitz' the electrician and the deckhands) an Indian (the First Engineer) and Portuguese (our steward 'Napoleon' and the cook). The crew totalled twenty-six, we were the only passengers and I was the sole female on board.

Officer Andressen, the Third Officer, was the first person we talked to. He came into our cabin to take care of the official business.

'Please sign these papers,' he said cheerfully as he handed us our embarkation contract. 'The passenger fee is twenty-five US dollars a day per person for four weeks.'

'Are we sailing for four weeks?' Nop asked.

'Maybe, maybe not. Can never be sure. But our rule is that you pay for four weeks and if we arrive before that time you get the difference back and if it takes more than four weeks you owe us.'

'Do you know where we're heading for?' I ventured to ask.

'Point Comfort, Texas,' he said. So, we were going to North America.

'How long does it take to reach Texas?' Nop asked.

'Well, we're first going to Guinea to load bauxite and *then* we cross the ocean, so it'll probably take a full four weeks.'

Wow . . . *four* weeks at sea!

*

Four weeks may seem like a long time to anyone who is used to the modern method of zipping around the world by air, shrinking the world to an unrealistic and ridiculous size. To us travel by ship was the *real* way to travel – to feel the distance between the continents and to have the time to adjust physically (the clocks are turned back a half-hour every day when you travel East to West by ship) and to have the opportunity to prepare oneself mentally for the challenge of an unfamiliar country. It makes so much more sense to travel this way, to appreciate the true size of the earth and to come face to face with the fact that no less than two thirds of our planet consists of water. Travel by sea seems to bring everything into perspective. Nop and I both agreed on this point – Nop had once been an engineer on board a Dutch ship and had sailed around the world and I was used to ships because my father hated aeroplanes and always made it a point to take home leave by ship (he especially delighted at the thought that he was out of reach of the Ministry of Foreign Affairs while sailing). We both loved the ocean.

Of course not all of the *Seascout*'s crew – especially those with families at home – would have agreed with us. On the one hand, take away the sea from most sailors and they're lost. First Officer Diadula, for example, loved the sea with a passion.

'The sea is like a woman . . . .' he explained one day to me in the typical manner of a man who had been sailing the Seven Seas all his life. 'It is unpredictable and moody . . . and can be very dangerous,' he said with a twinkle in his eyes. 'But I can't stay away from the sea too long either – I get so bored on land after a while.'

'How about your wife, don't you miss her when you're away for so long?'

'Of course I miss her, but it keeps the relationship fresh you see. You miss each other so you appreciate each other all the more when you reunite.'

10

'And how often is that?' I asked.

'Oh . . . I'd be at sea for three to four months at a time sometimes. Other times I don't see her for half a year.'

'Must be hard on her.'

'Yes, for her maybe. For me not. I have more than one wife you know . . . .'

Despite his nonchalant sailor attitude I couldn't help but like Diadula – he was a man who knew what the sea was and he was a patient and untiring teacher. We spent hours on the bridge while he was on duty in the mornings and in the early evenings.

After breakfast we got lessons in Morse Code (Diadula turned it into music for me: 'Just remember, Dee Da Da Da, Da Dee Dee Dee . . . ' he would sing cheerfully as he danced his roly-poly body around the bridge) and in the evenings when the sky filled with billions of dazzling stars, we got our astronomy lessons. And what a magnificent place to study the stars! I have never felt so humbled as when we stood on the deck of the *Seascout* looking up to the skies above us – the Milky Way was so clear and so full that it looked like a distant path we could cycle upon. We drew imaginative lines along the stars which marked the Big Dipper, Orion, Pleiades and Cassiopeia as we listened to Diadula's endless tales of the seas.

Officer Andressen gave Nop navigation lessons after giving up on my limited knowledge of mathematics – Nop soon proved to be an excellent student and was awarded a diploma when he could be taught no more. The diploma read:

TO WHOM IT MAY CONCERN

This is to certify that on this November 19th day of the year 1985, NORBERTUS VELTHUIZEN has been duly questioned and interrogated to ascertain His fitness and eligibility to fulfil the duties of a Third Officer Assistant. This certificate is limited as follows: Duties only to be performed on vessels of more than 2,000 feet of length over all. Ability of tea-cooking not proved. Wherefore we hereby ask all persons in charge to show the due honour whenever this certificate is shown by the legal bearer. This

11

certificate is issued under the authority of NEPTUNE, according to the following international rules which NEPTUNE has subscribed to:

    1. First International Convention of Professional Ship-Wrecking by Unable Staff (FICOPSUS 1963, Revised 1978)

    2. Deep Sea and other Waters Pirate Act (DOWPAC 1923)

    3. Passenger Entertainment Act (PEAC 1985)

Signed on behalf of NEPTUNE: Officer of the Examination: Uwe Andressen.

Ever wondered what bored officers did when crossing the vast oceans?

*

Our routine at sea was to be broken when we stopped in Guinea, Africa, to load bauxite. Coal had been unloaded in Hamburg when we had embarked and the place was still filthy with the black dust. For days, the crew had cleaned the decks and the enormous holds. The captain told us that cargo was almost always varied and that cleaning the ship was a gruelling job.

'Sometimes we load coal,' he explained, 'and after that we may have to load rice.'

Obviously coal and rice can't mix, but neither can coal and bauxite. So the crew's main job was to clean the holds of the previous cargo. I didn't envy the crew standing outside in the icy North Sea winds much of the day, hosing down the ship from port to starboard. No wonder they turned to alcohol and cheap video tapes at night and to women when they could finally disembark for a few hours.

The main crew which did the dirty work was a rather sorry lot of uneducated young Philippinos who spent most of their free time watching the same horrible *Rambo* videos over and over again in the lounge. And when the 'canteen' (local name for a ship's store) opened (by rumour rather than announcement), they were the first to arrive. They would rush to replenish their supplies of tobacco and alcohol in order to sustain them until the next rumour was heard.

We met the rest of the shy crew through our enthusiasm for table tennis, which we tried to play on a regular basis for exercise. The Second Officer, Abunalez, who was obviously of Chinese descent, was an especially dangerous opponent, and Nop played nasty 'smash' games with him a number of times. Unfortunately for Nop, Abunalez always won, as he did with whomsoever he played. I called him 'Abunai' – 'Dangerous' in Japanese.

But besides these occasional games or our joining the crew to watch *Rambo* for the umpteenth time, I never felt comfortable with them possibly because *they* felt uncomfortable with a woman on board. So I more or less stuck to my daily lessons on the bridge with Officer Diadula, my regular teatime chats with First Engineer Marwaha, my books and our meals with the Captain.

Our Captain was a rather serious chap with a pessimistic disposition. Our conversations during the – by the way excellent – meals dealt mostly with political subjects on which he held his own strong views. He reminded me of the type of professor timid students have a hard time approaching; demanding respect in a quiet yet forceful way (his mere presence hushed his crew whenever he entered a room). But once one overcame the stern impression he seemed to give newcomers, he was quite an amiable person. And anyway, how could a Captain who wore jeans and wooden clogs not be likeable?

*

There was nothing to do in Port Kamsar except watch the goings-on ashore below us and on the main deck where the local people came aboard to sell odd goods. We had been told to lock all doors since the locals had the tendency to try all the rooms and steal anything in sight. And indeed, no sooner had we docked, anyone and everyone simply came aboard and walked freely around the ship trying their luck at each promising door.

Port Kamsar consisted of one pier with a conveyor belt which transported bauxite directly from the factory nearby into the holds. Otherwise it was a dusty uninteresting place with bored-looking officials.

However, *our* normally bored crew suddenly came to life when we docked and immediately proceeded to haggle with the salesman who came on board with their African carvings, python skins and pitiful green parrot-like birds whose tails had been cruelly cut off to prevent them from flying away. Four or five of the poor creatures had been stuffed into a small box. When the salesman noticed me looking at them he took one out and pressed it to me. It was such a pathetic sight and all I could do was reprimand him with unimpressive gestures for his cruelty, but to no apparent avail. Some of the onlooking crew laughed and I couldn't help but despise them – not for laughing at me but for laughing at my concern for what they obviously couldn't care less about. And for the millionth time in my life, I was saddened by the basically cruel nature of human beings towards other living beings. This fact weighed heavily on me as we watched the bauxite being loaded onto our ship, covering everything with a fine film of red dust in the process.

*

It took us two weeks to cross the Atlantic Ocean and soon after the diversion of Port Kamsar, we were back into our routine of astronomy lessons and books. The temperature had turned to a balmy 70° Fahrenheit and every day we dutifully turned our clocks half an hour back. We especially felt 'ship lag' when we had to get up in the mornings!

Occasionally we saw schools of dolphins and flying fish, but nothing else until we neared the Caribbean. Then, all of a sudden, there were a lot of vessels in sight – especially sailing boats which Diadula almost always made radio contact with. Once he let me talk to a fellow only-female-on-board on a private yacht. They were heading for St Thomas. And on another day, as we were sitting on the port side reading our books and munching on some pears, a low-flying jet appeared out of nowhere and flew *at eye level* right at us. We almost choked to death on the pears we were eating and quickly went to the bridge to inquire about the incident. Diadula explained it was most likely a surveillance jet since we were in the vicinity of Cuba.

'They always do that,' he said, 'you know, fly low and probably take photographs of the ship. Maybe checking for dope or something like that.'

He added that the Caribbean was full of smugglers and even pirate ships. Excuse me, *pirate* ships? It sounded like an adventure story dating back several centuries but he assured me it was a present-day fact.

As we were sailing through the infamous Bermuda Triangle (we didn't know it at the time), we flew a delta kite from the open deck hoping to take our first aerial photographs on our trip. But the winds were terribly turbulent and before we knew it the kite dived for the sea and the line was immediately cut. It was goodbye to Kite No. 1. (Just four more to go).

'Are you two really planning to cycle around the States?' the Captain asked us as we were being piloted through the shallow waters of the Gulf of Mexico on our last day on the *Seascout*.

'That's what we intend to do,' I answered cheerfully.

'I don't know . . . ' he said, sceptically. 'It can get awfully cold this time of the year in Texas you know.'

'But it's almost 70° Fahrenheit!' I countered.

'I said it *can* be awfully cold. Last time we were here in December it was close to *zero* degrees mind you,' he said, still shaking his head.

'Well there is no turning back now, is there?' I thought sullenly to myself.

And so, before we knew it the four weeks were up and we were about to finally disembark at Point Comfort, Texas, and begin our trip with no destination. Speaking of no destination, the only map we had with us was an Interstate Map of the US which was certainly *not* going to get us anywhere in Texas. So, in order to obtain a map of Texas, our first destination would be a gas station. What could be a more appropriate place to start in the land of the automobile?

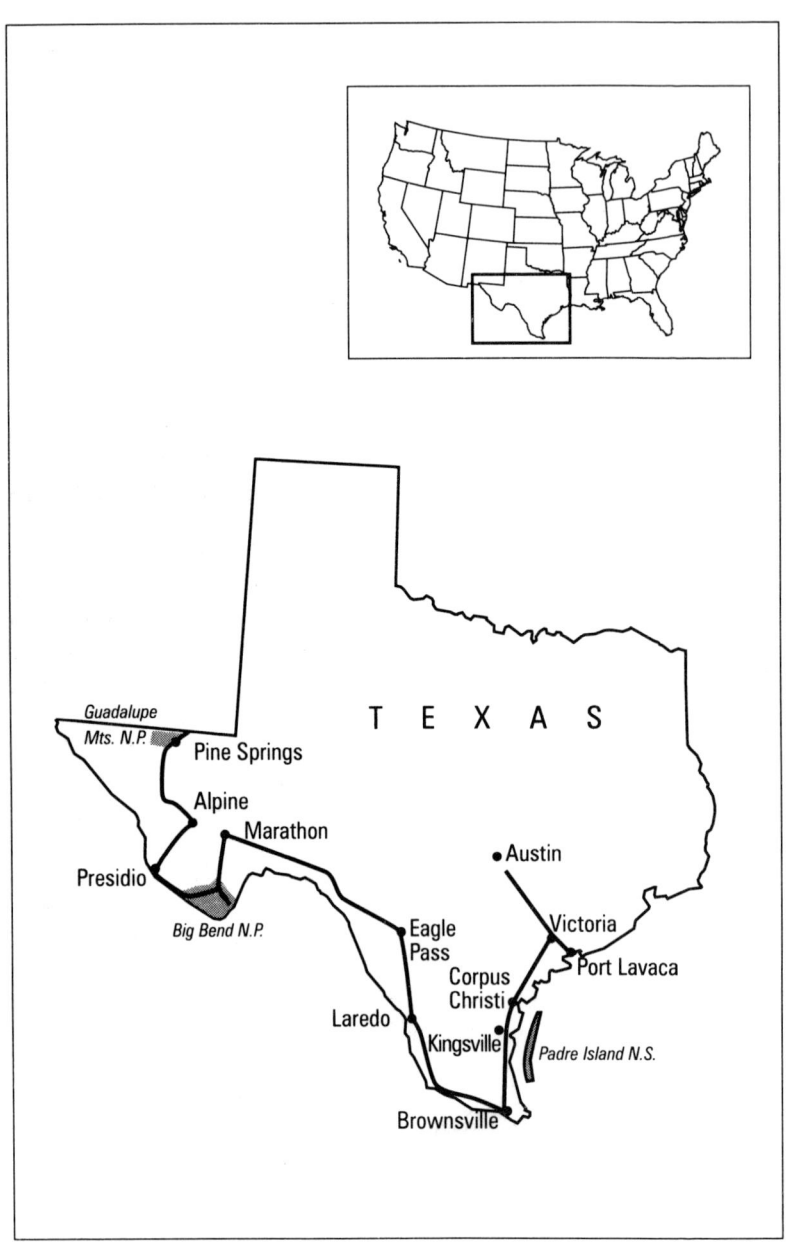

Guadalupe
Mts. N.P.
Pine Springs
Alpine
Marathon
Presidio
Big Bend N.P.
T E X A S
Austin
Victoria
Port Lavaca
Eagle
Pass
Corpus
Christi
Laredo
Kingsville
Padre Island N.S.
Brownsville

SNOWBIRDS

We were all packed and ready to go when we docked at Point Comfort. Enthusiasm notwithstanding, we had to hang around for several hours while the Captain and the local Sheriff/Customs Officer shared a bottle of whisky in the Captain's private quarters. Whether this was the normal 'port of call procedure' I will never know, but when the two of them finally emerged the Sheriff was in good spirits and hardly glanced at our passports and bikes. He wished us luck on our trip and drove away – rather unsteadily I must say – in an enormous car. I suppose I was rather apprehensive about the fact that he drove away after what must have been quite a dosage of strong liquor, let alone that he did so as an officer of the law. But I left my apprehensions behind when we found ourselves on solid land and ready to go.

But *where* to go?

We sadly waved our last goodbyes to the crew of the *Seascout* and pedalled our first feet in the United States and were covered in the fine red dust of bauxite in the process. It was only after we finally emerged from the small harbour that we found ourselves facing Texas for the first time and ... suddenly felt very lost indeed.

Quickly recovering from any doubts this created, we went searching for a gas station so that we could at least find ourselves a map of the state. An attendant obliged us with the first of the many free maps we would collect from gas stations throughout the US.

Incredibly enough, this single map covered the entire

19

state of Texas, the second largest state of the US. It is more than 800 miles across from east to west and from north to south and, I'm almost embarrassed to say, about ten times the size of the Netherlands (although I must quickly come to the defence of our country and add that is isn't quantity but quality that counts). Take any country in western Europe and one would find maps outlining the smallest of details of each and every province, yet in Texas one map sufficed – especially in the south and the west where there were so few roads anyway.

We made a quick study of the enormous state and decided to head for the nearest haven – a friend's home in Austin.

*

Because we had a late start, we had cycled only 20 miles from Point Comfort when it was beginning to get dark. We pitched out tent near the town of Port Lavaca (a local told us that Lavaca was the Spanish word for 'cow head') next to a fenced-in field off the main road and spent our first nervous night on American soil. I can still recall how strange it was to camp on unfamiliar land, and how utterly apprehensive I was about the whole journey itself. The first day and night out and I was already worrying whether someone would kick us off *their* land, whether a drunken driver would run us over, whether rattlesnakes would slither into our tent, whether we'd be harassed or threatened by someone with a gun etc. . . etc.

But of course none of those things happened and we 'survived' our first night out in the open.

*

The following day we passed the town of Victoria and got onto Highway 87 which took us through gradually undulating hills of farmland. We managed to cover 78 miles and were very pleased with ourselves. Being December, sunset was around 5 p.m., so we had to start looking for a place to camp at around 4 p.m. We were only at the beginning of the journey and packing and unpacking our gear still took time and we weren't very efficient with our homemade tent.

The trouble with Texas, we soon discovered, was that everything was fenced-in – a very inhospitable sight for a state that likes to call itself the 'Friendship State'. The sheer sizes of some of the farm and ranch lands were enormous and it was difficult to find the owner's house where we could otherwise *ask* for permission to camp. But perhaps it was just as well – the larger the land the less conspicuous we became.

In any case, that day we finally found a dirt road off Highway 183 which led to a small white house perched on a hill. It had some land around it which looked ideal for a tent, so I went up to the house and knocked. An elderly lady came to the door and looked suspiciously at me:

'Yes?' she asked behind the screened door.

I explained in the most friendly way I could think of that we were two cyclists looking for a place to camp, ridiculous as it sounded.

'Well, I dunno . . . .' she said reluctantly, 'I'd have to ask ma huzband when he gets back . . . .'

It was already getting dark, and who knows when this husband of hers was to return? I suggested we pitch our tent and talk to her husband *after* he got back. She hesitated but finally agreed.

We pitched our tent under a few trees and as soon as I saw The Huzband, I walked up to him and explained our plight. It turned out he wasn't in the least concerned about us camping on his land; he was concerned about the *fact* that we were camping.

'You wanna *camp* out here?' he asked incredulously.

'Well, yes, if you don't mind that is.'

'Ah don't mind, but did you know the're rattlesnakes out there?'

Gulp.

'I shot a big one right here a while ago. The critter was as tall as me!'

'Uh . . . well, our tent zips up so I think we'll be all right.'

'In tha' case, help yo'self,' he said.

It wasn't all right at all, but did we have any choice?

Later on in the evening we heard on the radio that a front was coming and as if to prove that fact, early in the evening we started to hear thunder rumbling in the distance.

We managed to sleep almost until dawn when we were awakened in the midst of a terrific thunderstorm. Water from the heavy rain was flowing directly under us, soaking the sleeping bags and us in the process. We soon realised we were freezing. Nop suggested we go to the house, but it was barely morning and I hesitated.

'You want to catch pneumonia?' he shouted at me.

So we grabbed what we could and ran across the slushing field to the house where an ancient poodle started to bark hysterically at us. This woke up the husband who came out, took one look at us and made us come in. He lit what must have been ten electric stoves scattered about the cluttered house, and his wife put the kettle on.

It was wonderful to be in a house with a hot cup of coffee in our hands, although we felt terrible for having awakened them.

'Ma name is Pink Brown,' the husband (not the wife) introduced himself, 'and this here is ma wife Portia.' We introduced ourselves and explained where we were from.

'The what?' Pink asked.

'The Netherlands.'

He still had a blank look.

Nop tried again: 'Holland.'

'You mean Holland, *Europe*?'

'Yes.'

'Ah'll be darned!' he said with a big smile. Perhaps we were the first Europeans he had ever met?

We talked about our two-day-old trip and sounded like utter fools when we mentioned bicycling around the entire

22

US, but despite our young trip, the Browns were impressed.

Pink told us that he and Portia had lived in Texas all their lives. They were both in their eighties although neither of them looked a day older than sixty-five.

'Back in the ol' days, this here used to be cotton country,' Pink said, 'and ma grandpa worked as a slave in those days, but most of the cotton is gone – it's mostly ranchland now.' Despite his age Pink was still working as a gardener at the cemetery in the nearby town of Cuero.

'What is it like being black in Texas?' I asked bluntly. I couldn't help but wonder how some of the redneck cowboys treated the blacks in this state.

Portia said, 'Not too bad. It's not as it used to be,' and with a chuckle she added almost with a hint of embarrassment at the memory, 'I remember a time when we used to get off the sidewalk whenever we saw a bunch of whites comin' the other way . . . but not any more.'

Pink asked us where we were heading for next. 'Gonzales,' we told him.

'Gonzales?! Ah wouldn't do that if ah was you!'

'Why not?' Nop asked.

'Cuz they got some mighty mean types up there in Gonzales. Yessiree, I wouldn't go up there for nothin!'

Well, if we heeded every warning we got from people we wouldn't even be in America in the first place ('America is so dangerous Michèle – people carry guns there!')

We assured Pink we'd keep an eye out for the 'mighty mean types'.

*

We realised as we packed our gear and said our thanks and goodbyes to the Browns that we were confronting our first northern front on this journey. The storm had let up but now it was terribly cold and we had strong icy headwinds as we continued up Highway 183 towards Gonzales. By the time we got to the outskirts of town, sleet was coming down and slashing our numb faces and hands and visibility was at a minimum. We saw a huge barn and headed for it. A woman who looked like a cowboy (not cow*girl*) with hat and jeans on was supervising the milking machines of the cows. We asked her if she knew a spot where we could pitch our tent.

'I live in the house up that hill. If you like, you can stay there. It belongs to the owner of this farm and he lets me use it for free. You're welcome to it, too.' We couldn't believe our luck – *anything* to get out of this shitty weather.

Cows roamed freely around the fenced-in house, and we had to push our bikes over a mass of slushy cow dung before we could reach the house. The interior was literally a pigsty; the kitchen was a mess and it looked like the dishes hadn't been washed for the last two weeks. The cowboy-woman who had introduced herself as Gloria had a roommate who was out. Obviously neither of them were interested in cleanliness. Both bedrooms were in disarray with clothes flung over every piece of furniture. It was a rather depressing sight, but it was a roof over our heads so I couldn't complain.

We decided to wait for the front to abate and spent the next two days cleaning up the kitchen to keep ourselves warm. There was no heating in the house except for a single electric stove in Gloria's bedroom beside which I would occasionally huddle in order to thaw out. Gloria's roommate, whom we met later on the first evening, was also of Mexican origin and, although she was a nurse, she too dressed like a cowboy with the usual hat, jeans and leather boots. I was beginning to think that this combination (a pick-up truck with a shotgun hung on the rear window as complementary accessories) was the compulsory 'cowboy look' uniform in this state.

Despite their spontaneous generosity for letting us stay, neither of them were particularly interested in us. Of course we were most grateful to be indoors, but it was depressing not to be able to talk to them on the same wave-length – it seemed there was simply nothing to talk about.

24

We finally couldn't stand the place another day, and decided to hit the road when the sun came out although it remained freezing.

We stopped in the town of Gonzales to do some shopping. As we got off our bikes, a man in his mid-fifties came out of the saloon.

'Hi there,' he said. 'Are those ba-cycles?'

Here we go again!

'Yes, they are.'

'Well then, where are the handlebars now?'

'Next to the seat,' Nop answered as he pointed to them.

'Ah'll be darned! You two travellin' far?'

How many times were we going to have to do this? We summed up our plans in three short sentences.

'Wha don't you two come on into this saloon here for a drink. It's one of the oldest buildin's in town, you know. Whaddya say I show you around Gonzales later? You can leave the ba-cycles here, the guys'll keep an eye on 'em.'

What the heck, we thought, it was too cold for pleasant cycling anyway.

He was right about the saloon. It looked like something out of a Western movie – a dark wooden interior with cowboys sitting sullenly around the tables, drinking in silence. But where were the poker games, the ladies of the night and the fist fights? I thought to myself as we were offered cokes. We felt completely out of place in our tight bicycle pants and jogging shoes. But our being from Europe seemed to be enough for people to ignore our odd appearance and open all doors for us. They were all eager to hear our story although it was a mere five days old. There was no sign of the 'mean types' Pink had mentioned.

Tom Tuss, our guide through Gonzales, drove us around in what I can only call a tank rather than a car – four people could have easily slept in the thing. He pointed out the old jail house and some other old buildings (although 'old' in the US is anything between fifty and a hundred and fifty years old), and then he took us to some turkey farms on the outskirts of town which were run by a friend of his. The smell of ammonia was overwhelming and stuck to us even as we drove away half an hour later.

Tom wanted us to come and stay in his trailer, but we declined after he rolled down his window and threw his beer can onto the street. This was something we just couldn't understand – here was a man proudly showing us around his native town and at the same time deliberately littering it. It put us off completely.

We had already come across quite a lot of litter along the sides of the roads in Texas which we considered a disgrace to the state – even the signs which warned: 'Don't Mess with Texas! $500 fine for littering' stood on heaps of garbage. Perhaps Texans littered so much because they considered any open space (which they had planty of) a public garbage dump. But it wasn't only the litter we had noticed (which consisted, by the way, mostly of beer cans) but also the number of dead animals alongside the road – birds, skunks, snakes, rabbits, even coyotes! As we travelled throughout the United States, we did become aware of the fact that the amount of litter alongside the roads often reflected the attitudes of the citizens of the state. I do not like to generalise, but our indelible impression was that Texans didn't appreciate land for its nature, only for its production value.

Back in town, Nop and I decided then and there that Austin was out of the question in the present icy temperatures and persistent headwinds, and that we should head for Mexico instead. So we turned around and with strong tail winds literally flew the 66 miles south back to the town of Victoria.

It so happened that our Hospitality Home List for cyclists mentioned a bicycle shop called 'Bill's Bikes' in Victoria. We found it and were welcomed by the Yearys who invited us into their meticulously kept home which had heating, clean beds and a hot shower! We were instantly revived and in the evening Bill and Fran took us out to our first Salad Bar Restaurant where we stuffed ourselves with tacos and fresh vegetables. It was great to talk to fellow bicyclists again and we could hardly believe how things could change so drastically from one day to another. Only five days on the road and we learned that bumping into the unexpected was precisely what this kind of travel was all about.

*

Six days and 250 miles later we reached the border town of Brownsville. Highway 77 from Kingsville to Brownsville was mostly one straight line. There wasn't much habitation of interest along the way and the one predominant ranch had been King's Ranch – some 823,000 acres – and every inch of it was fenced in. Occasionally there was a rest area next to it; wooden steps going over the fence were provided for those who really had to relieve themselves, providing they heeded the sign which said: 'Beware of rattlesnakes'.

The night before we reached Brownsville, we camped on a golf course which was part of some kind of millionaire village on the edge of Raymondville. A cop who was patrolling the village gave us permission to camp after jotting down our names and passport numbers. He (himself partly Mexican) warned us about going into Mexico:

'The peso is so low now Mexicans'll steal *anything.* I wouldn't go down there if I were you.'

Brownsville was ugly and the people were ugly. Everyone we approached refused to speak to us in English. I was beginning to wonder whether we were in Mexico or in the US. We had to use physical gestures to buy bicycle parts at a bike store run by a Mexican, and a gas station attendant ignored us till I probed into my memory (Spanish class from 8th Grade) and blurted out the words, *'Agua, por favor.'*

It was ridiculous. I thought this only happened in places like southern Belgium or Quebec! We were disgusted with the place except for the fact that the warm weather had finally returned. We now had second thoughts about giving up on the States so soon.

'Listen,' Nop said, as we pondered what to do next, 'why don't we try to make it to **Big Bend National Park** before the next front comes?'

I too didn't want to be defeated by this unpredictable Texan weather, and to visit a National Park seemed like good enough reason to head back north. Had the cold front continued we would have definitely headed for Guadalajara in Mexico and our trip may have turned out quite differently. As it was, the weather determined our route as it often would throughout our journey.

For the next two weeks we more or less followed the Rio Grande – the border between Mexico and the US. All along the way people warned us of the dangers of being too near the border where 'wet backs' (Mexicans) cross over illegally every day.

'They'd murder you for a couple of bucks,' they would say. Were they being paranoid? Well, it didn't hurt to be careful, and we always tried to camp away from the border towns and away from any roads. For the most part though, we usually ended up in someone's home, on someone's land or in a trailer park although Nop hated trailer parks mainly because they were so expensive – he always considered 'paying to sleep' a waste of money. When we left the Netherlands, a dollar was as much as three Dutch guilders, so we did have to watch what we spent our money on.

Yet I still wasn't used to camping in the wild or sneaking onto someone's land hoping they wouldn't see us till the morning and it would take me more than a month to pull myself away from this mental handicap. In the meantime though, Christmas was nearing and both of us felt slightly homesick, so a bit of company wasn't going to hurt and we decided to go for a trailer park.

Condit Park was the first park we stayed at along the Rio Grande, and it turned out to be the perfect place. The moment we pitched our tent a number of elderly people came up to us and immediately welcomed us with food and conversation. They acted as though we made their day – they were all retired people who had come down south for the winter: 'snowbirds' they called themselves. For three days we were taken into their mobile homes and fed and one day

28

the Condits invited us to cross the border into Presidio, Mexico, which was nearby. We were worried that Immigration would check our passports and have to reissue us visas, but the Condits just waved their hands and said, 'Don't you worry, they aren't looking for *whites*!'

Presidio was, I suppose, a typical border town, with the gap between the well-to-do Americans and the poor Mexicans quite conspicuous. It was a dusty place with a main road lined with stores and, surprisingly, huge American cars. The poverty in Mexico didn't seem to deter Mexicans from buying the oversized over-consuming vehicles.

We stocked up on coffee and cookies which were cheap, but other than that we found there was nothing to see or do in town.

On 24th December, despite the comforts of the Condit Park and the wonderful hospitality and affection our neighbours showed us, we decided to go on. They all fussed about us leaving on Christmas Eve but we really felt that we would end up living in Texas if we didn't discipline ourselves a bit. So, with tearful farewells we headed west along Highway 281. But 63 miles further, we ended up again in a trailer park – 'Oleander Acres' – which was bigger but no less hospitable.

We became, more or less, the grand attraction of the park; in no time we were surrounded by inquisitive but kindly snowbirds. Ed Welliver, the owner of the park didn't even know what to charge us since he never had people camp with a tent in the park. We suggested $3 and he agreed. Once we were settled, he invited us to join his family for dinner – his wife looked part-Mexican and was very beautiful. So were the children, who were so excited about our bicycles that we gave them rides around the park during our stay.

The next day was Christmas. Lucy – one of the snowbirds of the park as well as the secretary of the office – invited us to join the park in their potluck Christmas party. We happily agreed and literally *gorged* ourselves on vegetable and cheese quiches, potato, egg and bean salads, and half a dozen cakes and desserts including a delicious pie made from pecan nuts which was new to us.

After dinner an announcement was made about our presence and we were asked to give a little talk about our trip. We were rather embarrassed because we had only been on the road for less than three weeks; nevertheless, they all seemed to enjoy what we had to say and bombarded us with questions when we finished: 'How do you ride those bikes?' 'Where do you camp?' 'How do you like the US?' 'What do the Dutch people think of America?' etc . . . and to end the show, they passed the hat around and collected $75 for us. We were very touched by the gesture.

We spent the second day of Christmas lazing in our tent. Some of the snowbirds who had been shy earlier came up to us with all sorts of gifts: hand knitted socks, homemade cakes and cookies, fruit . . . our trailer was beginning to weigh a ton! But they were so friendly and sweet that we couldn't refuse.

We were also given addresses: 'Be sure to visit us when you get up north,' some said.

On 27th December we finally left Oleander Acres – most of the park members surrounded us and wished us well as they photographed us and waved goodbye. Our hearts sank at the thought that we may never see these kind people again.

*

Maps can provide extremely interesting reading and our map of Texas was no exception. We now knew that we were far away from all sizeable cities and that we were nearing the Chihuahuan Desert. The scenery, which had been mainly agricultural along the Rio Grande so far (carrots, cabbage as well as sugar cane), was now slowly changing into wilder prairie-like land, and the number of cows increased. We even spotted Brahman cattle – beautiful creatures with humped backs and long drooping ears said to have been developed from the zebu of India and therefore well-adapted to hot climates which are used for cross-breeding (for beef cattle). We made a short visit to the Santa Anna Wildlife Refuge, which contains various flora and fauna endemic to this region as it once existed before the advent of large-scale agriculture in the valley, where two men were intently looking through binoculars. When we inquired what they were observing they told us there was a grey owl in one of the trees:

'Texas is one of the best places for bird watching,' one of the men said. 'It's a crossroads for migrating birds. The variety of birds that pass through Texas is just *amazing*.' His enthusiasm was quite contagious as we borrowed the binoculars and watched the owl blink his wide eyes slowly. Now that we were moving away from large human populations and entering the *real* Texas it was gratifying to be able to finally concentrate on the nature surrounding us.

Following the Rio Grande inevitably reminded us that we were following a border – place names were often Spanish: Roma Los Saenz, Lopeno, Zapata, San Ignacio .... Laredo was the last large town we were about to pass through. On the way to Big Bend we had whiled away the day at Falcon Heights, a large reservoir owned jointly by Mexico and the US. As a result, we underestimated the distance from Falcon to Laredo and made the stupid mistake of arriving in Laredo – quite a large town as it is one of the major international crossings between the US-Mexican border – after sundown. We were stuck. We couldn't cycle on in the dark – drivers in Texas don't expect to see cyclists in the daytime let alone at night – so all we could do was look for a trailer park in the vicinity. We found one called Casa Norte which looked commercial and uninviting, but we had no choice. We pitched our tent next to a trailer from which a drunken couple emerged to welcome us. They kept urging us to have a beer, but our stomachs were so empty we refused. Then they insisted we join them for seafood. I was rather apprehensive that they wanted to drive to the restaurant (they were already quite drunk), but we couldn't very well suggest walking to Texans. We all squeezed into their pick-up truck – what else – and drove unsteadily to the restaurant. The food was spicy and delicious, but I was too tired to enjoy the food and their raucous behaviour didn't help either. They continued to drink even when we got back to the park, but we thanked them for the dinner and turned in early. We had covered 86 miles that day.

*

Continuing on Highway 83, which went inland after Laredo, we cycled 90 miles without seeing a single house along the way. It was one of the longest uninhabited stretches we had ever made on this journey, and it was *great.* The country seemed to be getting more barren, the ranches larger, and the landscape rugged. On the 30th December we came upon a free primitive campground at Carrizo Springs – just the thing for us. The view was splendid, no one bothered us and we were looking forward to Big Bend National Park more and more.

The following day we covered a rather hilly 63 miles passing the single town of Eagle Pass, and ended up camping on an empty campground called Bowman's Village near an invisible town called Normandy. We spotted the house of the Bowman's before we realised they had a campground. No one could miss it – two ancient trees grew *out* of their house.

'These pecan trees are more than sixty years old,' Mrs Bowman explained to us later as we sat by the fireplace and stared at one of the glass-enclosed trees which was literally standing in their living room. 'When we decided to enlarge the house we couldn't bring ourselves to cut down these magnificent trees, so we decided to build the house around them.' What a wonderful idea!

Later, I had the most interesting experience of sitting on the toilet while watching a squirrel scurrying up and down the other pecan tree, collecting nuts for the winter.

We spent New Year's Eve next to this unique house, and

Ben and Beverly Bowman treated us both on the eve of New Year and New Year itself to homemade food. On New Year's Day, Ben drove us to a nearby feed lot where 25,000 head of cattle were being fattened in a single lot. The smell was overpowering and I felt sorry for the fate of the poor cattle who had numbers stapled onto their ears and stood side-by-side squashed into this MacDonald Hamburger back-yard.

On the outskirts of Eagle Pass, Ben pointed out a pitiful community of Indians to us who were living in round shacks made of cardboard boxes. Their circular shape was perhaps reminiscent of the original indigenous dwellings.

'The government built houses for them, but they refuse to live in them,' Ben explained. Perhaps they were originally nomads and felt too claustrophobic in concrete buildings. How little people knew about some of the native tribes – we didn't even know the name of this one!

We had our first glimpse of what was to come in Big Bend as we stopped in the Amistad National Recreation Area and Seminole Canyon State Park – the first of the many canyon landscapes we were going to experience. At the tiny town of Langtry (population forty-five), we pitched our tent facing a magnificent canyon – carved out by the turquoise blue Pecos River whose sandstone walls glowed in the golden rays of the setting sun – a breathtaking sight for a front yard! Although we had easily crossed a bridge over the Pecos River to get to this wonderful camp site, the depth of the canyon reminded me of the terrific obstacles the pioneers had had to face when heading west. How on earth did they find a place to cross it let alone get their wagons across?

Every day the scenery was getting better and better and if all went well we would be in Big Bend in a couple of days. But then another northern front hit us just as we were about to turn south at the junction of Marathon and head for Big Bend National Park. This time we were really stuck because it snowed and the temperatures dropped to 20° Fahrenheit. We had to spend two miserable days behind the gas station at Marathon, shivering in our tent even with all our clothes on because we couldn't keep using our stove all day. For two days all we could do was shiver and wait. Besides boredom, not being able to warm up sufficiently was definitely one of our worst discomforts. Fortunately for us, the front lasted only a couple of days (and now we believed the Texan saying: 'If you don't like the weather wait three days') so once the snow melted we packed up our frozen gear and headed for Big Bend. It was still cold as we cycled south towards the park and new clouds threatened snow so we stopped at the next best trailer park (which turned out to be the last before Big Bend) to have better shelter in case of another storm.

As we were pitching our tent we were befriended by Bob and Betty Elmore, a retired couple who had sold their house and were travelling in a camper. They were accompanied by a cocker spaniel who I later nicknamed 'Crumple Face' because of the numerous folds on his face which gave him a perpetually worried look. They were also heading for Big Bend and were about to leave so we promised to join them at the Rio Grande Village in a few days' time.

The dog of the campground spent both nights with us in our tent – we didn't mind because it was way below freezing. The owner of the campground told us he was half-coyote and we believed him – he certainly looked it. Since the owner didn't have a name for him I decided to call him 'Wolf'. On our second day at the campground, Wolf joined us for a hike in the surrounding desert.

A jackrabbit sent Wolf bounding through the bush in pursuit. Outrunning his predator, the rabbit found a safe vantage point where he stood on his hind legs and stared at us. With the sun behind him we noticed how large and heavily veined his ears were. The jackrabbit radiates excess body heat through its nearly translucent ears, saving precious body fluid by eliminating the need to perspire. This enables it to live with little or no drinking water, subsisting on moisture-providing vegetation instead. This evening, however, the main purpose of the ears pointed so attentively upward seemed to be satisfying curiosity. Satiated, the

34

jackrabbit finally lowered them and disappeared into the evening's lengthening shadows.

Two days later we finally entered Big Bend National Park – it was an exciting moment for us because it was everything we expected it to be and more. Its sheer size was astounding – the size of the province of Zeeland in the Netherlands (imagine designating an entire province of a nation a National Park? Not a bad thought . . .). It was here that we saw the Chihuahuan Desert at its best: the desert lay empty before us devoid of humans and their habitations shining in the aftermath of the snow which still lingered on some prickly pear cacti and in the shade of the mountains. Eroded buttes jutted out of the ground in dignity, cacti lined the roads and the thorny arms of the Devil's Cane cacti were blooming in red. There were no cars and it was – could it be true? – *absolutely* quiet.

We were utterly content that evening as we sat in our tent at the primitive campsite of K-bar where we turned out to be the only visitors. It was very cold, but the sky . . . ! The stars were simply dazzling and seemed to occupy every inch of the entire universe while the Milky Way resembled a bridge connecting the northern and southern horizons. If we felt small in the desert during the day, we simply did not exist during the night when the skies took over so thoroughly. We were even able to see Halley's Comet with our newly acquired binoculars (compliments of Oleander Acres) and probably had the best view of it from where we were!

*

There was too much to see – we could have spent months exploring the diverse landscapes of this fantastic park. We wondered what gave places such peculiar names as Dugout Wells, Rooney's Place, Rice Tank, Mule Ears Overlook, Chimney's West, Burro Mesa Pouroff . . . .

We met Bob and Betty again during the three days we spent exploring the area around the Rio Grande Village. We shared meals and books and the love for the desert; they loved it the same way as we did, for what it was – harsh yet beautiful at the same time. One day, they drove us up to the Chisos Mountains in the centre of the park so that we could hike to an overlook called The Window. It was located at 4,500 feet and there was still snow on the ground. The trail was very muddy, but we managed to get to The Window, which was a small opening between two boulders and looked out onto the wide desert expanse – its edge was a 4,500 foot drop-off.

During the last blizzard, a lone hiker had died in these mountains. We had heard on the radio that a search party was out looking for him – they finally found his body that same day. Park rangers had said thet he must have left his camp site before the blizzard struck, then lost his way and froze to death. Even though we never knew him, it was sad to hear of the death of this man who must have loved these parts to hike it even under such precarious conditions. At least dying in nature seems preferable to dying from a car accident or from a disease. But the fact that the man died young remains an injustice.

On 14th January we headed once again to a primitive camp site of Croton Spring – this time at the western end – to enjoy the solitude such a camp site offered. Rio Grande Village wasn't bad as campgrounds go, but it had its extreme characters. Among the visitors had been a large convoy of campers and cars led by an enormous bus converted into some kind of super-deluxe home. When the convoy finally left the campground, the drivers had had the audacity to deafen the remaining campers with a cacophony of honking horns.

*

As we once again followed the Rio Grande west of Big Bend, we encountered an incredible 15% gradient hill. Both of us had to push our bikes up – especially Nop who had the trailer. It lasted a couple of miles and we were soaking with perspiration as we reached the top. But after that one gruelling hill, the road undulated alongside the river pleasantly and the view was marvellous; this road, known locally as El Camino del Rio (The River Road) runs parallel to an old Spanish trail which was first used to transport silver, but was later used to smuggle alcohol during Prohibition. To our joy this spectacular road was deserted. Only one camper had passed us (the couple in the camper waited for us at the bottom of one of the dips, waving cans of Pepsi to us so we would stop. We never refused drinks in the desert, but were rather annoyed that they didn't wait for us at the *top* of the hill).

It was such pleasant scenery that we decided to camp one last time alongside the Rio Grande – we found a deserted spot at a bend in the river. The only other person present was a college student trying our a new canoe. He invited Nop to give it a try so Nop, always open to new outdoor challenges, did. It was some kind of stunt canoe, and Nop soon found himself upside down, struggling for life. He looked a bit shaky when he came back to the shore.

The following morning, we flew one of our kites and took some aerial photographs of our camp site. We had made a deal with Kodak and Minolta that we would take aerial photographs from our kites as we travelled for them so that, in return, we would be provided with a good camera and all the slide film we needed. It was a good deal, and free film saved us a lot of money.

At Presido we finally parted with the Rio Grande river we had grown so fond of. We followed Highway 67 – which went straight through the desert until broken by the volcanic Chinati Mountains to the west – and arrived in the town of Marfa (altitude 4,688 feet).

Here we hoped to find spare tyres. For the past month our poor tyres had been plagued with thorns and a flat tyre a day was becoming annoyingly common. We were even out of patches. For the past few weeks, we had, out of desperation, been sewing on pieces of rubber which we had picked up from the sides of the roads (just shows how creative you can get under dire circumstances). The problem with Texas was that new tyres were hard to come by – this was a state for the pick-up truck or the horse and *not* for bicycles as far as Texans were concerned. It was no wonder that many a Texan would pass us in his pick-up truck only to screech to a halt to stare at us as if we had dropped from outer space. Of course, the recumbent was always a sight, but I always felt that Texans would have stared at us anyway even if we had been on conventional bikes or even on foot.

Marfa lay on the high desert (usually about 4,000 feet above sea level) and was dry and warm. We roamed the town looking for spare tyres, but couldn't find any. A man in a wheelchair came up to us on the sidewalk and asked us where we were from so we told him.

'Is that right? I'm of Swedish origin,' he added proudly. 'Where are you two staying the night?' he then asked.

'Haven't decided yet,' Nop replied.

'Well in that case, why don't you two come over to my place. You can sleep in my bedroom and I'll sleep in my trailer.'

We automatically thought of a hot shower we could definitely use and said yes.

The man, whom I shall call Duane, explained to us as we got to his house that he had had polio as a child. But he had nevertheless learned to walk although he still uses the electrical wheelchair for longer distances. At home he did indeed walk although not without some pain, every so often muttering 'ouch' as he walked around the kitchen.

Nop joined Duane when offered beer (I can't stand alcohol) but after the third round on an empty stomach Nop switched to coke. Duane went on with beer and I thought to myself, 'here is an unbeatable Swede'. After we were refreshed from our hot showers we offered to cook since we had done some shopping in town. But as we ate Duane hardly touched his food and stuck to beer. And the more cans of beer he downed the more raucous he became. We then were beginning to have second thoughts about spending the night in his house, but it was already too late to change our minds.

'You know,' he said, as he opened yet another beer can, 'I used to be an actor in my youth, but I got fed up with Hollywood and returned to Minnesota – that's my home state. There's quite a large Swedish population there you know.'

He was beginning to slur. 'I've never been to Sweden but I speak the language,' he said and then started to rattle on in (presumably) Swedish. For a while he wasn't aware that we didn't understand a word he was saying but suddenly he snapped out of it and switched to English and continued talking about himself. In Minnesota he had apparently worked for a radio station as an announcer and later he had become the Justice of Peace in his home town. Now he was retired and came down to Marfa in the winter months because of his arthritis.

'Marfa has great air,' he said. 'And the water here is among the best in this country.'

Duane went on to say that he had quite a command of languages: Swedish, Danish, Norwegian, German, Yiddish and even some Spanish. We talked at length about the history of the US, but by midnight our eyes were beginning to droop. It had been a long day and a long climb up to Marfa and it was way past our bedtime. But Duane kept on going, downing one beer after the other. He was oblivious to the late hour and became more and more sentimental as his drunkenness became more and more acute. Finally he was only muttering in Swedish and we gave up. We said good night, hoping that would make him go to bed too.

'Right. You two just go to bed. Have a nice sleep!' he mumbled.

Unfortunately for us, there was only a slight partition between his living room and the bedroom. We were now cursing our stupidity for not having put up our tent in his back yard instead.

Duane never did go to bed; hour after hour he went on. As soon as we had gone to bed, he put Swedish music on and started to sing along! At one point he burst into tears and started talking to himself. Then he put German organ music on, then Beethoven, and finally, towards daybreak, a cassette of singing birds.

Neither of us slept much that night and we were very grouchy in the morning.

'Good morning!' Duane greeted us cheerfully as we finally gave up on sleep and got up. 'Did you sleep well?' he asked cheerfully. 'I'm going to make pancakes for breakfast – would you like that?' What could we say?

Duane himself had beer for breakfast.

*

Route 90 to Alpine cheered us up. The sun was out, the sky was blue and we were glad to be out of that suffocating house and out in the open again. And on top of this we actually found spare tyres in Alpine – in a toy shop. Duane had given us the address of a Doctor Lockhardt whom he knew in Alpine so we were able to pitch our tent up behind his house in the middle of town and boy did we have a long good night's sleep!

The following morning we woke to the pleasant sound of birds; when we got up we found to our dismay that our tent was covered with pigeon dung.

*

The Davis Mountains, actually part of the long tail of the Rocky Mountains, were our first real mountains in the US. Fort Davis was a reminder of the by-gone days when this land was still wilderness and the Apaches were a threat to new settlers. One of the largest military forts at that time, Fort Davis had been recently partly restored to give the modern traveller an impression of the past. Times may have changed, but the land around the fort hasn't – it still seems untamed and uninhabited and the imaginary scene of Apaches ready to charge came easily as we looked around the monument.

It was a steep climb up to the MacDonald Observatory –

the highest point on this road – where we took a brief look at the Visitor's Centre – and then it was downhill into Fort Davis' State Park where we decided to camp. They charged us the astronomical fee of $7.

As we descended into the valley where the campground was located, we heard someone suddenly shout, 'Nop! Michèle!' As we screeched to a halt we saw, incredibly enough, Bob and Betty and sweet little 'Crumple Face'. It was like being reunited with family again.

*

On our last night in Texas we checked our map to add up the distances we had covered – in this state alone we had cycled some 1,875 miles.

I once read that Texans 'identify first with their region, then with their state and finally with their nation'; I couldn't help but agree when we spotted the exit sign of the State park which said 'Come back y'all'. We certainly felt like we were leaving a country.

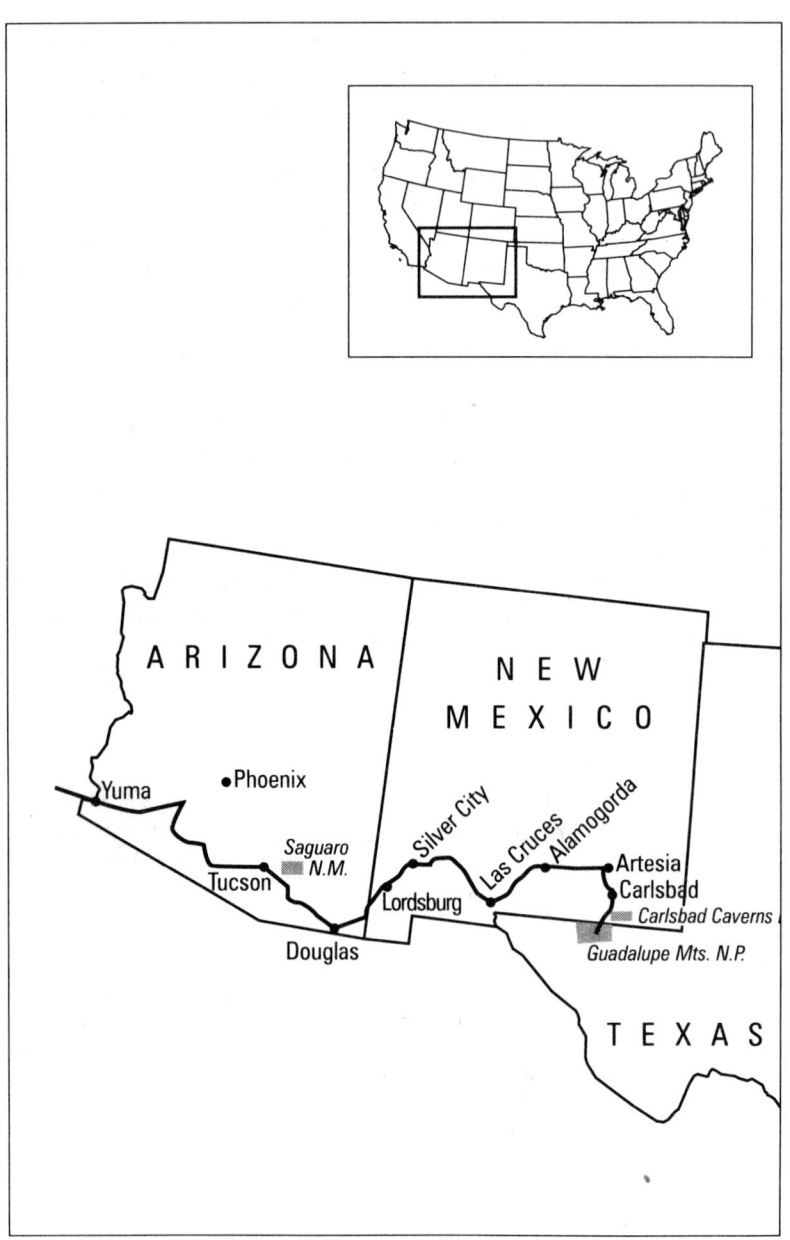

HIGH DESERTS

Crossing a state line in the United States is like crossing a border in Europe – there is no clear boundary, but the differences are somehow immediately noticeable. At the border to New Mexico we noticed, to our great annoyance, that the wide-paved shoulder we had enjoyed throughout Texas disappeared completely and that we now found ourselves having to share the road with speeding cars (interesting point 'cars' and not 'automobilists' – people somehow seem to lose their identity as living individuals the moment they step into their machines and close themselves off from their surroundings; I rarely think of cars with actual people driving them and unfortunately lump them together as 'cars'. But this is a well-known habit among bicyclists).

One look at our newly-acquired map told us that we would be confronting some serious mountain ranges in the high deserts of New Mexico – in fact two-thirds of New Mexico is lined with mountain ranges and we were heading west where most of them were situated. I (secretly) never failed to experience a tinge of anxiety whenever I knew we were going to cope with mountains – it was as though every mountain range was nature's way of testing my will and my physical capabilities. After all, I had never been a great athlete nor an ardent bicyclist before the trip and my instinctive tendency to worry about matters *beforehand* inevitably made me consider all natural obstacles a challenge.

It was 23rd January 1986 when we arrived in Whites City.

43

It is named after Jim White, one of the earlier explorers of the Carlsbad Caverns located a few miles up the Guadaloupe Mountains. Internationally famous as one of the Wonders of the World, the caverns are now designated a park. White City, however, was a tourist trap. The park offered no camping facilities and, as a result, the town had an enormous campground which charged bicycles and 30-foot campers alike the rip-off fee of $11. We wouldn't succumb to this highway robbery, but we couldn't very well miss the park either. Instead, we found some unfenced land nearby and pitched our tent. The owner gave us permission provided we did not build a campfire.

The following day we climbed up to the park entrance – a steady climb of about seven miles – through low-brush desert. The entrance to the cavern was one of those extravagant affairs typical of the over-visited national parks of this country. The sign reflected the pride of the park: 'Carlsbad Caverns is visited by more than ... million visitors a year'.

The entrance was packed with (judging from the diversity of number plates on the cars in the parking lot and the numerous languages spoken at the Visitor's Centre) visitors from all over the country and the world. Although we had to line up and join a group to descend the 85 feet down into the caverns it was well worth it. Once we reached the caverns we were free to roam on our own.

Having just recently come up the hot desert slopes of the Guadaloupe Mountains it was hard to believe that these cool, dark and enormous caverns existed just below them. Entering the caverns was like entering a fantasy world out of *Lord of the Rings*. In the partially lit caverns the sound of dripping water was consistent, accentuating the already damp atmosphere of the 'rooms'. Of course it was precisely the dripping water which, together with the minerals it gathered as it flowed down the cracks and vaults of the upper stone that caused new stalactites and stalagmites to form into an incredible array of shapes and sizes; ghastly monsters, rounded pyramids, unearthly trees, humorous

44

giants, colourful rocks as well as fragile and graceful coral-like flowers. It was a world away from the world of light and it was hard to imagine that some sixty-six other caves belonged to the national park site and that many more caverns had yet to be discovered. I couldn't help but wonder how frightening it must have been for the first explorers to penetrate these unknown dark depths of the earth. I suppose it wasn't dissimilar to experiencing the exploration of the dark depths of the oceans.

*

We had to blink several times to adjust our eyes to the light when we emerged from the caverns and found ourselves standing in the desert once again. Looking around us at the arid landscape in the heat made it hard to believe what we had just seen. Perhaps I was still daydreaming about these extremes as we cruised down the mountains to Whites City again, because before I knew it I just missed colliding head on into a deer and her fawn by a few inches. I hadn't seen them appear and they seemed just as surprised as I was when I flew past them – they froze where they were standing and stood blinking in my direction. I was so shaken up I had to stop for a minute or two and the three of us just remained in our respective positions staring incredulously at each other. And then . . . they were gone.

At the small town of Artesia, we headed west on Highway 82 in the direction of the Sacramento Mountains. At the tiny town of Hope we pitched our tent on the roadside town parkway since there was little traffic on the road and the town consisted only of a few houses. No sooner had we put up our tent when kids from the town surrounded us.

'Awesome bikes!' they excitedly shouted.

We soon found ourselves being invited into their homes so that we could tell them more about our adventures and explain the workings of our 'awesome-looking' bicycles. To this day I am not sure whether it was the kids who invited us for dinner or their parents but in any case we ended up having dinner with the large Whitings family.

Mr Whiting was the Minister of the nearby church in Hope and had seven children. Mrs Whiting was resting in her bed having only recently given birth to child number seven. Children ranging from ages three to thirteen and cats of various shades and colours seemed to be all over the place and the house was in total but obviously warm disarray. The fact that the Whitings had their hands full with all these children didn't stop them from being very hospitable – Mr Whiting laid two extra plates at dinner for us as if it was the most natural thing to do and we were touched by this sincere gesture. During dinner the children sat around us with open admiration and eager smiles as we described our trip so far and after dinner Nop went out with the older ones to let them try out our bikes. The rest of the children proudly displayed their toys to me – including *real* guns which they used, they told me matter-of-factly, to shoot skunks and snakes as target practice (mind you, these kids were no older than ten). And to prove it, they brought down their collection of rattlesnake skins. What could I say? I just couldn't imagine Dutch kids shooting the local ducks, seagulls and rabbits for target practice let alone being in possession of firearms!

Later in the evening we went to our other neighbour's home for tea and cake. Unlike the Whitings the Watts lived in a large meticulously kept house which used to be a hotel. They looked horrified when we told them we had just had dinner at the Whiting's home.

'Wasn't it a terrible mess there?' Mrs Watt asked us.

'Well, yes,' I answered, 'it was rather chaotic . . . .'

'And *all* those children!' she exclaimed.

We could have gone on gossiping all evening I suppose but we asked about the town of Hope instead.

'Hope used to be quite populated in the old days,' Mr Watt told us, 'but the river which used to run in these parts dried up for some reason and most people had to leave. There are only a few families left now.'

But the size of the town didn't matter to the Watts. Their

dream was to turn their house into a Bed and Breakfast for passing travellers. It sounded like a good idea. (So look out for a hotel next to the town park of Hope if any of you cyclists chance to pass by!)

After a good night's sleep, the Watts again invited us into their home the following morning for a huge authentic American breakfast consisting of pancakes, scrambled eggs, orange juice and coffee. As if that were not enough, they sent us off with home-made cookies and pecan nuts as well.

*

Cloudcroft was a ski resort located at the highest point of the pass (9,000 feet) over the Sacramento Mountains. We had been worried that the pass would be closed but fortunately there was only some residual snow along the sides of the road as we neared the top. The change in scenery as we climbed had been gradual but distinctive – we started at cacti level, moved up to junipers, from junipers to ponderosa pine and finally from ponderosa pine to log pine; and all in one climb. The descent on the west side into Alamagordo, however, was steep and quick – within half an hour we were back in the heat of the desert. Ridiculous.

The fact that the Space Shuttle had first landed at the Air Force Base in Alamagordo didn't change the fact that Alamagordo was simply a dull military town full of military personnel and army vehicles which used the nearby desert as a missile practice range. Here again the idea that the desert is a wasteland persisted . . . .

We tried a hospitality home number but the guy who answered hastily said he was on his way out. (No offence to people who volunteer their names for the Bicyclists Hospitality Homes List but I would hereby like to say that I think only real travellers who have experienced long-distance travel by bicycle should list their names - those who know what it's like at the end of a day of gruelling climbing to be given a spot to pitch a tent and to be offered a hot shower. They are the ones who understand that a

47

cyclist's needs are simple and few and would never refuse cyclists. The rest should honestly take their names *off* the list!)

It was too late to cycle further so we ended up pitching our tent in a park next to the Chamber of Commerce and spent a restless night next to the main road where the traffic never ceased.

*

The next range of mountains we had to cross were the San Andreas Mountains. We were told that Highway 70/82 passed through a missile practice range and that during such practices the roads were sometimes closed for several hours. We didn't wait around to find out when the next practice session would be and left Alamagordo first thing in the morning; because of this inconvenience we unfortunately had to skip White Sands National Monument which was right next to the missile practice range in the desert.

*

Las Cruces was definitely a university town – suddenly there were bicycles everywhere. Unlike our dusty recumbents, most of the bikes we saw were spotless racing machines ridden by mushroom-helmeted fashion-conscious riders. But bicycles they were and the sight cheered us up immensely.

We found a great bicycle shop in town where we could finally stock up on spare parts. But in addition to this luck the owner of the shop – Chuck Matthews – turned out to be a friendly and easy-going cyclist himself who immediately invited us to pitch our tent in his back yard. And in the evening, with borrowed clothes, we joined Chuck and his girl friend for dinner and later to a musical at the local university which turned out to be excellent. It had been a long time since we had 'gone out' and we thoroughly enjoyed ourselves.

*

Chuck had told us that the Black Range would be a piece of cake but he must have been Superman because I certainly didn't think so. It was a torturous, never-ending day of 66 miles before we finally reached the Percha Dam State Park in Arrey, and that was only one-third the way across the Black Mountains. I had to admit that the scenery was grand but the ascent seemed to take *forever*.

The following day we only covered 48 miles but camped on a wonderful spot next to a creek in the Gila National Forest. The only thing that bothered me in the stillness of the mountains was the occasional very unpleasant sound of hunters' shotguns going off and the barking dogs which accompanied them. I have always hated the idea of hunting down animals – especially in this age when there is ample food to be bought – but I especially detest those American hunters who shoot deer and then parade them around town on their pick-up trucks. To me they portray overgrown children who somehow have the stupid need to prove something by playing 'macho' among their buddies. The excuse for killing the graceful creatures was always the same: 'To keep the deer population down'. Right. And I presume they killed off all the natural predators because the predators were a threat and danger to man and his livestock? Yep, I've heard of that one too. It all boiled down to the usual reasoning of carnivorous people who somehow regarded humans as the most superior beings of all and who therefore felt they had the right to control all other beings.

*

The weather turned sour again as we camped in the Gila National Forest for the second time, this time south of Silver City. We had found a roadside park dotted with pine trees with a couple of other campers nearby. We managed to get water from one of them.

49

That afternoon, we actually made a campfire since our stove had conked out again and as a result our two pans were forever blackened. Nevertheless, we managed to bake some cookies. Being immensely proud of this feat, we decided to share the unique cookies with our neighbour, an elderly bearded man who looked a bit lonesome in his camper. When we approached him he invited us into his camper but once inside he took the entire batch of cookies without a word of thanks and placed them on a shelf above him. He didn't offer us coffee or anything else to drink for that matter and we quickly realised we would never get to taste our own tent-made cookies! We were furious but what could we do? We couldn't very well ask him to give them back so we sulked and made small talk with him instead. A few minutes later we were furious again – we found out he was a trapper who trapped rabbits and coyotes for their fur which he sold to a local fur dealer in Silver City. When we asked him how much he got for the fur he told us 'a few bucks'. How little value people put on animals, I thought. His attitude was enough for us to say a rude goodbye and leave him to himself again.

That evening a cold front hit us again and I was beginning to feel feverish – I was obviously catching the flu. We *had* to get down these mountains before it snowed again since our food supply was almost gone. So the next morning we loaded our bikes and headed for Lordsburg where we stocked up on food.

To get into Arizona, we were forced to take Interstate 10. There was no other road in the vicinity which went west. A few miles short of the border, a hailstorm broke out. My hands were blue and numb, and I insisted we crouch under the bushes till the hailstorm subsided, but Nop fortunately persuaded me to go on till the Inspection Station we could see a few miles further down the road.

Drenched, shivering and myself very sick, we arrived at the Inspection Station where we were greeted by a cheerful inspector who took one look at us and said: 'Training to become ducks, are you? Ha ha ha . . . .' Very funny.

Then another inspector came out, took one look at our bikes and asked: 'Did you build those recumbents yourself?' Our ears immediately stood up. What on earth was a guy who knew what recumbents were doing here in the middle of No Man's Land?

Jim Maender was his name and he made us come in so we could warm up. We were offered coffee and cake by other inspectors and Jim offered to drive us to his house (which was a few miles back into New Mexico and further south) after he got off work at midnight. He must have noticed how sick I was. We had planned to stay at a motel in the next town, but his offer sounded much better; we gladly accepted his invitation although it meant having to wait six hours. At least we were indoors!

While we whiled away the hours reading whatever magazines were lying around, a cowboy entered the room and said, 'Howdy.' 'Hi,' we answered, and returned to our reading. After a while we noticed he was looking strangely at us.

'Don't you know who I am?' he asked. Were we supposed to know the guy?

Nop and I looked at each other and said, 'No.'

I can't even remember what he said his name was, but he told us he was a famous country-and-western singer. In that case we were certain we didn't know him and 'Oh?' was all we could say with raised brows. He was apparently offended with our ignorance because he went stomping out of the place. Perhaps it was just as well we *didn't* recognize him for his fame.

The inspectors at this Station inspected fruit and plants on their way west and were very particular about fruit – Floridian oranges were prohibited in California because of some of the diseases they carried. People's cars and campers were inspected; sometimes whole cacti were found in peoples' possession which were taken into custody and placed in the room where we waited.

'You won't believe what some people bring across the border – all sorts of rare plants and hundred-year old cacti

51

as decoration for their living rooms or gardens,' Jim told us as he popped in to see how we were doing.

'The problem with these people,' he added, 'is that they are unaware that they're either ruining the desert environment or that they're bringing in diseases to other parts of the country – that's why this station is necessary.'

By midnight I was half asleep when Jim finally got off-duty; we loaded our bikes onto his pick-up truck and headed back through New Mexico to enter Arizona from the south. He was a careful and conscientious driver.

'There's a lot of nocturnal wild life out on these dirt roads when I drive home,' he told us. 'Look, there's a skunk,' he said as he slowed down to let it cross the road.

On one day we meet a trapper, the next day an environmentalist! A journey can be full of surprises.

Jim and Gloria lived in a rented house in the tiny town of Portal, which was situated next to the Chiricahua Mountains in Arizona. They rented the house from Jeanne Williams, an authoress who wrote predominantly about the southwest and who lived next door to them. We spent the next two days in their small, but comfortable home.

Portal, they told us, was a small town populated with a most interesting assortment of inhabitants: an authoress, a doctor, a traveller, a taxonomist and an artist to name a few. Jim and Gloria themselves were living in these parts because they loved the nature of the desert so much. The reason why Jim was a station inspector was because there was no other work around. He considered it boring work but felt compensated by the open desert and mountains which surrounded them. Gloria was an artist and sculptor who made jewellery based on a traditional Indian style. She too was an ardent naturalist; Jim and Gloria's combined knowledge about the flora and fauna of these parts was quite immense. This we discovered as we took a walk with them through the nearby mountains a couple of days later when Jim had a day off and the sun had come out again.

On the third day we felt we couldn't intrude any longer. Gloria worked in the confined space of one room which

52

served as living/dining and guest room and with us around she couldn't work properly. So, despite my flu, which I hadn't quite got rid of completely yet, we decided to go on.

I regretted leaving their home once we were on the road again – the wind was blowing so hard that tumble weeds (large round balls of thorned branches) were flying all over the place and we had to shout to hear each other above the sound of the howling wind. I was obviously in no state to go on under such conditions so we quickly decided to camp after only 13 miles. Thank goodness someone let us pitch our tent in her back yard.

But just as I got settled and tried to sleep off a terrible headache I had meanwhile acquired, I heard Nop talking to some people outside the yard. At first I thought I was drifting off to sleep and dreaming, but I soon realised I was hearing ... could it possibly be *Queen's* English? I couldn't resist taking a peek outside and lo and behold, there stood three ... *cyclists*? Not only were they cyclists, they were British!

They were just as surprised to see us as were were to see them. Apparently the woman who was with them had invited them to stay at her house and was leading them to it. Noticing our interest in each other she asked whether we would like to join them at her house too, which was a few miles down the road. Of course we said yes and packed up our stuff again and the five of us cycled together to the Turners' house while chatting excitedly about each other's trips.

The Turners' home was a large one-storied house with their own farmland around it. Mrs Turner assigned us all to various rooms with beds in them which must have once belonged to her grown children. She was the ideal mother to us and welcomed us all to stay for as long as we liked. This was the break I needed to get over my flu completely.

Mrs Turner was so considerate that she told us all to take a rest before dinner, and to give her all the clothes that needed washing. She certainly had a natural understanding for travellers' needs.

That evening was spent swapping stories about our respective trips; Jim, John and John had been on the road for the past four months and had already gone through seventeen states. They told us they lived on the ridiculous amount of $2 a day (we lived on five) and ate predominantly peanut butter sandwiches. They made up for their meagre diet by accepting any and all invitations from anyone to a free meal. They had been cycling in these headwinds for the last five days and had been fed up when Mrs Turner turned up and generously came to their rescue; so here they were, glad to be indoors, snug, warm and well-fed.

Mrs Turner was an ardent collector of Indian artifacts; her beautiful home was decorated with intricately woven baskets and Indian antiques. It was one of the prettiest homes we had seen so far; the dogs, cats and walls full of books made it the perfect home. But the Turners weren't without their problems. On the surface the lives of the Turners seemed idyllic, but they were farmers (who grew predominantly pumpkin and squash) and they were being hit by hard and insecure times.

'Costs are so high,' Mrs Turner told us during dinner, 'that we aren't really sure if we can keep on farming – every year the day we have to declare ourselves bankrupt seems to come nearer.'

On the second and last evening Mrs Turner invited Jim and Gloria for dinner too – Gloria and Mrs Turner were especially good friends because of their shared interest in Indian crafts. Jim and Gloria seemed surprised to find us still in their neighbourhood and were even more surprised to find three additional cyclists staying with the Turners. It was an appropriate get-together of people who were on the same wavelength and we all enjoyed the evening of good food and good talk immensely. All thanks to the generosity and hospitality of the Turners.

*

With the previous evening having been the ideal climax of

our stay at the Turners, the five of us decided to go on the following day despite the ever-unrelenting wind. At least the sun was out and I felt recuperated enough to go on. After saying sorrowful goodbyes to the dear Turners the five of us created a streamline by cycling in a line which helped break the wind. But I soon realised I wasn't used to the kind of competitive male pace these guys were going at and found myself lagging behind whenever I was at the tail of the line. It was a constant strain to keep up with the guys and one of the Johns sympathized with my predicament and told the others to slow down. The others (including Nop) were perhaps a wee bit irritated that a single female slowed the entire group down, but there wasn't anything I could do about it. I had my own limits and didn't feel the necessity to strain myself just to keep up with the males. I preferred to cycle alone in that case. In any event, I managed to keep up with them for quite some time until I ended up in the tail again and finally couldn't bridge the gap any longer and gave up. This seemed to cause an argument to erupt among the guys who were way ahead of me and when I finally caught up with them I found them sitting by the side of the road sulking. Later I was to discover that the two Johns didn't quite get along with Jim, and that there was an unfortunate crack in their relationship. It had nothing to do with me.

Fortunately they patched up their differences as we turned west (and got side winds instead of headwinds) and we arrived intact as a group, in the town of Douglas. Jim, a born diplomat, phoned a priest of an Anglican church and managed to persuade him to give us (pathetic cyclists worthy of the church's sympathy) a roof over our heads for the night.

*

The next day we headed west and because the wind was now on our sides and even occasionally on our backs we were all in a better mood. I especially enjoyed the English humour of the guys and practically laughed my way up to Bisbee (a very pleasing way to climb a pass I must say). One of the Johns (a PE teacher back home) had stuck two white paper cups onto his mushroom-like helmet and resembled an alien out of a comic strip. He was the wittiest of the three and kept cracking jokes the entire way.

The town of Bisbee was unlike any other town we had ever seen in the States so far. Narrow alleys on the hills were lined with quaint houses and pretty churches and resembled a north European town rather and an American one. The place had the air of a strongly health-and-environment-conscious community although it was also a mining town.

It was in Bisbee that we had to say goodbye to Jim, John and John. They were heading north for Tombstone while we were heading for Sierra Vista.

That afternoon, Nop and I tried out Jim's tactic and approached a Catholic church.

The young Irish priest who answered the door was kind and helpful and immediately said: 'You bet, you bet. Sure!' as we asked him whether we could stay in a church building for the night. He showed us into the school next to the church which had central heating as well as a kitchen we could use. It was perfect.

That evening it snowed; we were at 5,490 feet and were grateful to be indoors. I felt that Jim would have been proud of us. I wondered where they were that evening, and found myself missing their company already.

*

It was cold the next day but the skies were such a magnificent blue that we quickly packed up our gear and completed the climb up to the highest point of Highway 90. The snow had melted on the road, but the surrounding mountains were still covered with virgin snow and the vegetation glistened in the sunshine as if covered with jewels. It was so cold going downhill that we had to reduce our speed and every so often stop to warm our hands. I cursed myself for not having purchased gloves by now. But this was to be the last cold front we were going to experience in a long time although we didn't know it at the time.

In Sierra Vista we turned west on Highway 82 where the road undulated along ranch land with tall grass and juniper trees. We were still at an altitude around 4,000 feet and this would remain the same throughout our route in Arizona.

All the ranch land was, as usual, fenced in, with the typical unwelcoming signs of 'Keep Out' and 'Posted'. But occasionally we found a gate for ranchers which we could easily open. We would then enter through it, quickly locate an inconspicuous spot and camp on it. This we did in the evening after Bisbee – it was nice to camp again in our own cosy tent, away from people and the sound of traffic. As we closed the ranch gate behind us the following morning, a cowboy in a pick-up truck drove up to where we were but seeing that we were leaving didn't say a word and drove away.

We passed antelope grazing on the grasslands as we cycled to the town of Sonoita where we decided to have coffee at the local cafe. As we parked our bikes outside, a man came out and became very enthusiastic about our bicycles and our trip. He invited us to join a group of people who, he told us, belonged to a hiking club of Sonoita. After a hike it was the custom for the group to get together at this cafe and have lunch.

The others weren't too excited about us: 'How nice . . . ,' they answered, when Joel Brecheen told them excitedly that we had travelled 2,500 miles from Texas. You can always tell when people are indifferent. They usually make one enthusiastic remark and then change the subject to a more local matter.

But their indifference wasn't important; Joel kept asking us questions and insisted we 'Come stay with him and his wife Anne.' We had only cycled 16 miles that day, but he insisted.

'We live smack in the middle of the Coronado National

Forest,' Joel said, 'and have a spare room you could use. I only have to give a short tennis lesson this afternoon at the local high school, but we can load your bikes on the pick-up truck and go together!'

He was so lively and sounded so interesting (he told us he was a poet too), we decided to join him. The four of us squeezed into the pick-up truck and Anne drove. These were people who obviously had a passion for the southwest.

'We looked for the ideal place to live in for a *long* time,' Anne told us, 'and when we found this place, we knew this was it. We've never once regretted moving here. Isn't it beautiful?'

And so it was. They told us that developers had recently come sniffing around for land to build some industry or another on but the local population literally kicked them out. I liked that.

Nogales, where we were heading for, was a town further south on Highway 82 which passed through forest land the entire way. I could see why they loved the area.

In Nogales we watched Joel give an enthusiastic tennis lesson to the high school kids. He had been asked to do this by the local PE teacher, but apparently the PE teacher had done so on his own initiative for, no sooner had the lesson begun than an authoritative secretary of the school came up to the teacher and reprimanded him for not getting permission. But Joel went on with the lesson anyway.

Later, he said: 'You know what I call people like that? Beauro*cats*. I can't stand them. The moment some people have authority they just take advantage of it, or else they think it's their duty to make sure everything goes by the book. Ugh! I wrote a poem about them, I'll show it to you when we get home.'

After the tennis lesson, we visited a friend of theirs who was a retired cop and who now raised bees for honey. His house was perched on a menacingly steep hill.

Joel, who was driving, said laughingly, 'Every time I visit him I'm never sure whether the car will make it or not.' But somehow it did.

The house was tastefully decorated and there was a huge collection of Indian spearheads which the friend said he had found himself. The Brecheens were very fond of this man who was very content with his life and his bees.

'I don't have to protect my house from Mexicans who cross the border,' he told us, 'the bees do the job. I tell you, Mexicans won't come *near* this place!'

To get to the Brecheens' home, we backtracked to Sonoita, and from there it was almost 25 miles of dirt road which rose and dipped the entire way.

'Sometimes there are flash floods in the summer and these roads are impassable at the dips,' Anne said.

'How do you get to town then?' I asked.

'We don't,' they chorused.

Their house was indeed in the middle of the forest; the nearest neighbour lived several miles away. It was a great big wooden house with a wide verandah on the second floor. Horses roamed around outside, and it was intensely still. For firewood they collected dead tree trunks in the vicinity of their house which were plentiful. We took a walk up the hill behind their house which was full of juniper trees and manzanita bushes – a curious bush with maroon-red bark. A glance at the landscape was so fulfilling that words were unnecessary.

Back in the house we talked books; the moment we asked which books they recommended about the US, Anne, who had been otherwise quiet most of the day, lit up like a Christmas tree. No wonder, she was a librarian at a local school! Joel sold us his poetry book at a reduced price. *Peregrine Passage*, he had called it, and in it I found a small poem about the desert which summed it up nicely in just a few well-chosen words:

> *Desert*
> *Of this space, rigid angular,*
> *your calm,*
> *let me remember.*

59

*

We followed Highway 83 – a very scenic ride along the Coronado National Forest. But unfortunately it was spoiled when we got to the junction where the road met Interstate 10 which we had to follow to get to Tucson. With a sigh, we entered the city. Trafficwise it was worse than the map suggested. And this despite the presence of quite a number of bicyclists. We found the number of Joe and Charlotte Shields who were listed on the Hospitality Home List and who didn't hesitate to invite us to their home when we phoned them. They lived in a suburb on the east side of town with their granddaughter, grandson-in-law and great grandchild. They both worked even at their age because their granddaughter had become pregnant at the age of sixteen and her husband couldn't support her. The Shields didn't hide their resentment about this.

The Shields had done some extensive travelling on a tandem when they were younger – in their seventies that is – and they showed us a thick scrap book they had put together in memory of their travels. We had to admire their adventurous spirit and hoped for them that they could travel again soon – that is, as soon as their grandchildren finally got on their own feet.

The following day we made a loop around the northern part of Tucson where Saguaro National Monument was located. Here we saw thousands of the dignified Saguaro Cacti, some reaching dazzling heights. Once again in a preserve, we felt as free as the wildlife in them; we 'ooohed' and 'aaahed' pointing to the diversely shaped saguaros which began to resemble certain human movements.

'Look, that one looks like he's jogging; and that one, a policeman directing traffic!' and so on.

We visited the desert museum (which Gloria had recommended) which contained a variety of snakes confined to little glass cases. Most of them seemed to be fast asleep. Although I was glad to be able to take a close look at them (for future identification and warnings!) I couldn't wish even reptiles such a life of confinement – like visits to all zoos, I left feeling sorry for the plight of the animals.

The Shields had phoned a friend of theirs in Tucson, Suzanne Couvrette, who agreed to let us stay. She interviewed us that evening for a local bicycle club magazine.

*

The Papago Indian Reservation was the first Indian Reservation we were to cycle through. People always made generalisations about Indian Reservations: 'The Indians are addicted to alcohol, they're all unemployed, dangerous drivers, hate the whites, are all on welfare' etc. . . etc. . . and many Americans would rather detour hundreds of miles to avoid having to go through a reservation. It all sounded silly to us. Highway 86, the only paved highway which went from east to west in the reservation, passed through pure Arizona desert, and there was little habitation and no industry along the way. We were quite content about that; the only disturbing sites were the piles of huge beer bottles alongside the road and the number of crosses with flowers on them, which, if they did signify traffic accidents, were uncomfortably numerous. Perhaps the Indians' addiction to alcohol was true . . . ?

'There *is* a drinking problem here,' the pastor of the church in the town of Sells told us, 'a very *big* problem.'

We had approached a church on the reservation since we didn't know how the Indians would take to cyclists camping on their land. The pastor let us use an empty building next to his house, and after we had had our dinner, we dropped by to talk to him.

'You noticed the number of crosses along the side of the road coming up here?' he asked us. We said we had. 'Well, after someone dies in a traffic accident the crosses are placed there by the Indians here who are called Sonoran Catholics. When there are a number of crosses in a single place it means several people died there. The problem isn't

61

only a drinking problem, but also a drinking and *driving* problem. The government prohibits the Indians from having liquor stores on the reservations; as a result, there are bars and liquor stores right outside the reservations, so the Indians go there, get drunk, and then drive home.'

He went on to say that the Indians on this reservation traditionally, according to a ritual, got drunk once a year and that it was this ritual which made drinking something religious and, therefore, not shameful to them. I wondered about that . . . ; in a booklet about the Papago and Pima Indians I had bought at a Visitor Centre somewhere, I read that '. . . rain-making ceremonies were the most important of all . . . to make rain magic, the Papago make a liquor from the fruit of the giant cactus. The liquor was brewed with singing and ceremony and the men drank it, filling themselves with moisture as they wished the earth to be filled . . . this drinking is not a matter of pleasure but a very solemn ceremony.'

If this were true, then alcohol was not introduced to these Indians by the whites. So why prohibit it on the reservation? I sometimes found the attitude of the government towards the Indians to be exasperatingly patronising; must they forever dictate how and where and under what conditions the Indians must live? Yet I also felt that the Indians should also get back on their feet and stick to their traditions more adamantly instead of crying about how history has turned against them. (We later would come across a small Indian Reservation somewhere in the north where the Indians, who had been driven off their land and placed on a reservation forcibly, had fought against the injustice by *buying* back their own land and moving back to their original homes!)

*

Right outside the Indian Reservation was the small community of Why. Why it was called Why, I don't know. We camped at the Coyote Howl's Park for the reasonable fee of $3.60; we were in desperate need of a shower after a dusty 66 miles from Sells. People we met on the campground couldn't believe we had survived *cycling* through the Indian Reservation. What biased preconceptions people sometimes had!

Ahhh . . . another wonderful national park. We spent two days camping and hiking through Organ Pipe Cactus National Monument just south of Why. Spring was already in the air in the Sonoran Desert, and flowers were blooming everywhere. We camped in the wild, and we felt snug and protected amidst the giant saguaro guardians, and the only sounds we heard were those of birds.

The Ajo Mountain Drive was a dirt-road loop of the southeastern part of the park, but it was 21 miles long, so we hitchhiked to the beginning of the Estes Canyon trail. A couple from San Diego, in a jeep, gave us a ride. We weren't used to the enclosure of a car anymore and felt like we were suffocating. Worse, the scenery just passed by us without us being able to smell, see nor feel it. And in addition to that horror, the yuppie couple *reeked* of the city. They had taken a couple of days off work to see the park, but they only spent two hours in it of which only five minutes were spent outside the car when we stopped at an overlook. Even then the scenery didn't matter to them. Another car was parked at the same overlook which happened to contain fellow – San Diegoans.

'You're from San Diego *too*? Well, what do you know! What parts are *you* from? No! We must be practically neighbours!'

Without having taken one look at the surroundings, they got back into the car and looked disdainfully at us as they drove on – perhaps we didn't look civilised enough with our burnt skin, chapped lips and faded clothes? We were relieved to get out of the car and go on our hike. It had been an effort to thank them for the ride.

We climbed up to what was called 'Bull's Pasture' and were rewarded by a magnificent view of the land below us spreading far and wide under the blue sky. We could have sat there forever, gazing at the rugged landscape and enjoying the emptiness and the peacefulness of it all.

*

Highway 85 which started at the southern tip of Organ Pipe Cactus National Monument, went on north till it hit Interstate 10, and the entire trip to the junction was beautiful and quiet. Then we were once again on the awful Interstate which shot through the rest of the state like an arrow; it was boring and wide and contained monstrous-looking vehicles which should never have been invented. The traffic drove on monotonously by us, as we cycled on and on, oblivious to the distance we were covering. And just as we thought we would fall asleep any moment if we didn't stop, we saw in the distance what appeared to be a dog sitting peacefully on the shoulder of the road. Next to him was parked a bicycle, but no cyclist. Were we hallucinating? But no, it was a golden retriever all right and it was sitting on the shoulder as we had seen it from afar. It wagged its tail as we approached but otherwise it didn't move. Then, a guy came jogging across the Interstate.

'Hi,' he said.

'Hi,' we answered, but felt like scolding him instead. 'Weren't you afraid your dog would follow you across the road?'

'Uh-uh. He wouldn't do that. He does exactly as I say.'

'Where are you heading?'

'San Diego. I came from Phoenix. This is my first trip by bike.'

Adam was only seventeen and wanted to see what San Diego was like. So he had simply packed a backpack (mainly with dog food), bought himself a mountain bike (had only oil for maintenance), and without knowing he'd be crossing the desert, put his dog 'Toe-cutter' in a box behind him and took off.

'Man, the first night we were *so* thirsty I thought we'd die!' he said, 'And so the next day I bought these jerry cans and filled them with water.' The jerry cans dangled from the side of Toe-cutter's seat.'

'What were you doing on the other side of the Interstate?' Nop asked him.

'Oh, I was taking pictures of some wild flowers.'

We told him we'd be camping somewhere off the Interstate at the next exit and that he was welcome to join us.

The map said Sentinel but it wasn't much of a town – a gas station and one house which had a campground at the back. So we camped there and waited for Adam and Toe-cutter, who joined us a while later. Toe-cutter and Adam were inseparable; he was right about how Toe-cutter listened to him.

When the owner of the campground told Adam to keep the dog chained, he whistled to Toe-cutter and said: 'Bring your leash, Toe-cutter,' and the dog grabbed the leash in his mouth and brought it! Adam loved his dog; he told us that he thought about going abroad but decided not to when he found out Toe-cutter would have to go through quarantine and that they couldn't travel together.

Adam fed his dog first before thinking about food himself. We offered him dinner, but he declined saying he only ate out of cans.

That night, as we were sleeping, we were rudely awakened by a truck which had driven in and made a lot of noise first braking and then taking off again. When we zipped open the tent the following morning, we found a mountain of oranges in front of our tent! The truck must have braked too fast, causing the oranges to tumble over. So before the owner of the campground awoke, we gathered as many oranges as our trailer could carry, and Adam filled his backpack too (at least he ate fresh fruit).

As we were about to leave, the owner of the gas station offered us more oranges; we couldn't refuse since she didn't know we had already taken our fill.

Adam had told us he usually cycled only thirty miles a day, so we parted at Sentinel. We continued on boring

Interstate 10. But it didn't stay boring all day; after cycling for about 44 miles and stopping at a rest area, as we continued on the shoulder of the Interstate, an enclosed pick-up truck pulling a long camper passed us but then started to behave very strangely. At first I thought the driver was drunk because the camper at the back started to swerve from left to right; but it continued to do so until it was fish-tailing uncontrollably; the driver then made the mistake of braking whereby both car and trailer swerved off the road directly in front of us, toppled over a couple of times and ended up on its side.

The camper was smashed to pieces, but at the moment of impact a dog managed to jump out safely, although it was barking pathetically, presumably from shock. We parked our bikes and ran to the truck to see if anyone was hurt. The driver was an elderly woman with curlers in her hair – the curlers were full of glass, But she wasn't hurt.

We helped her out, and as soon as she saw the wreck she became hysterical and started to cry, 'Oh my God! Oh my God!'

Her husband also came out unhurt except for a cut on his head and started to walk around the mess with a half-smile on his face. He was in some kind of daze. No sooner had this happened than a crowd gathered and the police came and we were told to wait as witnesses. We waited in the ninety degree heat for *four* hours during which time others began helping the couple collect the things which had survived the crash. The woman in curlers remained hysterical and told the police in tears that she was driving on the right side of the road when she saw us; she then moved to the left too abruptly when the trailer started to fishtail. She made it sound like it had been all our fault.

Finally, after dehydration was beginning to set in, we told the police what we had seen and were allowed to go. After 13 miles we got off the road and camped in the bush, too shaken up and tired to go any further.

Some of the events of our journey were becoming too much for me. That evening I started writing a journal.

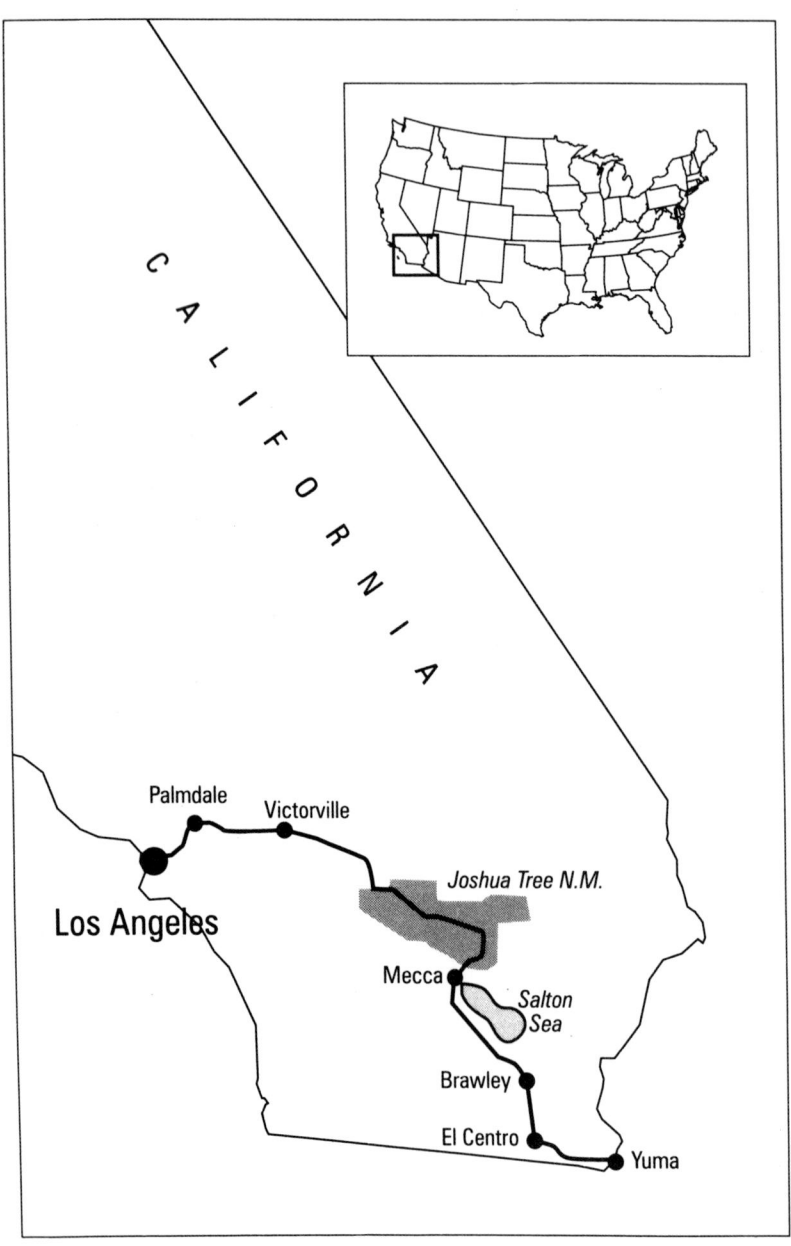

HEADING WEST

It was hot and windy as we continued on Interstate 10, crossing the Colorado River to enter California at the town of Winterhaven where we tried to find a map of California but without success. We went back onto the Interstate despite signs prohibiting bicyclists and in no time at all we were stopped by a black cop who very politely told us that we had to get off the interstate.

'Sorry, no bicycles allowed on the interstate here,' he said.

'But there is no other road for us to take,' Nop argued.

'If you get off at the next exit, Sir, you will find a frontage road which runs parallel to the interstate.'

'Does the frontage road run parallel to the interstate the whole way?' I asked.

'No. The frontage road will continue for approximately three miles, then you'll have to cross over the interstate on an overpass to get to the frontage road which will continue on the other side. Four miles further up the road you'll find a sign which will state that bicyclists are allowed on the interstate again. There you go back onto the interstate and five miles later you'll see a sign telling cyclists to exit where you'll find another frontage road which you can take . . . .'

Right.

*

About sixteen miles into California we suddenly entered a

landscape of pure sand dunes. There were some campers at the base of the dunes who told us we could camp there for free. All of them seemed to camp in the dunes for the weekend in order to ride their ATCs – a kind of three-wheeled motorcycle with fat tyres – up and down the sandy slopes. Even the smallest of children had ATCs to match their size – part of their parent's idea of education I suppose. The buzzing ATCs continued on until it was too dark to see anything any more.

*

The next hot day was spent figuring out where the damn frontage road started, where it ended and on which side of the interstate it was, if it was there at all. At one point the surface of the road was in such bad disrepair that the asphalt was cracked open and weeds had taken control. Nice to know that nature can take over asphalt after all, but it was hell riding it. The road looked like it hadn't been maintained since the last earthquake hit. We were no longer even sure it *was* a frontage road but we couldn't be bothered about where we were. It was just too hot. We drowsily went on in the direction of Holtville, the next little dot on our map, where we were hoping for some shade and cold drinks.

But before we could reach Holtville, we spotted a couple actually taking a *walk* on the road ahead of us. Were we hallucinating, was it a mirage? Why on earth would anyone take a walk in this heat, I wondered, as we passed the elderly couple and mumbled a sleepy 'hello'.

'Hey, Hollanders!' the man shouted a few moments later. We screeched to a halt and looked back. Of course! Who else would be out in this heat for the sake of its warmth but Dutchmen!

Hubert and Anne Huizinga – Dutch Canadians – had noticed the NL stickers on our trailer. They bombarded us with questions the moment we stopped. It took us a while to switch to Dutch after all the months we had communicated together in English, and it was even harder to understand Hubert who spoke eastern Dutch with a Canadian accent! They told us they were camping at Hot Springs, a free campground up the road and that we should join them. So we went ahead and pitched our tent next to their camper and refreshed ourselves in the hot springs which gave the campground its name.

The Huizingas treated us like long-lost children and fed us with loads of food and good (Dutch) coffee. They lived in Winnepeg but, like many retired people from the north who were either sick of ploughing the snow year after year or suffered from arthritis or rheumatism, migrated south every winter. They always came to this particular area because of the guaranteed sunshine, the free campground (how Dutch can you get!), and of course, because of the area's accessibility to much of the spectacular scenery found in the southwest. But they also spoke about Canada with a passion.

'It's so spacious and beautiful in Canada,' Anne said, 'I could never live in the Netherlands again.'

The Huizingas were one of the many couples who immigrated abroad after the Second World War when opportunities for the then large families in the Netherlands were extremely limited. There was a large influx of Dutch immigrants to Canada, New Zealand, South Africa and Australia at the time and, like many first generation immigrants, the Huizingas still spoke Dutch. Hubert, in particular, still felt an old affinity for the Netherlands and returned regularly to visit his relatives. But Anne, on the other hand, had only returned once and never wanted to return again, finding the Netherlands too crowded after Canada.

'It's not only the physical crowdedness of the place,' she complained, 'I noticed that these days everything is so regulated; you need ninety-nine different diplomas in Holland before you're qualified to do *anything*! At least in Canada it's what you're *capable* of doing that counts and not the kind of papers you have.'

71

She was right in a way but her arguments seemed a bit simplistic so I came to the defence of our little country and countered that, from what she was saying, I got the impression that in Canada, as in the US, it was 'the survival of the fittest' so that if you happen *not* to be capable you simply lose out in society. I found it hard to dismiss a country like the Netherlands which has attained one of the best social welfare systems in the world and, despite the exploitation of the system by a minority, gives the weak and disabled a chance to survive. And to myself I added, 'Tell me which society *isn't* drowning in its own bureaucracy?'

Anne's attitude was actually quite a common trait I found among immigrants from small European countries to large countries such as Canada, the US and Australia. I suppose one couldn't blame them – I had to admit that when we first experienced the great expanses of the southwest in the US we could easily sympathize with their feelings of independence, freedom and the breathing space such a large country offered. But then again, the thought that a car would be almost essential to live in a country where the distances were so huge was more than enough to deter us from wanting to settle in the US, much as the country had to offer in terms of opportunities, spaciousness and wilderness (although we didn't come to this conclusion until the end of our journey).

*

Despite our differences on the matter of the ideal country to live in, we would never forget the hospitality and the company of the Huizingas who, even after we parted, continued to write to us to find out how we were progressing (Hubert even went so far as to write to our parents personally to reassure them of our whereabouts and safety).

Throughout our travels in the US, Hubert became a fatherly figure to us and always ended his many extensive letters to us with the reassuring words 'if you are *ever* in trouble, just phone us'. And we knew he meant it.

Our short encounter with the Huizingas turned into an everlasting friendship which didn't wane even after we returned to the Netherlands. To this day we still correspond regularly with Hubert. Sadly, Anne passed away a few years after our first encounter in Hot Springs, leaving Hubert to struggle through life on his own.

*

I couldn't imagine what the desert was like in the peak of the summer. It was only January and yet so terribly hot that I was beginning to develop blisters on my legs despite the sun cream I kept smearing on.

From Holtville we headed north on Highway 86. We had our first experience of having to share the road with Los Angelites out on their Sunday drive (although 'Sunday race' would have been more appropriate!) Motorcycles and cars alike drove by at such high speeds and with such recklessness that one would think they were carrying dying passengers to the nearest hospital. They certainly risked *sending* people to hospital.

We got off the road at Salton City and found our way to the shore of Salton Sea, a great expanse of salty water in the middle of the Mojave desert just south of Joshua Tree National Park. We decided it was a good spot for a two-day break and pitched our tent as far from the last camper on the gravel pier overlooking the water as possible. Gulls were everywhere, chasing each other in flight and fighting over morsels of food right in front of our tent. It was an ideal spot.

Ideal until the evening that is, when our peace was disrupted by the ever-growing line of campers and trailers parking on the pier. Finally the line reached our isolated spot and a group of yuppies parked right next to us, placed their foldable chairs in front of their camper and started to exchange complaints about their respective jobs and drown their problems with hard liquor. Maybe it was their way of relaxing in the weekend before returning to the city and to the jobs they despised. But it wasn't their gloomy talk which irritated us; it was the fact that despite the full moon they had to switch on a generator to keep a single light bulb in their camper going until they finally went to bed.

Fortunately for us the next day was Monday and most yuppies returned to their lives and jobs in the city – we were left to laze contentedly in our tent and enjoy the racket the seagulls were making again. And that evening we were treated to a glorious rise of the moon above the water in front of us as the sun went down behind us; the sky turned deep purple and the moon was a huge yellow ball which cast its long rays on the water. And at this most magnificent moment an entire flock of pelicans which had been resting on the water in the moon's reflection took off in perfect formation and flew across the moonlit horizon in a single snake-like line.

*

The road continuing north was congested with trucks that had diverted to our highway because of construction on Route 51. The drivers of these monsters drove like maniacs deliberately out to kill us, passing us with only inches to spare. Fortunately, we turned east at a town called Mecca, whoever gave it *that* name.

We passed irrigated, agricultural land used for growing grapefruit, oranges, dates and grapes. Thousands of ripe dates were lying under the trees begging to be eaten, so Nop went to gather a bagful while I kept watch. They were sweet and delicious and gave us instant energy as we started the long climb up to Joshua Tree National Park's entrance. There wasn't a tree in sight and it was unbearably hot – it must have been close to 100° Fahrenheit. The only shade we found was behind the brick park entrance. But it was shade, nevertheless, and there we conserved our energy and water by taking a short nap until the worst of the heat was over and we could cycle again.

Construction was going on in the park itself, and the eight mile climb up the unpaved road was both frustrating and very tiring. By the time we got to the Visitor's Centre we were both in a foul mood and started to argue about where to camp. I wanted to camp on the campground, but Nop refused: 'I'm not paying $5 when they don't even have showers!' he said stubbornly. He wanted to camp on an arroyo in Cottonwood Spring.

'Suppose it rains?' I argued, 'An arroyo can turn into a river!'

He looked at me as if I was an imbecile: 'Does it look like it's going to *rain* to you?'

It was beginning to get dark, so I grudgingly followed Nop down the trail and helped set up camp. He was right about one thing in the end: it didn't rain.

As the name implied, Cottonwood Spring was dotted with cottonwood trees (usually a welcoming sign of a stream or river in the desert) and Californian fan palm trees which had apparently been planted by miners in the late nineteenth century. The place used to be a popular stopover for travellers because of the available water, but today we were its only occupants and the silence was overwhelming.

In the morning we were awakened to the pleasant chatter of birds. We left at 7 a.m., hoping to make use of the cooler morning hours. It was a long descent into the Pinto Basin, a region of arid desert with dry rugged mountains surrounding it, and then a hot, painful climb up again. Upon passing 4,000 feet, Joshua trees started to appear, their numbers increasing as we gained altitude. The Joshua Tree (*Yucca Brevifolia*) belongs to the Agave family and is said to have acquired its name from the Mormons who were on their way to California. The Mormons had encountered these trees in Nevada and, because they thought the branches resembled the arms of Joshua beckoning them to go farther west, they gave the trees the name Joshua. Looking like a cross between a tree and a cactus these trees are endemic to the higher elevations of the Mojave desert which spreads itself across parts of California, Arizona, Utah and Nevada. Some had slight stumps with single branches whereas others were truly imposing trees with a multitude of branches, but it was the magnificent backdrop of the plain and arid hills which made them stick out so grandly.

We were happy to be in a national park again. National parks are the only places in the US which are devoid of heavy traffic (except in certain parks in certain seasons), electricity poles, billboard signs and (thank heaven) the ugly, gaudy towns consisting of a gas station and several fast-food joints of which we were beginning to get tired of in this country.

Here we could let our imaginations run wild; we could dream about how this vast continent must have once been before the advent of industry (including the invention of the automobile), development, pollution and overpopulation. The Mojave desert had a rugged beauty of its own; it was its harshness I loved best – the desert had a way of putting man in his proper place.

Jumbo Rocks was a cluster of enormous rocks; the spaces between the rocks were decorated with the lovely Joshua Trees which offered shade, comfort and privacy to campers, birds and squirrles. We set up camp next to a Joshua Tree which was occupied by an antelope ground squirrel scurrying up and down the tree for its last-minute shopping before settling down for the night, and several cactus wrens who hopped gaily from branch to branch chatting noisily with one another about . . . the day's events? None of them took any notice of us, their neighbours for the night. We were happy as can be on the so-called 'primitive camp site' where no facilities like flush-toilets or water was available. It was just the jumbo rocks and us.

In the late afternoon, as the sun hit the trees and cast long shadows on this fairyland, we climbed onto the rocks and took some aerial photographs with a kite before the wind died down completely.

*

The following day we cycled a record 100 miles. This feat was accomplished partly because there was no water between Joshua Tree and Lucern Valley and partly because deep inside us we were eager to hear from home – we had given a friend's address in LA for mail. Perhaps we also wanted to get the visit to the *big city* over with as soon as possible – after the peace and quiet of the desert the past two months, we weren't all that excited about having to pass through a sprawled-out polluted megalopolis like LA.

To get to the coast, we first had to cross the mountains of Angeles National Forest which rise to about 5,000 feet. We spent our last night under the stars in the mountains only some 38 miles from the city, yet incredibly enough, we heard the sounds of barking coyotes and their pups all through the night.

*

We couldn't see a thing when we reached the highest point on the road before descending into LA the next morning.

I said, 'Look at that smog Nop, you can't even *see* the city!'

'Michèle . . .' Nop said with a sigh, 'it's not smog, it's *fog!*'

*

We descended swiftly down the mountains and were soaked by the time we reached the outskirts of LA. We passed a cyclist coming up the other way who cheerfully waved to us – it was only after we waved back and passed him that we realised the man only had one leg.

*

Actually we found LA not too bad for cycling. We bought a

detailed map of the city and simply followed the suburbs. Our eyes feasted on the proliferation of subtropical plants and flowers in the gardens and parks lining the road. We hadn't seen so much green vegetation for so many months that it came rather as a 'vegetation shock'. The climate was different too – the humidity immediately hit us like a damp cloth and we were soon drenched in perspiration which stuck to us like glue the entire ride to my friend's home in Encino.

*

Ellen was one of my oldest bosom friends from Japan where we had shared the uncertain years of puberty together in the same neighbourhood. She now lived with her husband, Fred, in what was locally called 'The Valley' where they had started a thriving gold business only a year ago. Having one's own business in LA meant cutthroat competition and hard work and it took us a few days to get used to their rather hectic way of life and understand just what it was they were trying to achieve in their lives.

Fred's day started at five a.m. every day because he had to be in his office in time for the opening of the gold market in New York and he only returned home late at night. Ellen had her own department in the office and dealt mainly in gold coins from China with panda bear engravings on them. But it wasn't only the office which took up most of their time; both Ellen and Fred participated in many coin shows all over the world so they were away a lot of the time as well. It was a life I couldn't understand at the time yet I found myself also in a few years later (although I eventually put an end to it).

Despite their busy schedules, however, Ellen tried to make some time for us, meeting us for lunch and taking us out to dinner most nights at her own expense. Her younger sister, Karin, who lived in San Francisco, was also on a visit, so the three of us did a lot of chatting and reminiscing about 'the old days' in Japan. For the next ten days or so in LA, we reorganised our possessions, sorted out the slides we had taken so far and simply enjoyed what we considered a well-deserved break from the rigorous three-month-old journey during which we had covered some 3,000 miles.

We also had a chance to catch up on mail – there was sad news from home; our dog, Happy, whom we had left in the care of my mother had meanwhile died at the age of fifteen. The news broke my heart and I cried in the bathroom as I read the sad news from my mother.

*

We now knew we had to get rid of the trailer – it was too cumbersome and heavy and it wasn't fair on Nop who did all the pulling. So we decided to switch to two sets of panniers instead so that we could distribute the weight more evenly between the two of us. We sent home several packages containing bulky clothing, books and maps and half of the kitchenware we never used. We were now down to the basic necessities. It was a good thing we did this when we did it because the *real* mountain-climbing was yet to come. Nop made aluminium racks on the front wheels so that we could each take two two-litre plastic bottles for water. We also made an invaluable discovery at a nearby bicycle store – thorn-proof inner tubes for our tyres – which, we discovered, could withstand glass and thorns alike as long as the outer tyre was changed before it became worn out. This 'wonder' tube proved itself by lasting all the way from LA to New York! (For sale in K-Marts as well).

*

While we were reorganising our gear Ellen's mother also came for a visit and the house was beginning to get crowded. We could feel that with all these people around Fred and Ellen couldn't relax in their own home after a tiring day's work and it was beginning to take its toll on their nerves. I soon found this out when one day, wanting to do something in return for their generous hospitality I made the foolish mistake of cleaning up the house, including a room containing Fred's prized collection of Beatles memorabilia (which, despite its worth to him, was in total disarray). I was severely reprimanded by Ellen who became furious when she returned from work and saw what I had done. Apparently Fred didn't allow *anyone* to touch the stuff.

The only thing I could do was to suggest to Ellen that we put it back in disorder and hope Fred wouldn't notice. This we did and fortunately ended up laughing about the whole thing as we threw the last magazine on top of the disorderly pile and became friends once more. We certainly were reliving our teenage years.

But the incident did somewhat sour our otherwise pleasant stay and although it had been my own silly fault perhaps it had been a cue for us to get moving again . . . .

*

We made one more stopover on the other side of LA in Hollywood, where another old friend of mine lived. Greyland was an old roommate of my brother in Japan and had remained a friend of the family ever since. He was an artist as well as a very talented musician, but to make ends meet he had to work as a security guard on a university campus. He lived with a Japanese roommate, Hideki, in a rather small flat, but didn't mind us camping on the floor.

Greyland had a curious background. He was from a large black family in Detroit but when he was in his twenties he one day decided he wanted to go to Japan and simply took off, leaving his family and friends in Detroit flabbergasted. In Japan he somehow managed to enrol as a student at Sophia University in Tokyo where he met my brother. Chaotic as he was, he was always short of money and never seemed to have a proper visa for Japan so he ended up coming to Seoul, Korea, in order to be able to re-enter Japan on a student visa. It was in Seoul that he met the rest of our family. My father took an immediate liking to Greyland who was always hilariously funny and he soon became a 'mascot' of our family.

While his visa was being processed, he took to walking the streets of Seoul on his own, always returning half a day later to spill out his experiences in great humorous detail to us. He stayed with us for several weeks and when the time came for him to return to Japan we were all very saddened and the house suddenly became empty without his presence.

I warned Nop about Greyland's eccentricities, but I had nothing to fear – Nop liked him as soon as he met him and we certainly spent a lot of time laughing during our stay in Hollywood. I was glad to see he hadn't changed one bit.

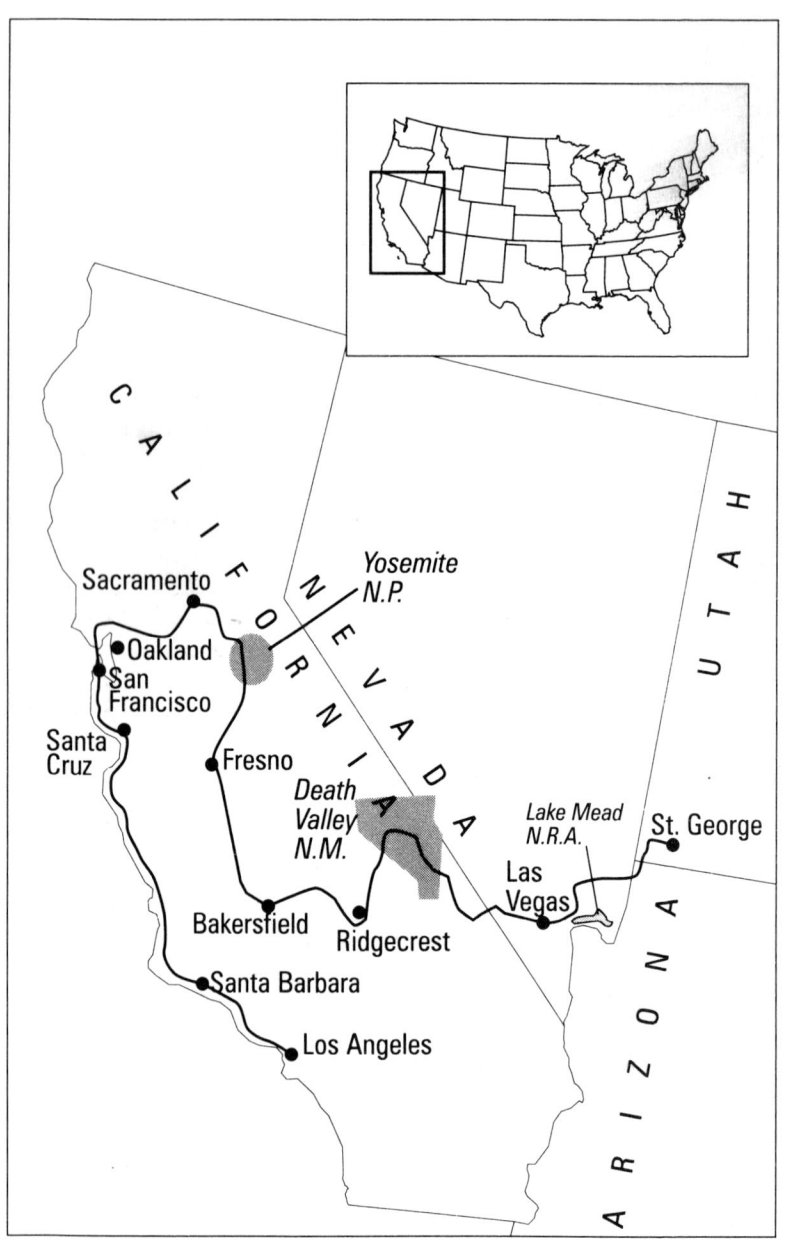

GOLD SEEKERS

The Pacific Coast Highway was to be a fabulous stretch of cycling despite some of the tortuous climbs along the way. As we finally put Los Angeles behind us, the hair-raising congestion lessened and we were soon enjoying the blue Pacific Ocean to our left and emerald green hills with carpets of yellow flowers to our right. We cycled past the pleasant town of Ventura which was full of bicyclists and had a boulevard along the seaside. This reminded us of our home town of Scheveningen, which is a seaside resort. Only here, a charming wooden pier jutted out to sea, in contrast to the ugly concrete structure I have always disapproved of back home.

As we were nearing Santa Barbara after a number of steep climbs we suddenly found a blond cyclist pedalling next to us, saying, 'Hey, did you two know there's a storm coming?'

We certainly did not and could not imagine it since it was great weather so far. But he persisted and said, 'It might be a bad one – they're even expecting tornados. Why don't you come and stay at my place in Isla Vista till it blows over?'

Before we could give him a proper answer he said, 'Ask for Simon's place in Isla Vista – I live near the local Co-op,' and off he went as fast as he had appeared.

I thought it was a rather curious way of being invited into someone's home, but on the other hand we certainly didn't want to get stuck in a storm by the sea. We followed a number of bicycle paths – yes, *bicycle paths* – to the town of Isla Vista as he had suggested. Isla Vista turned out to be a small town located right next to the campus of the University of Santa Barbara. It was a quaint town and rather European I must add – students were sitting on cafe terraces enjoying the weather (which was still fine) and the town was compact so that everything was a walkable or cyclable distance – a wondeful relief after sprawled-out LA.

We found Simon, the cyclist who had invited us. He turned out to be British although he looked more like a stereotype Californian beach bum to me – tall, bulging biceps, tanned, blond and baby-faced. He told us he was an 'illegal' and had been so for the past six years. New laws about to be passed in the US would allow illegals who have been in the States for more than five years to become American citizens. He was counting on it and was certainly adamant about never wanting to return to Great Britain again.

'Why should I go back to rain?' he said, as he fed us home-made tortillas with a spicy red sauce he called 'Simon's Salsa'.

'California has everything – sun, sea, mountains, desert. It's the perfect place to live,' he insisted.

Yep, and his view was most likely shared by the rest of the 23 million inhabitants of the State. If they discover something beautiful, humans have the habit of overrunning and ruining it. But if I was being critical, I wasn't being fair. Simon was obviously not in California to suck the blood out of the State like many entrepreneurs were doing. His needs seemed to be simple and few and he had respect for the nature the State offered. There was nothing wrong with him wanting to live in a mild climate with accessible and varied nature around him. Perhaps if more Californians shared Simon's way of life the cities wouldn't be such a horrid mess
. . . .

Simon shared the apartment with three students from the University of Santa Barbara although Simon himself wasn't a student.

'What do you do?' Nop asked him out of curiosity.

'I play,' he answered with a beach boy grin. We both raised our eyebrows. 'Play?' I asked.

'I work part-time at a bicycle shop in town, sometimes I'm a referee for the local soccer team, I help out at the local Co-op. I go avocado hunting and sell whatever I can't eat myself, I go and collect my own drinking water from the mountain after it rains – it's great water by the way!' he explained.

In other words, he lived a carefree life and enjoyed himself. We could understand that. Simon had also done some extensive travelling through the US by bicycle but had inevitably returned to California.

'No place beats California,' he repeated. He now rode a flashy, yellow, lightweight racing bike which had aero-dynamic bright yellow discs covering the wheels. What with a matching yellow shirt and glistening black bicycle pants he certainly looked like someone out of the year 3000.

*

Isla Vista had the pleasant atmosphere of a laid-back Californian student town where everyone either surfed or bicycled and seemed to be generally health- and environment-conscious. We found the Co-op nearby which offered a wide range of health foods including peanuts which clients could machine-grind into delicious fresh peanut butter themselves. We also found a second-hand bookstore and spent half a day browsing, stocking up with reading for the road.

We ended up staying at Simon's place for three nights. As he had warned us, the storm did come with quite a fury so we were glad to be indoors.

'Bad luck for you guys,' Simon said when the storm was at its climax.

'Why's that?' I asked.

'After a storm like this, you're going to have some pretty bad headwinds going up the coast,' he said. So what's new?

On the second day, after the rain let up, we could see waterfalls in the mountains even from where we stood on the coast. We joined Simon and a couple of his friends – Michael and Rick – for a slippery hike into the mountains. When we had travelled as far as we could in Michael's van (which was also Michael's home – he worked as an airline steward and because he flew most of the time he kept the van at the airport as a mobile home) he took out what looked like an opium pipe, lit it and passed it around. Why some people need to get high on stuff like that when the surroundings were enough to make one ecstatic was something I couldn't quite understand.

The forest was dripping from the aftermath of the heavy rains and the trails were quite muddy, but the vegetation smelt fresh and renewed. Simon had obviously been here before and we followed him until we got to a gushing river which I refused to jump over. It wasn't a large jump across, but the current was obviously very strong and I didn't feel like ending my life just yet, so I – the sole female – told them to go on without me. I directed my attention to a curious-looking lizard, which froze under my gaze, until the rest returned. Simon was the first to come bouncing back, happy with his new supply of drinking water.

On the last evening in Isla Vista, Simon organised a small pot luck party where we met some more Isla Vistans, one of whom was Tod, also an ardent bicyclist. He was going to Moab, Utah, to work in the spring. There we would meet again.

*

On 17th March we left Isla Vista to brace the headwinds and continue up the coast. But by the time we got to the town of Lompoc the winds had turned to gale force so we decided to call it quits. Fortunately we found the Leroy's home – one of the Hospitality Homes for bicyclists – where we were given a warm welcome, a hearty meal and some tips about the roads to come.

The following morning we set off with renewed high spirits as the wind had mercifully dropped. The scenery became more spectacular by the minute as we continued up Highway 1. It was also getting quite hilly and I was slowly and painfully beginning to discover muscles in my legs I never thought existed before.

As we were picnicking off the road on a slight incline a lone cyclist cyled by but came back as he realised we too were on bikes and joined us for lunch. His name was David Beattie, a Canadian returning from a year-and-a-half journey around the world!

We were so glad to have finally met a 'world cyclist' as there were hundreds of questions we wanted to ask him about cycling through other parts of the world. Since we were going in the same direction, we cycled the next few days together until San Francisco.

On our first evening together, we camped at Morro Bay State Park which offered $1 campsites for Hikers and Bikers; we could even take showers! David told us that this was the case along most of the coast – very good news indeed.

In between cycling we enjoyed each others' company through long talks about cycling long-distance, swapping information and tips (which came mostly from David, obviously). We also talked about means of getting sponsorship for such trips – we told him how we got our cameras from Minolta (in exchange for aerial photographs we took along the way) and film from Kodak (in exchange for a few articles about our trip). David, however, had acquired quite a number of sponsors during his travels and Kentucky Fried Chicken was one of them.

'How did you manage to get so many sponsors?' I asked.

'Oh, it's easy,' he said. 'Just walk up to a company manager and tell him his company *needs* you. It almost always works,' he said with a sly grin.

David was obviously a born entrepreneur – he actually managed to convince Kentucky Fried Chicken that they could promote their company wherever David cycled in exchange for providing David with meals at any Kentucky Fried Chicken restaurants he wished to stop at. He proved himself right when he sent back numerous newspaper cuttings from many regions about himself and his travels in which the name of the company was always mentioned. He now had a booklet which contained several pages of stamps from Kentucky Fried Chicken restaurants all over the world. He did likewise with other companies – when he reached Australia he went up to a company which not only produced beer but also owned a whole chain of hotels and got a similar deal as that with Kentucky Fried Chicken. Except this time he could drink all the beer he wanted in a hotel bedroom. In Australia David had travelled light and had slept like a king!

*

We undulated along a rugged coastline topped with lush green plateaus on which cattle were peacefully grazing. Cars became scarce and we soon found out why. A sign said: 'Road closed 15 miles north of San Simeon'.

We decided to ignore it since most obstacles on a road don't apply to bicycles. ('We can always walk if we can't cycle,' was our motto) and we took a lunch break by the sea just below Hearst Castle before proceeding to find out just what the obstacle was.

Hearst Castle was a peculiar building which, we were told by passing tourists, contained an enormous collection of art from all over the world. It had become a major tourist attraction, but the magnificent view of the sea in front of us was more inviting than mundane art, so we chose to remain where we were, calmly watching huge sea lions basking in the sun only a stone's throw away from us. The colossal creatures occasionally opened their eyes to make sure we didn't get any closer but otherwise remained where they were.

As we cycled along the Padre National Forest the road

started to become steep, occasionally reaching 900 feet, then descending briskly to sea level, only to climb once again. The road continued in this up-and-down manner all the way to Monterey, some 113 miles to the north.

As we neared the obstacle which was the cause for the 'Road Closed' sign, a man in a jeep stopped as we cycled up and said: 'The road's closed man! There's *no way* you're going to get through on your bikes man. Better turn back and take another road man!'

We told him we'd see for ourselves whether we could get through or not and he said, 'You're crazy man!' and drove off, shaking his head. I suppose he didn't know that most bicyclists don't particularly enjoy backtracking.

And then we finally saw it.

'God, look at that!' we chorused as we slowed down and stopped in front of *it* – an enormous mountain slide. One side of the mountain had simply collapsed, burying about 150 feet of road with what must have been millions of tons of rubble in the process.

We sat on some rocks for a minute and pondered what to do. As we sat discussing how to climb over it we saw other cyclists arriving at the other end of the slide who simply unloaded their bikes and started carrying their stuff across. So we did likewise (although I had second thoughts whenever some remnant rubble came down while we were crossing – as usual, the precarious situation didn't seem to bother the others – or they simply didn't show it). When we met halfway across the slide Nop and David helped the other cyclists with their stuff and they with ours. Nop even stopped to chat in a relaxed manner with one of the cyclists in the middle of the rubble, disregarding the imminent danger the slide posed. My legs were shaking by the time I reached the other end.

'How's the road further north?' David asked one cyclist before he crossed for the last time.

'Not too bad,' he said. 'There's only one more slide a few miles up. It's a muddy one compared to this one, but road workers are already clearing it up so you should be able to get across.'

We had to admit that there was one advantage to such slides – we had the entire road to ourselves. And by evening we found an isolated clifftop off the road where we had a grand view of the setting sun and could hear several sea otters frolicking in the waves some 600 feet below us.

All morning the next day we cruised along Highway 1 with the satisfying experience of knowing there would be no traffic to have to watch out for or spoil the peace we were enjoying. It was wonderfully quiet save the occasional sounds of seals barking below us. Their barks rebounded off the cliffs to our right making them sound like they were in the nearby mountains rather than the sea.

We stopped to look down one of the drop-offs and saw what must have been at least a hundred seals sunning and resting on a small inaccessible beach – from where we were standing they looked like little brown sausages lined up neatly on a kitchen counter.

When we reached the second slide we were told by the workers to wait a while before attempting to cross – the slide was very wet and muddy and every time the bulldozer cleared away the muck on the road, more came sliding down. It was obviously dangerous work.

'Every spring we gotta close this road off cuz every year we get these darn slides,' one of the workers told us as we watched them clear the rubble.

'I tell ya,' he continued, shaking his head, 'one day they'll just close the road for good cuz it just costs too much to keep patchin' the road up!'

We had lunch as we waited for the worst of the rubble to be cleared away and when we were given the OK sign, Nop was the first to push his bike across. But he immediately became stuck in knee-deep mud. One of the workers yelled at him to move on since the slide could shift at any moment, so with all the strength he could summon he pushed his bike one last time and got it across. Both his legs and panniers were covered with muck.

Just as I was wondering how the hell I was going to get

across, a pick-up truck brought three bicyclists across from the other side. David and I had the good fortune to receive a lift across as well. The truck skidded precariously but managed to get us across safely.

Streams were gushing down the mountain side so Nop was able to wash off most of the mud. He had to make do with cycling in wet shoes the rest of the day.

Highway 1 continued to be a strenuous but spectacular road all the way to Big Sur State Park where we camped among large Redwood trees. But after that we hit 'civilisation' again and had to cycle through traffic in the towns of Carmel, Monterey and Santa Cruz – not bad as towns go, but in Santa Cruz I was quite taken aback when a guy rolled down his car window and shouted, 'Get off the road, asshole cyclists!'

Having passed the unwelcome town, we found a side road at the town of Watsonville which designated itself as being part of the so-called 'Bikecentenniel Route' for cyclists. This is supposed to be the scenic route for cyclists up the coast. We followed it for a while only to end up at a closed-off bridge. So we cursed the sign and hauled our bikes over the barriers only to find a sign at the *other* end of the bridge which pointed out the detour we could have taken instead.

We camped at a Hiker and Biker campground at Sunset Beach State Park and the following morning we went to the town of Capitola where David treated us to coffee and cake at a popular cafe called 'Toots Coffee Shop'. David suggested we look for the local newspaper to 'tell our story'. We weren't used to seeking publicity ourselves (it came looking for us often enough) but we joined him anyway to see how he went about it.

A woman reporter from the Santa Cruz Sentinel came out to talk to us but wasn't very interested in out trips – she only lit up and started writing when David mentioned some of the local places we had passed, including Toots Coffee Shop! She was the first reporter we met who didn't send us a copy of the article.

We went on north until we found a dirt road heading off Highway 1, and camped once again facing the sea. It was our last night with David; we would be heading east the following day to Portola Valley where my sister lives and David would be continuing north all the way to Canada. It made us all rather sullen – I was going to miss David's good humour and company.

We said goodbye to David at the junction where the road headed for La Honda; it was like saying goodbye to a close friend although we had only been on the road together for a mere five days. But the five days had been wonderful and had shown that we three had a lot in common, and that each day had been memorable in some way or another.

*

Since LA we had covered 500 miles up the Pacific Coast Highway and they hadn't been easy. I was glad we could take a break and that I could rest my leg muscles which, although they were getting stronger by the day, still felt like they were about to burst from the strain of having to push the new load I was carrying.

Karen, my sister, and her husband, Mark, live in Portola Valley, which is located south of San Francisco, near Stanford University where Mark works as a cardiologist. Their home is situated in a beautiful suburb surrounded by hills shrouded in mist most of the time. For five days we delighted in the luxuries of hot showers, good food, good wine, good books and the company of the lively family members I could finally meet. They were the only real family we had on this huge continent but it was a comforting thought to know that they were a telephone call away if we ever needed them. Just the thought made a difference.

We promised to be back the following year when we returned to the west.

*

Because it was too early in the year (and too wet) to be heading north along the coast to the states of Oregon and Washington and also because we were already missing the dry, warm deserts, we decided to head east to Yosemite and from there skirt the mountain range south and head for Death Valley instead.

The Golden Gate Bridge had a wide pedestrian path to accommodate both strolling tourists and bicycles so we had a chance to stop halfway to look back at the city. We realised that San Francisco wasn't at all bad for a city. The hills were lined with pretty pastel-colour houses, the business section with its skyscrapers was confined to one section of the city and the shimmering Bay itself was filled with ocean-going vessels as well as white pleasure-craft. And on this particular day the sun was out and the air was clear, obliterating the layer of smog which unfortunately normally hangs above the city like a filthy blanket.

We followed a complicated network of bicycle paths which, much as they were meant to provide a safe way for the cyclist, were in actuality quite a nuisance. The route was inconsistent, often ending as a dead-end or as a time-consuming detour. So finally, after having got lost for the umpteenth time we changed our strategy and decided to head for the sea one last time. But how stupid could we be! We had forgotten it was Good Friday and that half of San Francisco was out for a drive, swerving up and down the mountains to the coast as if they were in a Grand Prix race. Drunk kids literally hung out of their cars and shouted profanities at us as we slowly struggled up the steep climb to Mount Tamalpais State Park.

By evening, however, all was quiet again and we found a Hiker and Biker camp site which more than made up for the day's bad luck.

*

Within three days we arrived in Sacramento where we surprised an old classmate of mine, June Cochrane, from

Seoul American High School whom I hadn't seen since our graduation in 1976. As it was late in the afternoon we simply waited on her doorstep till she got back from work. We had told her we would come by but we didn't tell her when.

We spent the next few days reminiscing about our school days and June showed us a lot of the sights including Lake Tahoe, since we were in the vicinity. It was strange *driving* up a mountain instead of cycling up it – I felt guilty, like we weren't doing the mountain justice by not having to suffer to appreciate its height. I suddenly realised that cycling was really beginning to have a deep effect on my way of thinking. Had Lake Tahoe retained its original beauty I would have probably felt worse about the drive up, but as it turned out, the place was one big ugly tourist trap of a town with horrible fast-food restaurants, bill-boards signs and 'Instant Wedding Service' churches lining the main road. I didn't want to think what the place was like during the peak season, but I kept my mouth shut so as not to offend June who was enjoying every bit of the outing with us and proudly explaining how Lake Tahoe functioned commercially (through its instant wedding services and gambling services). The only consolation was that at least parts of the Lake were safe from the surrounding commercialism by being designated State Parks or nature preserves.

Despite our differences in outlook on life it had nevertheless been good to see June again and we promised to meet again when we got back to California. June filled our panniers with loads of M & Ms (our staple source of sugar) and repeated what she had said since we reunited – that she *still* couldn't believe we were actually doing what we were doing.

Well . . . sometimes we couldn't believe it ourselves.

We were soon in the Napa Valley which reminded us of the rolling hills of France. Highway 16 followed a scarcely-inhabited area and the paved shoulder of the road made cycling very pleasant. In the town of Surry Creek a man at a garage kindly gave us some detailed maps of the area and told us to take a road known locally as Stony Creek Road which led to Pardee Dam. The road was as scenic as he had promised and was totally devoid of cars. It didn't have a great surface and we had to watch out for occasional potholes, but otherwise it undulated like a roller coaster along green meadows full of yellow spring flowers. We were like children as we 'whooped' and 'weeeed' up and down the hills.

*

Pardee Dam had a campground but we were told that seven miles further up the road there was a free campground at Hogan Dam Reservoir. It turned out to be a rather desolate place with several dilapidated campers inhabited by scruffy-looking semi-permanent inhabitants. The surroundings were nice enough but I was disgusted to have to clear away a mountain of litter before we could even put our tent up.

No sooner had we made ourselves as comfortable as the place permitted, our neighbour – a grumpy unkempt old man – repeatedly came out of his camper whenever his dog started barking and shouted, 'Shut yo goddamn mouth, dawg! Now git!' followed by a pitiful yelp from the dog.

Our neighbours to our back were no better. They were an unruly bunch of drunken youths who played their cassette recorder at full volume way into the night. The music was so loud they even had to shout to hear each other.

*

The hills turned into mountains as we followed Highway 49 and towns were getting fewer and smaller. We were approaching the foothills of the Sierra Nevada Range which runs along the eastern half of southern California from north to south with some of the mountain peaks reaching up to 13,000 feet. We were hoping the roads into the valley floor of Yosemite would be open – one could never tell at such high elevations.

At one of the last tiny towns called Chinese Camp a rancher gave us permission to camp on some grassland.

'Watch out for poison oak, now,' he warned us as we went looking for an appropriate spot. He pointed to the ominous plant and said, 'This stuff is terrible if you touch it. I once knew some kids who had made a campfire on the stuff by mistake; one of 'em had to be hospitalised cuz he inhaled the smoke.'

'What's the best remedy if you do touch it?' I asked.

'The only thing that'll probably help is hair spray,' he said.

'Hair spray?'

'That's right. It won't stop the itchin', but it'll stop it from spreadin'. But you have to apply it as soon as you touch it,' he added.

I also asked the rancher when the snakes would be coming out of hibernation.

'Aw . . . they should be out by now,' he said nonchalantly.

Right.

*

It was one of the most gruelling climbs I can remember; about 50 miles up to the highest point on the Old Big Oak Flat Road which was the upper western entrance into Yosemite National Park. It took us two days to climb. The weather wasn't much help either; by the time we got to the park entrance it was drizzling and very cold. The campground looked wet and depressing so we pushed ahead until we got to a track which led to Merced Grove. Although camping wasn't allowed beside the trail we considered our situation an emergency.

We pitched our tent under some trees at the bend of the trail where we weren't too conspicuous. I was no longer concerned about snakes in this cold – now I was worried about hungry bears. Spring was supposed to be the season bears came out of their winter hibernation weak and

96

hungry. Because food would be scarce until the beginning of summer they would go for any kind of food, including whatever we may have in our tent. The only thing we could do was to place our food bags away from our tent by hanging them from a tree in the forest and hope the bears would be diverted to the bags and not to us.

Whether bears had actually appeared or not during the night I will never know but the following morning we awoke to an eerie silence. And it was only when we zipped open our tent that we found ourselves in a fairyland of white virgin snow. The silence was simply overwhelming – no birds, no people . . . just the two of us in a sleeping world.

It was clear that we couldn't go on till the snow melted so we decided to take advantage of our position and go for a hike down to the grove of Sequoias instead. Quietly we descended the trail and spotted some very tall trees; first we thought these were the Sequoias, but we were mistaken. A few hundred yards further down we finally saw them: the unmistakeable giants of the world. Five grandiose Sequoia trees stood clustered together at the end of the trail – each tree must have had a circumference of at least fifteen feet. Standing next to these dignified grandfathers we felt timid and insignificant. We also felt like trespassers in an untouched world. They undoubtedly demanded respect and got it because they deserved it. After a long time I finally gave them a last hug and we left them in peace.

The image of those grand trees in the snow has forever been imprinted on my mind. I don't think I would ever visit the grove again lest I destroy the magnificent memory of that day.

*

Not only did this enlightening experience brighten our spirits the following day, but so did the sun which came out and was rapidly melting the snow. We quickly packed up and got going, eager to get a view of the valley floor before the final descent. And to our surprise the highest point was a mere one or two miles further from where we had camped. We were rewarded for our efforts with the most magnificent view of Yosemite's valley below: towering granite cliffs, snow-capped mountains, glistening domes and . . . the waterfalls! It was all too breathtaking to take in at once, and we didn't dare cycle down too fast lest we miss some of the wondrous scenes along the way.

Even from where we stood on the top we could see that the silvery lines in the far distance were in fact very tall waterfalls and as we slowly descended into the valley every corner of the road offered a waterfall, a gushing stream, a cascade. Wherever we went there was water, water and more water. And finally, we were down in the valley itself where we could hear the tremendous roar of the surrounding waterfalls. We had certainly arrived at Yosemite at the best possible time of the year – in the spring. The snows on the higher ranges were beginning to melt, flooding the streams and rivers and causing the waterfalls to gush down full force. At no other time on our journey did we feel the force of nature's seasonal transition so strongly as when we experienced Yosemite that spring.

*

We pitched our tent at the Sunnyside Walk-in campground which cost $2 per person. However, we never paid since the ranger always came to collect the fees while we were out hiking. For five days we hiked the walls of Yosemite starting with the Upper Yosemite Falls early on the first morning. It was a steep climb up to the top of the falls, then the trail continued up until it finally levelled somewhat at the snow-line. It was strange walking through the snow in shorts.

The following day we explored part of the North Dome Trail. We had just counted the 106th switchback when we heard a thunderous sound across the valley and saw a huge chunk of snow detach itself from the mountain and go tumbling down into the valley – we had never witnessed an avalanche at such close range.

*

The valley floor itself also had many interesting spots to discover. We went to see all the falls there were to see, observed climbers clambering up the sheer granite walls of El Capitan, went to ranger talks, and did some domestic chores like shopping, cutting each other's hair and keeping the blue jays and squirrels (not bears) away from our food. At one ranger talk, we learned that there were only a few peregrine falcons left in these parts due to the continued use of DDT in some parts of South America. Some of these rare birds nested high upon the granite cliffs of the park and each spring climbers would climb up the cliffs to replace the eggs with dummy eggs so that the real ones could be hatched safely in a laboratory (the shells of these eggs had become extremely thin and fragile because the falcons were at the top of the food chain where the concentration of the pesticides was the highest). Once the eggs safely hatched the climbers returned the chicks to the nests to be reared by their parents. As long as DDT continued to be used this tedious process would have to be maintained in order to guarantee the survival of these birds.

*

As I was cutting Nop's hair and beard in the campground on our last day in Yosemite one of our neighbours came by and asked if I could cut his hair too – he was about to go for a job interview in the park. As I did so, I asked him whether he was applying for a ranger job.

'Nah,' he said, 'just some odd labour job. I'm a park bum.'

'What's a park bum?' I asked.

'People like me who go from one national park to another – sometimes we work in the parks sometimes we just live in them for a while and then move on. It's an OK life.'

*

We took our time as we cycled out of the park taking the southern route which passes the Mariposa Grove of Sequoia trees. It wasn't the fault of the trees, but Mariposa Grove just couldn't compare with the experience we had had at Merced Grove. Everything was wrong here; the road to the grove was too wide and accommodated large crowds during the peak months. Even now there were too many tourists milling about noisily and there were too many signs. It was more of a tourist attraction rather than a nature preserve, hence my disappointment.

We followed Highway 41 – a continuation of the park road – and filled our water bottles at Fish Camp. We camped on top of fresh pine needles in the forest and found magnificent long cyclindrical pine cones covered with a sticky inflammable sap which literally ignited with a single matchstick flame.

*

It was sunny and hot again as we cruised down to the San Joaquin Valley – a long flat valley which stretched south parallel to the Sierra Nevada Range. The road was rather pleasant till the town of Oakhurst where we were suddenly confronted with truck congestion once again – the park had given us respite from such traffic and we had forgotten how awful it was to share the road with monstrous motorised vehicles.

As we neared the town of Fresno, the mountains from which we had descended gradually turned into rocky, grassy hills, then into hilly vineyards, and finally even these disappeared and we found ourselves in the flat dusty valley.

Fresno was quite large (population 200,000) and sprawled out. We did some shopping and managed to find spare generators for our lamp and our stove (both were meant to function only on white gas, which was hard to come by so we used unleaded gas most of the time which eventually clogged the generators after a few months).

We sat outside a gas station eating ice cream, a custom we were beginning to get used to in the heat, when a guy on a motorcycle came by and stopped to talk to us. He invited us to camp on his land in Selmo, which was about 14 miles south of Fresno.

Dan lived with his wife and baby in a house next to a vineyard and he worked for the county. We quickly sensed that Dan had invited us because he was eager to hear about travel; he had the typical hungry look of someone who felt he had missed out on the opportunities to travel and now had to resolve his regret by hearing someone else's story.

We tried to persuade Dan that he could still travel if he wanted to. We suggested he could always rent or sell his house – after all a house is only an object – and that he could always take his child along as long as he was still small. We told him that we lived off $5 a day – which was a bit of an extreme case (the dollar's exchange rate was extremely high when we first set off) – but that anyone could travel cheaply as well as comfortably as long as they gave up certain luxuries.

Our words encouraged him somewhat and I sincerely hoped he would fulfil his dreams one day.

*

Highway 43 was one long, straight road through the San Joaquin Valley – it was the one road on this trip where I thought I would literally fall asleep while I cycled. In the hot sunny haze we could barely make out the Los Padres range to our right while the Sierra Nevada range to our left was completely invisible. The road ran parallel to a railway track and occasionally a train would pass us – the conductor would wave to us from the front of the train and minutes later (some of these trains were extremely long) the brakeman would wave to us from the last carriage of the train. A passing train became the diversion on this dull road.

Then, in the middle of this wilderness we came upon

101

Colonel Allensworth State Historical Park (where we were the only visitors) – we were glad to get off the monotonous road.

It was a rather desolate place, but interestingly enough, the park had once been a bustling community of blacks who had come to get away from the rat race and bigotry of the big cities. The town was founded by a black Colonel called Allensworth and had been a successful community until, unfortunately, the water level dropped and was finally found to contain arsenic making the place no longer habitable.

The park offered free camp sites so we pitched our tent for the night amidst the rather unnerving stillness of the ghost town.

*

If the previous day was dull, then the next day was ugly. After the town of Shafter, we headed east, where truck traffic picked up, and came upon a most peculiar area of brown hills (near Backersfield) where hundreds of oil pumps nodded their heads in the non-stop extraction of oil. As if to compensate for these unsightly rigs, a grassy green park had been placed next to the complex. Even now, I always think of that hideous area of rigs whenever I hear the name Backersfield.

We continued east, this time climbing the tail end of the Sierra Nevada Range which was rocky and dry. As we followed the Kern River through a gorge, we found a forest campground. It was partly occupied by some 'park bums' who greeted us and invited us to drop by once we got settled. A couple occupied one van, which had been converted into a permanent home: the floor was covered with a tattered carpet, and a huge kettle stood on a wooden stove whose chimney protruded through the roof of the van. The other van was occupied by a single man. They could all have been anywhere between forty and sixty years old – it was difficult to tell with their overgrown beards, unwashed bodies, decaying teeth, unkempt clothes and spaced-out looks.

The man (of the couple) offered us a beer, but our stomachs were still empty so we declined.

'You don't drink?' he asked incredulously.

'*He* does,' I said, pointing to Nop.

'But not on an empty stomach', Nop added.

'Man, you *don't* drink . . . ?' he repeated without seeimg to hear what we had just said.

The woman then offered us some coffee in two filthy cups which we reluctantly accepted instead. The man was still pondering why we didn't drink.

'Well, if you don't drink, then you *must* smoke, huh?' he said hopefully taking out a pipe made of deer horn and filling it with pot.

'Uh . . . no, not really,' Nop said, hoping not to offend him.

'You don't *smoke*?' he asked again. 'You don't drink, you don't smoke . . . man, what *do* you do?'

Now that was a difficult question.

'We travel,' Nop suggested.

'On 'em weird lookin' bikes?'

'That's right.'

'Man . . . they don't smoke an' they don't drink! I can't believe that!' Then, changing the subject, he looked slyly at us and said: 'Wanna know somethin'? We here are *gold seekers.*'

'You're looking for gold?' I asked, raising my eyebrows. 'You mean *here*?'

'Sure,' he said, 'I'll show you.' He disappeared into his van and came out with a tiny tube containing some liquid and what was evidently a few tiny chunks of gold, 'See?' he said.

'How much is that worth?' I asked.

'Aw . . . not much. Probably a few dollars. But there's gold out there all right and we're gonna find it one day.' I could see the dollar signs in his blurry eyes.

He told us they had wandered all over the country trying their luck. They showed us their picks, shovels and sieves.

103

Gold seekers indeed! I thought they had become extinct.

*

Isabella Lake was a cool and inviting sight after the hot climb up Highway 178 to about 1,800 feet. However, we couldn't find a single spot which wasn't given that most annoying of American designations to be seen all over the country – PRIVATE PROPERTY. We looked all around the lake for a patch of empty 'no man's land' but to no avail, so we settled on a piece of land which looked suspiciously 'private' but which was obviously not being used at that moment.

We continued to follow the Kern River the following day when a car drove by us only to stop a few metres away. Out came a man with a video camera who proceeded to film us as we climbed the mountain. He then hopped back into the car, drove on and stopped once again to film us as we cycled past him. Then it was back into the car to film us from his rear window. Finally he stuck his head out, shouted 'Merci!' and drove off leaving Nop and I laughing uncontrollably on our bikes.

A little while later another car passed us and the driver looked at us with some concern and said, 'It's still a *long* way up, you know,' and Nop and I burst out laughing again.

*

Walker Pass was 5,250 feet high and we were once again in the high desert, joined by cholla cacti and Joshua trees. We enjoyed the view as we had our lunch at the top, then we held onto our handlebars to brace the strong side winds which threatened to blow us off the road as we descended into the town of Ridgecrest. In town we did some shopping and treated ourselves to the usual triple-cone ice creams from Thrifty's. There a kindly woman came up to us, introduced herself as Del. 'How would you like to come up to our RV park for the weekend? Our Good Sam's RV Club members are getting together at Johannesburg – it's a bit out of the way, but you're welcome to join us.'

We would have liked nothing better and we immediately accepted; our greed for another potluck dinner got the better of us. Did she say it was a *bit* out of the way? Johannesburg was a good 20 miles from where we were – which was not a *bit* after getting dehydrated and burnt through 56 miles of desert heat! Worse, it turned out to be all uphill. But we made it all right – it's amazing what the thought of food can do to grumpy, exhausted cyclists.

*

As usual, the senior citizens showered us with their affection and good-will and filled our stomachs with a wide range of delicious food. The next day, after a breakfast of pastries and coffee, one of the couples, Charlie and Neva, took us on a drive to Landburg, an old mining town in the vicinity. From there we headed into the desert to witness a convoy of antique cars – with drivers and passengers all dressed up in the style of the 20s – drive by. In the evening the RVers (RV stands for Recreational Vehicle) organised a Hawaiian night (everyone dressed in tacky moomoos and flowery shirts) and we once again were invited to huge plates of nourishing food and good-humoured games. Senior citizens (what a wonderful name for elderly people) often reminded me of happy children – they were so uninhibited in their relationships with one another and seemed to be beyond the strains of responsibilities which usually plague the working middle-aged.

*

I suppose many people would consider Highway 178 heading into Death Valley a desolate stretch. Except for the small town of Trona, with a smelly chemical plant, there is no human habitation whatsoever along the way. But we enjoyed it although it was *terribly* hot.

We stocked up on water and food at the supermarket in

105

Trona and were joined by a lone cyclist – Robert – who had cycled from San Jose and was also heading for the park. The three of us waited till it was cool enough to cycle again and at sunset we camped in the desert near Dry Lake. Unlike the cold nights we had experienced in the desert during the winter months, we now found ourselves feeling hot even in the evening.

To get to Death Valley from the west we had to climb about 4,800 feet and cross the Panamint Mountains. The road was in a terrible state and the climb was quite steep. The worst part was that there wasn't a single patch of shade in sight and we literally roasted.

As we were climbing, a car stopped and the driver asked me if I had enough water. I said I did and that we would be getting to Wildrose campground soon where there was water but I thanked him anyway.

When we reached the campground, Nop and Robert went up to the Ranger Station to get water and information, but when they got back they were both fuming.

'What happened?' I asked.

'It's a dry camp,' Robert said.

'Doesn't the ranger station have any water?' I asked.

'The ranger,' Nop said with disgust, 'said there isn't any *potable* water here – apparently it turned bad some years ago. She suggested we go on to Emigrant campground!'

'How far away is that?'

'Twenty miles,' Robert said between clenched teeth.

'Did you tell her we were on bicycles?' I asked.

'Of course we did,' Nop snapped.

'She couldn't care less,' Robert added. 'And you know what? All that time we were standing there obviously showing signs of dehydration, she was drinking an ice cold can of coke right in front of us. I couldn't *believe* it.'

'What was her name?' I asked, hoping one day to take revenge on this woman (as I am doing now).

'Mary something.'

Therefore note: be wary of Mary of Wildrose Campground, Death Valley!

106

We found a cluster of trees in someone's front yard (which we hoped was Mary's) where we sat down to eat something and collect our thoughts. There was even a hose so we watered ourselves down although we couldn't drink the water.

There were a couple of campers parked at an unshaded picnic site nearby, so we decided to ask them for water. One of the men sitting at the picnic table went inside his camper and returned with a small plastic cup of water which he handed to Robert. The three of us just stared at the guy, and another man nearby said, 'Come on Tom, fill up their bottles will ya? Can't you see they're on ba-cycles?' The man grudgingly took our bottles and filled them up for us.

Don't get mad, I kept telling myself. Remember the driver who stopped to offer water – there are people and then there are people.

*

The sun was already quite low as we finally reached Emigrants Pass at 5,315 feet but we only had to ride down into the valley to get to the campground. Nop and Robert were cycling ahead of me when I suddenly saw Robert waving his arms in the air towards me – he was trying to tell me to move to the side of the road. In the nick of time I saw what he was pointing at – a long brown snake, covering the entire width of the road which made it to the bushes just as I passed it with an inch to spare.

'Was it a rattlesnake?' I asked, as we all stopped to watch it's tail disappear under the bushes.

'I think it was a gopher,' Robert said. Gophers resemble rattlesnakes but aren't venomous. Nop walked to the bush to get a better look.

'Nop, please!' I pleaded.

'OK, OK. I just wanted to make sure.'

The desert is never so beautiful as when the sun is either rising or setting, and Death Valley was no exception. As we slowly descended into the valley the sun cast its beautiful rays on the curvatures of the alluvial fans located at the base of the surrounding mountains. The vegetation which was normally brown and dull by day turned into a magnificent array of pastel colours accentuating each and every thorn on every bush at sunset. Sometimes the beauty of the desert was simply overpowering.

The campground was empty but there was water. We were delighted at the privacy and once again hosed our sun-scorched bodies down with the wonderful water we could drink as well.

We had dinner under the full moon, and because it was so warm we only pitched our inner tent. Nop didn't even want to pitch the inner tent but I refused to share my sleeping bag with any snake – rattler or non-rattler.

Just as we were feeling secure at the thought that we would have the campground to ourselves, a car pulled in with three guys and a girl who proceeded to pitch their tents. It was a while before we realised they were speaking Dutch. Instead of going to bed early as we had planned we ended up sharing their wine and chatting about home. They told us they were students and that they were on vacation.

*

We got up at dawn to make use of the cool morning hours but no sooner had we turned south the wind picked up and it was like cycling into an oven. We came across an area called Devil's Cornfield, where rows of bush formations resembled neatly stacked triangular bundles of hay – hence its name, and in the far distance we could see some sand dunes and a large salt flat shimmering in the heat.

Furnace Creek was, despite its name, an oasis, and although it was suppposed to be part of the national park, it was a commercial village; it had a hotel, a golf course and a swimming pool catering to ... whom, I wondered? To people like us, I suppose, since we were invited by a man named Al from the general store to use it free of charge. Robert had quickly made friends with Al since they discovered they were both University of Berkeley graduates. So it was actually Robert who was invited to use the pool while we were the ones who merely tagged along.

It was only when we put on our bathing suits that we realised how brown we had become and how utterly ridiculous we looked – our arms were brown up to the shoulders, our legs two-thirds up to our thighs, part of our necks (it depended on the direction we had been cycling whether the left or right of our necks were burnt) and our faces up to our foreheads because we usually had visors and sunglasses on. The rest was pure white.

*

We got up early the next morning to cycle to Badwater which was about 20 miles from Furnace Creek and for the first and only time on our travels we actually *saw* a coyote at close range. It had yellowish fur, large ears and was quite skinny and shabby-looking. He stopped for a second look at us and then disappeared.

By 8 o'clock in the morning we were roasting. We got to a salt flat called Devil's Golf Course (everything in Death Valley, as the name suggests, has been associated with the Devil because of its harsh environment) and took some aerial photographs of it with one of Nop's kites. Seen from afar, the salt flat had looked white, but at closer range it had a rugged grey surface on which it was almost impossible to walk. The booklet we had acquired at the Visitor Centre explained that the salt pinnacles were 95% pure table salt and that some 2,000 years ago the flat had actually been a lake. As the water dried up salt precipitated and formed the rugged surface we were looking at.

Badwater was a pool of water which, although it wasn't

109

poisonous to drink, didn't look very tempting either. We were supposedly standing about 300 feet below sea level on the hottest place on earth – the hottest recorded temperature had apparently been 134° Fahrenheit. I didn't doubt it for a moment.

*

Back at the campground we met a couple from Washington – Bud and Ardis – who kindly invited us for a sunset drive through the park. Bud was a geologist and as we drove to Zabrinsky Point, Mule Train Trail, Dante's View, Artist's Drive and Golden Canyon he explained some of the geological features of the park. One of the most striking areas at sunset was Golden Canyon; the hills were illuminated by the sun's rays and, as a result, the alluvial fans became incredibly pronounced, clearly showing how erosion had affected the formation of these beautiful mountains although it was difficult to believe that rain – infrequent as it may be – does fall in sudden downpours in these parts, causing gushing streams to push everything down the mountains in their wake.

Robert decided to cycle out of the park that evening because there was a full moon and he wanted to make use of the strong tailwinds he expected. I thought he was crazy to ride at night, but he was adamant and even Nop agreed that the conditions were ideal. We said goodbye to Robert after dinner at Al's place. Al was very sad to see his fellow Berkeley graduate go and didn't seem pleased to be stuck with us non-Berkeleyites and so he chose to ignore us for the rest of the evening.

We remained another half day at Furnace Creek, talking to Bud and Ardis, visiting the Borax Museum and writing letters. When the oven-wind lessened in the afternoon we decided to go on.

Fortunately it was easier getting out of the park than it had been getting in; we took the road west and covered some 31 miles till we got to Death Valley Junction which consisted of a few run-down houses and what we were told was an opera house. If anything, the place looked like a ghost town.

*

It was 25th April and my mother's birthday so I decided to give her a call; that is, if we could find a phone in the desert to call her from. We finally got to a small town called Shoshone which consisted of a store (which was closed) and a phone (which worked).

I called her collect.

'Happy birthday!' I said, as soon as she accepted the charges.

'Michèle! How nice of you to call! Where are you?'

'In Shoshone.'

'Where?'

'Near Death Valley.' No, that sounded ominous so I quickly added. 'We're almost in Nevada. How's everything back home?'

'Don't worry, everything and everyone is fine here. Conny, Erny and Hanny,' (my aunts) 'are all here having coffee with me. We just got back from an Indonesian restaurant where we celebrated my birthday.'

I looked at the dry arid landscape around us and couldn't quite picture an Indonesian restaurant . . . .

'Michèle,' my mother was saying, 'is everything all right?'

'Yes, yes. We're both doing great. We just wanted to wish you a happy birthday.'

'Can I send you anything? Do you need money?'

'No, no. We're fine.'

'Well, take care and here's Tante Conny for you.'

'Hi, Michèle! How's life?'

God was I homesick all of a sudden.

'OK Con.'

'When are you coming home?' she laughed.

'Not yet, Con.' I laughed too.

'Take care and have a good time. And say hi to

111

Noppie.'

'I will. Bye.'

I wished my mother Happy Birthday again and hung
up.

'Well?' Nop asked.

'They had just come back from an Indonesian restaurant
. . . .'

We looked at each other and sighed.

*

Welcome to Nevada, the Silver State, the sign said. This was
our fifth state and we were now five months on the road.
Longer than any vacation I could remember. I suddenly
realised this was no longer a vacation but a way of life.

At the summit of Spring Mountain (6,500 feet), I looked
down and asked Nop: 'So where *is* Las Vegas?' It was very
hot again, and there wasn't much to see through the midday
haze. 'I thought Las Vegas was a big bustling city.'

'I think I see it,' said Nop, pointing to a cluster of buildings
he discerned vaguely in the far distance. It looked like a
hump of concrete to me. What a place for a city!

We descended the mountain in a blasting hot headwind
which burnt us quite badly and got to the town of Arden
where I phoned a friend and got directions for Henderson, a
suburb at the southeastern end of Las Vegas where she lived.
As we got closer to the city we finally saw the skyscrapers
which had looked like a lump of concrete from afar. Close-
up the gambling city looked drab and not at all glamorous
in the daylight.

*

Misong was an old classmate of my sister's from Seoul who
now lived in Henderson with her husband, Carl (also a
Seoul American High School graduate), who was a PR
manager for the Imperial Palace (one of the huge casino-
hotels) in Las Vegas. We stayed in Henderson for four days

112

and were shown the sights from the inside, so to speak, since Carl worked in the midst of the craziness of the gambling halls. Las Vegas may be dull by day, but at night it transforms itself into a bustling town of incredible neon lights, noisy gambling halls, rows and rows of armed bandits clinking with the sounds of coins, music and people – everywhere. The place certainly reeked of money. I tried a nickel machine and lost $4 and Nop won it back playing Black Jack.

Las Vegas was definitely an *interesting* place. I wouldn't know what other word to use – extravagant, ludricous, flashy? It was certainly a town which reflected the innate greediness of people.

'I've seen many people get ruined by gambling,' Carl told us as we sat pondering the place after tramping around for hours and were still dazed by all the noise, sounds and colours.

'Take this Korean student I introduced to you a while back. He's come to Las Vegas for the third time. The hotel pays for his room, even his flight, so he comes back time and time again only to gamble away more money. When gamblers start losing heavily they get the urge to win it back, but they always lose more in the end.'

We asked Carl if he ever gambled.

'No way!' he said. 'Just look around you. Notice how there aren't any windows or clocks in these gambling halls? It's even a psychological game. The owners of these joints don't want you to know what time it is. Those women at the slot machines? They sometimes go on for 48 hours without being aware of it! It's all terribly addictive and the place caters to addicts like them.'

*

We now had Dutch flags fluttering on our flag poles (which had come in a package for us from Holland) as we put Las Vegas and its gamblers behind us. We cycled in the direction of Echo Bay which was located on Lake Mead National

Recreation Area, about 53 miles from Henderson. What a relief it was to be out in the empty desert again!

It was a very pretty ride despite the heat; so much so that when we saw some beautiful red hills with gorges between them we decided to take aerial photographs of them. Actually it was a foolish thing to do in the middle of the day when the desert heat was at its worst but the scenery seduced us. And as a result, in the process of taking the aerials we unconsciously drank most of our water and were on the verge of serious dehydration by the time we managed to reach Echo Bay's campground. Never have I experienced such thirst as on that day and we never fooled with the desert again.

Lake Mead was not a natural lake – it had been created by damming the Colorado and the Virgin Rivers. Under the lake lay the 'lost city' of Moapa Valley and with it a wealth of Indian artifacts and village sites which archaeologists never got a chance to dig up and study. And now with the lake above it, the site, with all its buried wealth of information, was lost forever. This wasn't the only man-made lake we were to come across in the deserts. Cities like Los Angeles, Las Vegas and Phoenix with their thirst for water didn't really belong at all in the desert where water was scarce. Yet there they were and they were only getting bigger. The only way to supply these ever-growing desert cities with water and electricity was to dam the rivers and create large lakes at the expense of the environment. What annoyed me most was the fact that so much of the precious water was actually wasted in the form of filling swimming pools, keeping lawns and non-endemic plants alive and golf courses green.

St George was surrounded by purplish red mountains and although it was a small town we found a cyclists' hospitality home and, to our surprise, the hospitality home turned out to belong to Reverend and Mrs Wilkie of the American Baptist Church! Reverend Wilkie surprised us even more when he told us we were the third and fourth cyclists to come by on recumbents to his home.

'The last recumbent cyclist who came by was in fact a

woman travelling on her own,' he added. He told us she had been on a tricycle recumbent with a faring around it. Why was it that *we* never saw any of these touring recumbent cyclists?

After treating us to dinner, which he prepared himself, Reverend Wilkie took us on a drive to nearby Snow Canyon to show us the black rocks of an extinct volcano. The entire area around St George was very picturesque; in fact the whole ride from Mesquite to Shivwits – a detour we had had to make earlier in the day because we weren't allowed on the Interstate – had turned out to be quite spectacular too. I had a feeling we were going to like Utah – we were already beginning to appreciate it for its unique nature, rather than ponder whatever silly preconceived notions we may have had about Utah before we even set foot in the Mormon State!

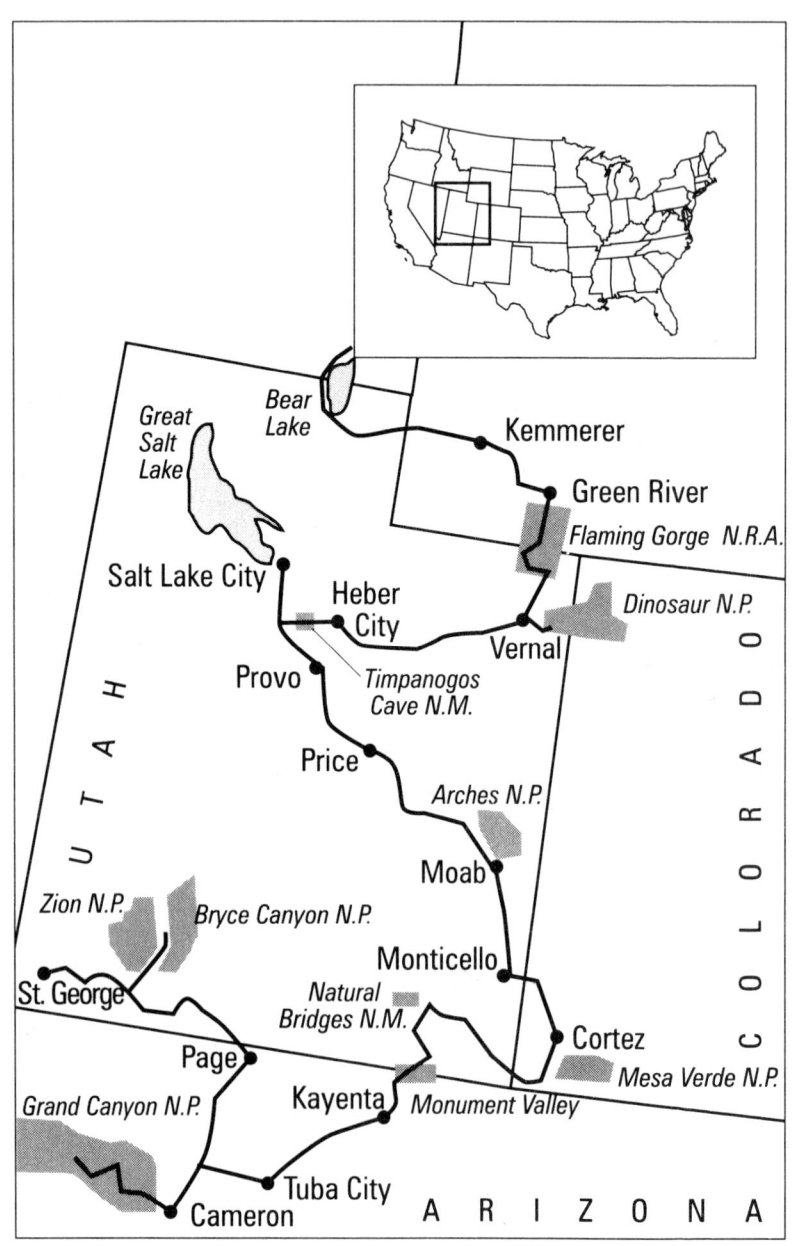

LANDS OF CANYONS AND MESAS

In the month of May alone Nop and I cycled to and explored nine different National Parks and Monuments. It wasn't because we wanted to break any record but because this particular region of the United States – Utah, Arizona, New Mexico and Colorado – offered such a *wealth* of national parks. This was a region of incomparable beauty: canyons, mesas, mountains, gorges, wide open spaces, rugged rocks, varying elevations, diverse vegetation, Indian ruins, the bluest of skies and fabulous cloud formations. For us, this region was the most memorable part of the journey as far as nature was concerned. And even now, as I write this on the island of Schiermonnikoog in the dead of winter, the memories come back vividly; I feel as if it were only yesterday that we were pedalling unknown paths of the deserts . . . .

*

Zion was the first of these national parks, located only 47 miles east of St George. It was a gradual climb as we followed the Virgin River which eventually split into two smaller rivers. The road ran parallel to the north fork of the river and as we neared the entrance to the park the valley narrowed into a gorge. We were already at an elevation of 3,585 feet as we entered the park to settle down at the campground.

In the late afternoon, as the last sun rays illuminated the

peaks of the tall canyon walls, we took a small hike up the Watchman Trail. Before we got onto the trail, however, I spotted a huge kingsnake in a grass patch. The kingsnake isn't venomous although its black and white rings give it an ominous appearance. I was more awed by it than scared – not a bad sign for someone who had always been terrified at the mere thought of snakes. My attitude must have been improving . . . .

The view of the valley within Zion Canyon was magnificent, and the red Navajo sandstone of the walls of the canyon glowed in the soft sunset light. This Navajo sandstone, a red porous stone, is present throughout most of this region. It is a soft stone and vulnerable to erosion, yet it is precisely this erosion which has allowed the creation of the oddest looking rock formations we were to come across time and again.

I felt sick the first day in the park and couldn't do much except chat with a cyclist, Brian, whom Nop had invited to share our camp site. Brian didn't move much that day either – he wasn't sick, he said, he just didn't cycle on Sundays (?).

We spent the next two days clambering up Angel's Landing – a 1,200 foot high rocky protrusion through the valley, enjoying the clear song of canyon wrens who sound like piano tuners as they repeatedly try out the entire music scale. We also explored the valley floor all the way to the narrows where the gorge closes to form a narrow corridor with its walls soaring up into the blue sky. We cooled ourselves at Emerald Pools (a delightful water hole which gets its water from a source directly above it: a water curtain with a backdrop of green moss). We examined vegetation – particularly the delightful slickrock paint bushes which were blooming in profusion between incredibly narrow rock crevices and cottonwood trees which managed to find space between the canyon walls and catch some sunlight. We laughed at scurrying little squirrels and we were totally mystified in general about the 200 million-year-old geological history of this place as we gazed at the awe-inspiring stone masses of the canyon.

*

Bryce Canyon National Park was 71 miles from Zion, an easy two days of cycling. For the first time in ages it was overcast and quite chilly – I didn't feel like going on just yet but Nop managed to persuade me.

We took the Zion-Mount Carmel Highway, famous for its switchbacks, out of the park. When we got to the tunnel we waited for a car which might escort us through the tunnel with its headlights since it was several miles long (and pitch black) and our lights didn't work any more. We had no luck with the first car we waved at but the next one did stop and the kind couple guided us through.

Directly outside the tunnel we stopped to take a short hike off the road which led us to a panoramic view of the entire park.

A couple passed us as we were heading down the trail, and the woman asked: 'Were you the ones on the bikes in front of the tunnel?'

When we said we were, she apologised, 'Oh, we're *so* sorry we didn't stop! It was only after we passed you that we realised you needed help getting through the tunnel. We felt *so* bad afterwards.'

Well, whadya know!

*

The scenery was definitely becoming weird as we continued along Highway 9 – we passed a mountain of sandstone called Checkerboard Mesa which was indeed a cone-shaped white mountain with a checkerboard pattern on it.

We had stopped at a viewpoint to appreciate Checker-board Mesa from the other end when a couple on motorcycles stopped. Ron and Sue were from California and were riding around the country for three months. They took an interest in our bikes and our travels so we chatted a while. We found out they were heading for Bryce Canyon as

119

well so we promised to look out for them when we got there although we weren't going to make it to Bryce Canyon that day since dark clouds threatened.

Sure enough it began to drizzle by the time we got to Mount Carmel Junction. We continued on after some pie and coffee at a cafe which warmed us up (by then it was freezing) and found a KOA campground just beyond the town of Glendale. But they charged an exorbitant fee of $9.95 for a tent, so we went up to the house across the KOA instead and asked the woman who opened the door whether we could camp on her front yard.

Once we got settled we decided to take revenge on the KOA that evening; when the attendant locked up and left, (there were no campers that night which served them right) we sneaked in and took hot showers.

*

The weather the next day was no better than the day before; in fact it was quite cold so we decided to wait another day and hike in the vicinities instead.

A beautiful German shepherd dog whom the woman of the house had named 'Dog' followed us on our hike. She must have been quite young since she was very playful and cheerful – we gave her the more dignified name of 'Cheery'.

We weren't anywhere near the park yet on our hike we got a clear idea of what to expect – the mountains in this particular region had eroded to such an extent that their remaining shapes were that of strange-looking tall rock formations with a peculiar combination of pink and orange tints. The colours were accentuated when the sun shone, giving the landscape a fairyland-like atmosphere.

The woman, called Bessie, who let us camp on her front yard, was a widow and lived alone. As she fed us dinner that evening we got to talking about Mormons. She didn't have many positive things to say about the Mormons – I suppose she would know since she had been married to one!

120

'Ma husband was a Mormon,' she said, 'and the biggest darn hypocrite as well. Mormons are always saying one thing and doing otherwise!'

We asked her whether bigamy was still prevalent in Utah.

'You bet it is!' she said. 'If you see a house where extra rooms have been added on it's most likely to belong to a bigamous family.'

I asked her why they practised bigamy and she said, 'Oh, some of those old men are just lustful and lecherous. They do it in the name of their religion but often marry very young girls. It's really disgusting.'

She went on to tell us that it was quite common for young girls who were forced into such marriages to run away but they usually got caught and were brought back again. Some who persisted in running away were often found dead.

It all sounded like something out of a film, but Bessie was dead serious as she related the stories to us.

But we also talked about books and about preserving food. She showed us a storeroom in the back of the house which contained rows and rows of jars filled with an array of colourful jams and every conceivable fruit and vegetable – she had preserved them all herself as was the custom in Utah (as well as of the Mormons, I should add).

'Now that the kids are grown and out of the house I don't make much anymore,' she said modestly as she presented us with one of her strawberry jams.

Bessie lived alone but didn't seem lonely. In fact, she seemed to enjoy the solitude the magnificent surroundings offered her – she certainly could do jolly well what she pleased since she couldn't even see her nearest neighbour.

*

We would be backtracking from Bryce Canyon and would see Bessie when we passed by again so we didn't wake her when we left the following morning. But Cheery, who was wide awake and who was eager to join us as she had on all our walks, followed us.

'Cheery, stop! Go back!' we kept saying, but she wouldn't listen. We tried cycling away quickly but she loved it thinking it was one of our games and ran just as fast.

'Go home, Cheery!' we repeated, but no, she was determined to come along.

'What do we do now?' I asked Nop, as she kept following us.

'She'll probably head home in the end,' Nop said.

But we were already on the main road and I was getting worried. She kept following us so we finally stopped and decided to take her back and have Bessie tie her up till we were well out of sight. But as we were getting off our bikes a car came up from behind us and Cheery, who had also stopped, turned her head towards the sound of the car – at that split moment the car sped by her, hitting her head in one powerful clap. The bastard just drove on, not once looking back.

I was suddenly in hysterics as poor Cheery lay there convulsing as blood spattered out from her ears and onto the front of my bicycle and my shoes. Within a few seconds she finally lay still and was dead.

We couldn't believe what had just happened and I was sobbing as we went back to Bessie's house to give her the bad news but a man who had apparently witnessed the whole thing already had gone in to tell her. Bessie consoled me with coffee while Nop and the man who had witnessed the scene went to bury Cheery near the road. I was too upset to help them.

*

At the time I felt that this single incident marred our entire journey – I felt terribly depressed and listless when we finally left Bessie's house and continued on to Bryce Canyon. I kept thinking of Cheery and cried most of the way to the park although I had to wipe away my tears when a car stopped and a kindly woman handed me two bananas.

Further on we met some cyclists coming the other way who turned out to be Dutch. They were businessmen who had, after having completed whatever business they came to do in the States, took some time off to cycle around the countryside – they stayed in motels which explained their meagre luggage. Still unable to get over Cheery's death I hardly joined in the conversation.

It was cold and windy by the time we reached the junction into Bryce Canyon National Park and as we climbed to the plateau it started to snow. We quickly headed for a building we saw in the distance – Ruby's Inn – with one side of our bodies completely covered with five inches of snow. We were still dripping as we stood next to the stove in the hallway trying to warm ourselves when in walked Ron and Sue, the motorcyclists we had met in Zion.

We must have looked quite pathetic to them since they invited us for a warm hearty lunch at the inn's restaurant. They told us where they were camping in the park and suggested that we should join them when the snow let up. This we did.

Unfortunately Ron and Sue were already leaving the park the following day, so we spent the best part of the evening chatting and getting to know each other better. They gave us their address and told us to come by when we hit the west coast again – a promise we kept.

*

I hung up a little note in the Visitor's Centre inviting others to share our camp site and the fee of five dollars. Before I knew it a German guy in a car drove up and asked if he could pitch his tent next to ours. Then Nop brought back a cyclist – Bill – who also pitched his tent on our site and finally a VW van drove up with two Dutch girls, Gerrie and Inneke, who were sisters, who also joined us on our site. Even later a Swedish girl and her Dutch boyfriend, also in a

VW van, dropped by to say hi and left us some wood for a fire that night – they were going to camp outside the park in the forest. I suppose my note worked!

The conversation around the camp fire that night was basically centred around travel and was conducted in a potpouri of German, Dutch and English. Gerrie and Inneke had been on the road quite a while and made money by collecting interesting objects as they travelled and selling them with a profit at flea markets in towns. Bill, the cyclist, was from Minneapolis, and was heading north as we were planning to do.

*

We could hardly believe the view in front of us: we were standing on the edge of the Colorado Plateau we had recently climbed in order to get to the park (which was around 7,800 feet high), overlooking an impossible, almost supernatural, landscape of thousands of rock formations. Each rock had an individual shape and size tinted yellow, pink, orange, white and vermillion. We had never seen anything like it and were truly surprised that nature could take on such a bewildering form.

We followed the Navajo Loop and Queen's Garden Trail which led us down and into this fairyland of eroded rock. The entire walk evoked long-lost images of fairy tales from my childhood. The rocks took on the forms of monsters, of giants, of wise old men, robed monks and princesses with crowns on their heads – they were sure to come to life the moment we turned our backs!

The following day we took the Fairyland Trail – an apt name – which wound through the strange landscape for eight miles. The impressions along the way were almost too much for our imagination. Deep down in the valley we spotted several mule deer and higher up on the trail we examined a lone twisted pine tree which seemed to have endured years of harsh weather and strong winds. Some of the rocks had natural windows which invited peeping through them and from such holes the grandeur of the park took on a different perspective.

*

On the last day in the park, we followed the 'scenic drive' to the southern end of the park and watched tourists roll down their car windows, take a photograph, and drive off. Some way to see a country . . . . We tried to take aerials at a viewpoint but ended up spending half the day trying to rescue our kite (without the camera, fortunately) from one of the cracks between the rocks below, where it had got stuck after a turbulent gust of wind had made it plummet into the canyon.

*

Five days later we were back at Bessie's home. The ride back reminded us once again of Cheery's sad death and there was little we could do to brighten up the mood – it was just too soon. The following day, we said goodbye to Bessie for the last time and headed first south to the town of Kanab (where we were told at the courthouse that we would have to go to Salt Lake City personally to extend our six-month visa) and then headed east towards the town of Page.

The highway ran parallel to an empty stretch of land dotted with juniper trees, so we pitched our tent away from the road under one of the trees. The rest of the way to Page was a gradual descent and, for once, we had tail winds. Page was located next to Lake Powell – another one of those man-made lakes in the desert. Houseboats floated near the shore of the lake, and it was clear the lake was used for recreational purposes. It was depressing to think how much of nature had been sacrificed when the Colorado was dammed . . . .

There was no visible habitation whatsoever along Highway 89. We found water in Bitter Springs which was merely a cluster of unfinished buildings without a soul in

125

sight. We were now officially on the Navajo Indian Reservation according to the sign we had passed at Page, but to us it was merely a continuation of the desert.

The wind had picked up and was doing its best to keep us from descending into Cameron. There was a gas station and a few houses; we asked at a house if we could camp on their land and an Indian boy of about fourteen just nodded an OK and pointed to his front yard.

*

We had horrific head winds as we climbed Highway 64 into Grand Canyon National Park. We stopped to take aerials of the Little Colorado River gorge, then went head on into the wind, struggling up the steep road. Clouds threatened rain and thunder was rumbling in the distance, but fortunately nothing came of it.

When we finally reached the entrance of the park, a ranger who came out of the office took one look at us and said: '*Anyone* who comes up *that* mountain on his *own* power definitely does not pay an entrance fee! Have a nice trip!' and waved us on.

*

We cycled on towards Mather Campground which had Hiker and Biker campgrounds. The road undulated along the rim of the canyon through thick pine forests, but once in a while we caught glimpses of the canyon from the viewpoints and rest areas along the way.

In preparation for a three-day hike down into the canyon we did some odds and ends the following day and chatted with other bikers and hikers at the campground. We met a biker called Erik who came from Santa Rosa. He was riding a pink bicycle and told us what a hard time he had been having because of the colour of his bike – apparently quite a number of rednecks assumed he was gay just because he rode a pink bike. He had been hassled constantly by idiots who shouted profanities at him as he cycled.

We also met Raymond and Roeland, two Dutch guys hitchhiking their way across America, and finally, a German cyclist called Stefan, who came limping into the campground because of some blisters caused by his shoes. All the while he was pitching his tent (which took forever) Stefan was cursing to himself in German.

When we asked him what was wrong he said, 'These bloody bicycle shoes . . . and the bloody dezert! I hate cycling in ze dezert; it is soooo boooring and soooo hot!'

*

We were anxious to know whether we could get a permit to hike and camp down in the canyon as there seemed to be an awful lot of people waiting in line at the permit office. Thankfully we succeeded and as soon as we had our permits we went to rent backpacks. The guy at the rental shop was nice enough to let us leave our bikes in a container behind the store for safe keeping while we hiked. And then we were ready to go!

Three guys drunk from beer – and getting more drunk by the minute – were sitting in front of the Permit Office waiting for a shuttle bus that had already left long before. We were heading for the trail head on foot.

'I think you missed the bus,' Nop said to them as we walked by.

'Shit . . .' they chorused back.

*

We started our hike at Yaki Point and followed the Kaibab Trail. It was a steep descent and we passed a number of people coming up the trail looking exhausted. Some people chose to ride mules instead of walking through the canyon – I noticed that some of the poor beasts didn't look very happy carrying these artificial cowboys and cowgirls in the heat. As we passed one such group of tourists on mules coming up

127

the trail I saw that one mule carrying a middle-aged woman had his tongue hanging out of his mouth as if he was dying of thirst and exhaustion. The woman riding the mule was utterly embarrassed by the state the mule was in and was trying to explain to the hikers she passed that the mule had stuck his tongue out ever since they left the rim. What she was really saying was that it wasn't *she* who caused the exhausted state the mule was in. However, it was the *mule* who evoked the sympathy of the passers by.

At a junction we headed west on the Tonto trail which was deserted and looked like it hadn't been used very much – the vegetation was pretty overgrown in parts.

'Watch it, Michèle!' Nop said suddenly as he hiked ahead of me.

'What?'

'Be careful, I think a rattlesnake just went under those bushed. Just walk quietly past it.'

I held my breath and quickly caught up with Nop. Of course I was now aware that snakes were more afraid of humans then humans are of them, but nevertheless my fear of venomous snakes wasn't easy to restrain.

It was getting hotter by the minute as we descended further into the canyon. In the middle of a hot day, the canyon doesn't possess the colourful grandeur it has on most posters hanging on the walls of travel agent's offices in the cities – it is basically desert country and therefore brown and hazy in the midday sun; even the sedimental layers are not very distinguishable. When the trail levelled out on a plateau we passed a tall blooming century plant and a prickly pear cactus with yellow flowers lining its head –these were the only bright colours we saw all day.

In the midday heat we fortunately arrived at a wonderful shaded spot with a small stream of water – one of the two rare sources of water along this trail. We carried our own water with us, of course, but it was essential to know the whereabouts of these spots in case of emergency. Four months in the desert had taught us that it was important to drink constantly even if we weren't thirsty – the dryness of the desert was deceiving and dehydration could occur so easily if one forgot to drink. A ranger at the permit office had warned hikers about this.

'We once found a hiker dead from dehydration,' she had said. 'The ironic thing was that the guy's water bottle was still full when he was found.'

*

We arrived at Indian Garden campground in the afternoon. It was a pleasant shaded area with water. Here we pitched our inner tent and hung up every edible item on a designated pole so that the squirrels wouldn't get to them. In such national parks where tourists have the bad habit of feeding wildlife, the animals have become so bold that they literally snatch food out of people's hands. In Bryce Canyon National Park we had once forgotten to put our plastic peanut butter jar in the inner tent; when we got back from our hike, the jar had been bitten open by a squirrel and we could see the claw marks on the leftover peanut butter. And in Yosemite we had hung up our food on a similar pole against bears and squirrels yet in the end it wasn't the squirrels nor bears who got our muesli but blue jays!

We hoped our food would be safe this time – we had had to carry it down the entire trail and didn't want to have to starve while climbing back up.

Indian Garden was located on a plateau just about halfway down into the canyon. At sunset Nop and I took a walk to Platform Point which was a high drop-off at the edge of the rim. There we could see the silvery line of the Colorado River cutting through the canyon floor, and could also finally enjoy the spectacular colours of the hundreds of sedimentary layers of the canyon walls of the northern rim.

As we walked back to the camp site I suddenly tripped and knocked over a rock under which a baby kingsnake had been sleeping. It quickly slithered away. Then, as it got darker and we neared Indian Garden, a bat flew right at me,

129

or rather, it flew right in my direction but stopped just short of my nose, literally made a 180 degree turn and flew away again.

*

Leaving our tent where it was, we made the final plunge down to the Colorado River which was an impressive sight at close range. The water roared by with incredible force as we crossed the bridge and went on to Phantom Ranch where we treated ourselves to some coffee and Orios – it was Nop's birthday and although there were no cake and no presents, the unique location did make it a birthday to remember. After all, how many people could claim they spent their birthday next to the Colorado River with a spectacular view of the heart of the Grand Canyon?

We climbed back up to Indian Garden and later in the evening as we were having dinner we saw Roeland and Raymond come jogging up the trail.

'Don't tell me you guys hiked all the way down today and are now heading all the way *up* again?' I asked incredulously.

'That's right,' they said as they wiped their perspiration from their foreheads. 'We couldn't get a permit to camp, so we had no choice really.'

We felt sorry for them so we fed them some peanut butter sandwiches.

'Just what we needed,' Raymond said gratefully, stuffing a third sandwich into his mouth, 'now I *know* we'll make it!' and off they went jogging up the trail as if it was a routine work-out for them.

Our load was a lot lighter without food although we still had to carry water. But it was a pleasant, if not a bit strenuous, climb back up. I still couldn't believe those guys went up and down the canyon in a single day!

As we worked our way up during the cooler morning hours we came to a cliff of switchbacks from where we heard someone singing his way up. His powerful, baritone voice

130

rebounded off the cliff wall and echoed all the way down to where we were walking. When we finally caught up with him we noticed the first black hiker we met in a national park. He was in no hurry and seemed to be enjoying the hike immensely, greeting everyone he came across on the trail.

'Beautiful ain't it?' he kept saying, followed by more singing. There was something very pleasant about hearing someone singing while walking *up* hill – he must have cheered up many a hiker sweating up the trail that hot day although he probably didn't know it.

Back at Mather Campground we celebrated Nop's birthday again – this time with doughnuts and coffee – with Raymond, Roeland, Stefan and a new arrival, a cyclist called Steve.

The winds were just as bad when we left the park as when we had come in. On the way down – cycling *down,* that is – we passed a German couple pedalling up the other way. The woman was furious about the wind and was cursing in German. When they saw us she desperately asked me (in German) whether they sold wine at the park shop. I said they did (in English) and that seemed to cheer her up a bit. But I didn't dare tell her it was still a *very* long way to the shop from where they were since she was threatening to throw her bicycle over the mountainside at any moment.

The wind was unrelenting even when we left the park premises; it was blowing so hard my sunglasses blew off my face every time a truck passed us. To make matters worse, I was beginning to have trouble with the seat of my bike. Our seats were made of straps (used for seat belts) which ran horizontally across the chair, and part of my spine, which got pushed between two of the straps, was beginning to get sore. Nop tried adjusting the straps but it didn't help. Arriving hot and tired in Tuba city, we saw some people at a church and asked if we could pitch our tent; one of the men invited us to camp in his back yard. After a refreshing shower (the single most important thing for revival next to food), we chatted with Mr Nelson over coffee. Mr Nelson was a Mormon teacher at a nearby high school for the Indians of the reservation. He told us that the biggest problem was that the kids didn't speak English properly. They would go back to their families deep in the reservation in the summer vacations and come back to school in the autumn with the English they had learned the previous school year already forgotten. When we asked him whether some Indians were Mormons, he said there were and explained how the Mormon church converted them.

'The Indians are told that for every generation which becomes Mormon the following generation will be born with lighter skin; eventually, therefore, the Indian race could also become Caucasian.' It was the most ridiculous religious tactic for converting people I had ever heard.

But even more absurd was that all good Mormons had a two-year supply of food stashed away in a cellar or store room in the event of Armageddon which, he added, was supposed to happen quite soon. The Mormon church was extremely powerful, partly because all faithful Mormons contribute approximately ten per cent of their income to the church.

Mr Nelson told all of this to us matter-of-factly, so we couldn't tell whether he himself was a faithful Mormon or not. And we didn't probe.

*

It was 66 miles to Navajo National Monument, an area which is owned by the Navajo Indians but which is run by the National Park Service. Again, there was almost no habitation along the way – most of the Indians seemed to live inland, a good way off the main highway. At the campground of the monument, we shared a camp site with a man in his early fifties – David Cooper – who turned out to be a great enthusiast about the desert like ourselves. He told us he spent a lot of time in the desert, hiking and photographing it at its best at sunrise and sunset. He was a professional photographer, he explained, and sold his slides mostly to advertising agencies. What a wonderful way to make a living, I thought!

But David's professional relationship with the desert was only secondary in importance to him – he really loved the desert with fervour and his enthusiasm was definitely contagious. I suppose he realised we were genuine enthusiasts too because he later asked us whether we had read Edward Abbey's book *Desert Solitaire*.

When we said we hadn't, he went into his camper and came out with a copy and said, 'This book is a must if you love the desert. I keep a supply of his books with me all the time so I can give them away to people like you.'

The following day we joined David on our hiking tour to the Betatakin Cliff Dwellings down by the valley floor – the dwellings were ancient Indian ruins in an enormous natural alcove in the canyon wall. Indians had apparently lived in several such alcoves because they not only provided shelter but were also situated in valleys where fresh water was plentiful. David explained that the Indians who inhabited such cliff dwellings were generally called Anasazi Indians meaning 'the ancient ones', and that they had dwelled in such alcoves up to about 700 years ago when, for some unknown reason they suddenly seemed to have abandoned them. Whether it was because of draught, disease or war archaeologists still don't know. The ruins consisted of several two- and three-storied stone buildings clustered together and several round rooms called 'kivas' which had been excavated and partially restored. The kivas were supposed to have been used for social gatherings and religious ceremonies.

I tried to imagine what it would be like to live in such an alcove – the view was certainly grand. The lush green vegetation of the valley floor was an inviting Garden of Eden and the canyon wall which ran along the opposite side of the valley seemed to provide ample protection from the elements of the higher mesas. All in all it looked quite comfortable, but perhaps I was forgetting the harsher aspects of reality.

The hike had been in the morning; at noon we said goodbye to David and promised to rendezvous at Arches National Park in ten days.

As we continued on Highway 160 we passed an Australian cyclist who was heading west; we stopped briefly to chat with him and, I must add, promptly forgot about the meeting until two years later when we received a letter from a certain Peter Conroy who refreshed our memory about the meeting. In fact *his* memory had first been refreshed when he coincidentally camped at the very same Condit RV Park in Texas where we had camped a few months earlier. There he met the Condits and some of the other senior citizens of the park who described us in detail to him. It was then that he realised we had indeed met. That had prompted him to write to us and we have corresponded ever since!

Kayenta was a most strange town – in fact it wasn't a town at all since it consisted of just one large supermarket with a huge parking lot in front of it. People seemed to come from all directions of the desert to get to this supermarket – perhaps it *was* the only store around. But then again what was a 30 mile drive to a supermarket for some Americans?

Most of the customers were Indians from the reservation. Other than their distinctive features, they otherwise resembled the stereotype American citizen who frequents cheap supermarkets – obese to the extent of being grotesque and wearing clothes which seem to accentuate the excess fat rather than hide it. The obesity of a third of the American population betrays the poor diet of this nation, the source of which was readily to be seen in the enormous shopping carts these Indians also pushed to their pick-up trucks – they were filled to the brim with junk food such as ice cream, potato chips, TV dinners, (Diet!) Pepsi, candy bars, sweetened cereals and loads of frozen meats.

Once we hit Highway 163 we could already see the pinnacles of the rock formations of Monument Valley in the distance. I couldn't help but be reminded of the TV commercials which frequently use Monument Valley as a backdrop for car commercials: a business-man driving through the desert at sunset and the scene is accompanied by some silly comment like 'With this model you feel like taking the long way home'.

At the junction to the Navajo Tribal Park (where, we had been told, there would be a campground facing Monument Valley) we saw a cyclist resting by the side of the road.

We greeted him with the usual 'Hi, which way are you heading?'

But he didn't give us one of the usual biker answers like 'East' or 'West'. Instead he said, 'Actually, I was waiting for *you.'*

'For *us*? How did you know we were coming this way?' I asked, perplexed.

'Another cyclist told me you were heading this way,' he answered.

We couldn't remember passing any other cyclist except the Australian we met near Navajo National Monument.

'You mean an Australian?'

'That's right.'

'But we met him going the *other* way so how could he have told *you* we were coming this way?'

'Somehow he knew he would meet you,' he said with a shrug. 'Maybe someone else told him.'

It seemed like a ridiculous discussion in the middle of the desert, so Nop said, 'Want to join us? We're planning to camp at the tribal park.'

'OK,' he said.

As we headed for the park we soon discovered that we were going to be cycling with a comedian who began his never-ending jokes with:

'Guess what? I saw this T-shirt the other day ... know what it said?'

'What?'
'The wind doesn't blow, it sucks!'

*

We couldn't have enjoyed a better front yard: our tent literally opened out to the monolithic rock towers of Monument Valley below us and at sunset we were rewarded with a grand closing of the day when the sun's rays struck the buttes, turning them into a fiery red. They resembled proud giants gracefully ageing in the open, oblivious to the world around them.

*

Randy was the longest cycling companion we had on our journey – from the day we found him 'waiting' for us at the junction to Monument Valley, we ended up cycling for about a month together. He was a student from Phoenix, Arizona, and was travelling around for the duration of his summer vacation which had already started. Like us he wanted to see as much of the desert as possible and then head north when the heat became unbearable and the Rockies became passable.

From Monument Valley, we headed for Goosenecks which was 34 miles further north. Again, it was terribly hot, and when we got to the trading post of Mexican Hat (named after a rock in the vicinity which resembles a Mexican man wearing a Sombrero hat) we each ate an entire pint of ice cream. We then filled our bottles and took a side road to Goosenecks, so called because the San Juan River makes four incredibly tight, symmetrical bends, each of which looks like the rounded neck of a goose.

We wanted to take aerials of the curvatures of the river but unfortunately the wind died down completely by the time we reached the viewpoints. This was a constant frustration for us – hauling our kites wherever we went (usually in head winds) only to encounter turbulent or no winds at all when the scenery for aerial photography was perfect.

By the time we arrived at the viewpoint, there were two women cyclists – Jan and Cindy – who were already getting settled to camp at the covered picnic site. Since we immediately felt a feeling of comradeship (as it was rare for so many cyclists to meet in such a region) we sat together and chatted while we all cooked and ate our respective meals. There was only one motor camper at Goosenecks but to our great annoyance the inhabitants decided to start their generator as soon as it got dark, spoiling the peace of the place. Why some people deliberately come to such lovely spots only to put on their damn television set is beyond me. They could just as well have stayed at home if they weren't interested in the stars or the magical stillness of the place. At 10 o'clock, when we were all ready to hit the sack (no tent this time), Randy finally went up to the camper and politely asked them to turn the damn thing off.

*

Jan and Cindy went on to Mesa Verde, while we went on to Natural Bridges National Monument, 56 miles from Goosenecks. How wonderful it was to cycle from one park to another in a single day with very little traffic and no ugly towns to spoil the ride! This was perfect bicycling country, and Nop and I were now *very* glad we had decided to go south after Yosemite. What can I say ... Natural Bridges was *also* spectacular (I feel like I'm running out of adjectives to describe all the wonderful national parks of this region); what was unique about the Natural Bridges was, of course, the natural bridges. Nature's forces of flowing water which had eroded, percolated and finally broken through the sandstone walls formed peculiar spans of stone 'bridges' across the valley. Some of these natural bridges extended some 180 feet across the valley and were particularly striking when the sun hit them: they looked as if they were made of solid gold.

*

The Grand Canyon is said to be one of the seven wonders of the world because it is one of the largest canyons in the world; but the expression is also rather bizarre in a land *full* of canyons. Ever since Zion National Park we had passed canyon after canyon and to me each and every canyon was 'Grand' in its own way. If someone now asked me whether I had been to the Grand Canyon during my travels through the US, I would take the question as either coming from someone who was ignorant of the American desert or from someone who hadn't taken a better look at America when driving (and therefore daydreaming) through it.

The road through the canyonlands we were now traversing was typified by long stretches of flat mesas followed by steep descents into canyons and immediately followed by steep ascents back onto the next mesas. The road continued in this manner for hundreds of miles and it wasn't easy cycling with the sun pounding down on us and the wind relentlessly blowing into our faces day after day.

Towards sunset one day when we were climbing yet another canyon wall little insects started to bite me all over.

'What on earth *are* these buggers?' I said in annoyance, while trying to get them out of my ears and nose.

'Gnats,' Randy said as he too swatted yet another one from his face.

The only way to get away from them was to cycle at a relatively steady speed but this was impossible when we had to climb steep slopes and as a result we were literally eaten alive at every ascent.

When we reached the small town of Montezuma Creek we asked at a church whether we could pitch our tent on the churchyard. The Pastor and his wife invited us to stay in a church building since the gnats were so bad. They also let us take showers for which we were very grateful since it had been a long hot day – we had covered 72 miles in the heat and were so exhausted we could hardly eat anything. But at least we were protected from the damn gnats . . . .

*

The state lines of Utah, Arizona, Colorado and New Mexico meet at a junction called 'Four Corners' but it was a 10 mile detour we didn't feel like taking in the merciless heat so we headed for Cortez instead. We now entered the state of Colorado.

Nop was having stomach cramps – posibly because of all the cold drinks we couldn't resist along the way – so we took a long break at a gas station which had the only shade we had seen for miles. When he felt better we went on to Cortez where we decided to stock up on food before climbing into Mesa Verde National Park.

I was sitting in the shade of a supermarket by our bikes while Nop and Randy were doing the shopping when a guy came up to me and started asking the usual questions.

'Are those your bikes?' he asked.

Tired and fed up with having to answer the same old questions again and again I curtly replied that they were. But when I looked up I saw that there were two *other* recumbents against the wall.

I jumped up and this time *I* asked, 'Are those your bikes?' and when he said they were I said, 'Could you keep an eye on our bikes, I won't be a moment!' and went dashing into the supermarket and dragged Nop and Randy out: 'Look!' I said excitedly, 'Recumbents!'

The guy introduced himself as Mark, and his wife, as Barbara.

'A friend of ours saw you coming into town and gave us a ring,' Mark said.

He and Barbara lived in Cortez and they immediately invited us to come and stay the night. It goes without saying the Nop was especially happy to meet someone who also made his own recumbent bikes and by the time we got to their house (half of which was a workshop) the two of them

139

were in deep discussion about tools, material and designs, swapping ideas and basically getting into heavy bicycle jargon that none of us lay people could understand.

Mark's experimental recumbents were quite different from Nop's: he had made handlebars up front, shorter frames and very high pedals. We all tried out each other's bikes, and for once we were pleased to see that Randy was in the minority with his conventional bike.

Nop made use of Mark's workshop to do some maintenance work on our bikes and Barbara let me take whatever clothes we needed from a pile she said she no longer needed. This included a couple of tight-fitting woollen sweaters we would be eternally grateful for once we hit the Rockies, and some shorts to replace the once-upon-a-time shorts we had been wearing.

Barbara missed travelling, she told me, as she put her son, Scot, to bed. 'God, I envy you guys,' she said.

'But you've done some extensive travelling yourself,' I said. 'Aren't you satisfied about that?'

'I am . . . but seeing you guys like this, it reminds me so much of how wonderful it is to travel.'

I knew what she meant.

'I was so angry when I got pregnant,' she went on. 'And until the very last day before Scot was born I *cried* you know, because I felt my freedom to travel was finally lost forever.'

'But you can still travel *with* Scot,' I suggested.

'Oh, I know, but it's not the same. The funny thing is, as soon as Scot was born I did change – now I can't imagine *not* having had him since I love him so much. Still, I miss the kind of freedom you guys have . . . .'

*

In the morning we all had doughnuts and coffee. Mark got a phone call from someone and came back smiling to say that he had just been offered a full-time job. Barbara was exhilarated and gave him a big hug. They had been having a hard time scraping together a living with odd jobs till now so this was very good news indeed. We were happy for them – they certainly deserved the wonderful news.

Randy went to see whether his money had arrived at the local bank; meanwhile, Nop and I did some more shopping in town, In the afternoon, we sadly said our goodbyes to Mark and Barbara and went on to Mesa Verde National Park. At the entrance, our Eagle Pass card, which was supposed to give us free entry into any national park, or at least give us a reduction on the entrance fee, was rebuffed by a bureaucratic woman ranger who said it only applied to one 'vehicle' and that the other two people would have to pay. My argument was that it wasn't fair that bicyclists had *each* to pay a fee when huge campers with five passengers *and* bicycles attached to the roof were allowed to enter with one pass; it fell on deaf ears, and she refused to let us in until we paid.

We had to climb several long switchbacks to get to Morfield campground. Nop and Randy, ahead of me as usual, waited for me after some strenuous bends, only to go on by the time I arrived.

'That's not fair,' I complained.

'We *had* our rest already – while waiting for you!' Nop joked.

'You guys always rest longer.'

'That's cuz you're so slow,' Randy teased as he went around the next bend and did his usual number of 'Andele andele . . . . Woooopoooopooopooo' at the top of his voice.

He's crazy, I thought, not without affection. Randy sometimes made the most idiotic sounds when climbing particularly steep ascents – he was especially adept at imitating the sounds of geese or crows and now he was doing his crow act again. It never failed to amaze me where he and Nop got all their energy from. Sometimes it was a pain in the neck having to cycle with two hyper-energetic males.

*

We left our tent at the campground the following day and cycled up eight miles of dirt road (due to construction). We were certainly glad our bikes were unloaded.

Mesa Verde's Indian Cliff dwellings were, unlike the alcove we saw at Navajo National Monument, located high up the canyon walls – a somewhat precarious location considering the fact that the inhabitants had to practically scale the canyon walls to get to their homes. Fortunately the Park Service had created a network of narrow stairways and ladders to make the cliff dwellings accessible to the public. It was also the first national park we came across which actually prohibited overweight citizens from taking certain tours to the cliff dwellings. And when we joined a small group led by a ranger to the cliff dwelling called Balcony's House we saw why. We had to climb a thirty-foot-high ladder. ('Whatever you do, don't look down,' the ranger had warned) and had to squeeze through and climb a very narrow stairway as well as crawl on all fours to get through a low, cave-like entrance into the alcove.

The view out into the immense valley was very impressive from the alcove and with the help of our binoculars we could see several more niches at the other side of the valley which were also cliff dwellings. These cliff dwellings were much larger than those of Betatakin; not only were the alcoves higher and wider but they were also much deeper, and the buildings had more floors. It was obvious that quite large communities had lived there – one alcove seemed to represent an entire tribal village. But here too the mystery remained as to why the Anasazi's abruptly abandoned the dwellings.

We visited the museum, the 'Spruce Tree' and 'Cliff Palace' dwellings and then treated ourselves to ice cream and drinks before descending back to the campground.

*

Back in Cortez, we temporarily said goodbye to Randy, who was going to detour to the Rockies while we went to Salt

Lake City to extend our visas – we agreed to rendezvous in Dinosaur National Monument on June 12th – two weeks later – and from there cycle together again up through the Tetons to Yellowstone National Park.

For the first few days it was strange cycling without Randy – he had become such a part of our trip that we found ourselves missing him and the ridiculous sounds he made.

Thunder rumbled in the distance as we headed for Monticello on Highway 666. At the border between the states of Colorado and Utah, lightning started to thrash around. So we took cover under a roof of a bar which seemed to be located in No Man's Land – it stood literally between the two state signs.

We arrived in Monticello at 8 p.m. just as it was getting dark and camped behind the home of the minister of the 'Community Church' who, upon opening his door, said, 'Oh! You're the ones we saw in Natural Bridges a few days back!'

This sort of thing was happening more and more frequently these days, possibly because most people headed for the same national parks on the few roads which led to them.

*

The ride to Moab on Highway 163 was very scenic, especially the last part. As we descended into town we saw quite a few peculiar-looking red rock formations along the way but unfortunately the wind was blasting away again, somewhat diminishing the fun of the ride down.

In Moab we dropped by Rim Tours Cyclery where Tod – whom we had met at Simon's place back in Isla Vista on the west coast – was supposed to be working. He wasn't in at the time so we collected the mail which had been waiting for us (mostly for Nop!) and bought some new chains for our bikes. The two guys (brothers) working at Rim Tours were very friendly and gave us a discount. We left a message for

Tod saying we would be heading for Arches National Park which was some 20 miles away.

The road was deserted most of the way and the scenery absolutely breathtaking. The sun was beginning to set and we knew we wouldn't make it to the campground before dark but for once we didn't mind. Cycling through the main part of the park at sunset gave us a chance to see it at its best – it was absolutely majestic and we could see why Edward Abbey had been so protective of this particular region. This region was formed some 150 million years ago when sandstone and other layers, which had hardened into rock, were lifted above ground and slowly began the process of erosion in wind and rain. The constant erosion caused cracks to form in the exposed sandstone which then widened into narrow canyons separated by 'fins' – vertical walls of rock. Perforations then began to appear in these fins with the continuing erosion until large 'windows' took their place. Even further erosion enlarged these windows and finally graceful arches were created (differing from the formation of natural bridges in that arches are formed by erosional forces like wind, rain and sun rather than by the forces of water from a river).

The most interesting aspect about the park was that all stages of this long erosion process could be witnessed, whether it be fully-fledged arches like Delicate Arch, fins which were just beginning to get holes in them or vertical walls which had yet to become fins – all of this with the wonderful backdrop of the snow-capped peaks of La Sal Mountains in the distance. And as the stars came out and we cycled on in the silence of night when the silhouettes of the canyon walls, domes, balanced rocks, arches and fins took on eerie shapes, I couldn't have wished to be anywhere else in the world, the landscape was so hypnotic.

It was pitch black by the time we finally reached the campground where we went in search of David's camper. By chance David had passed us just before we went to Rim Tours, and there he had given us specific directions as to where he was camped. It was good to see David again, especially here in this park which he had spoken so passionately about; after dinner the three of us pored over the map of the park and made plans for several hikes together. We pitched our tent snugly between two huge boulders where we had a nice tree for shade and a picnic table to sit at.

The following morning, the three of us hiked for about five hours through Devil's Garden which led to various arches and entire hills of the elongated fins which here we could definitely see resembled shark's fins. The setting was absolutely perfect for a picnic lunch.

In the evening David cooked a delicious pasta dinner for us and with wine which accompanied the dinner we celebrated the 10,000th kilometres (6,250 miles) of our journey. We were now seven months on the road and had grown so accustomed to this new lifestyle that it was becoming harder and harder to imagine what it was like to live in a single place any more . . . .

*

David drove us to the trail heads of Window Arches, Double Arch and later that of Delicate Arch from where we could walk through the rock formations and enjoy the desert and peace. In Desert Solitaire, Edward Abbey vividly described the puffy cloud formations in the cobalt-blue skies of the desert which serve as the perfect backdrop to the magnificent nature of this region. Edward Abbey had been, at one point in his life, a park ranger at Arches National Park before the roads to the park had been paved. He detested everything that had to do with development and growth and subsequently he was a strong defender of America's natural environment.

I had to sympathize with him since the roads of the park did get paved in the end and now most lazy drivers can easily enjoy the park in 'comfort'. This was unfortunately true in almost every national park we cycled through in this country – they now all seem to have what they call 'Scenic

Drives' – a paved road which usually leads to the main sights and viewpoints where tourists no longer need to make the effort and get out of their cars to take a photograph.

It was a pity America was so car-oriented. I often wondered how many people would actually even *consider* giving up their car. Perhaps depriving an American of his car would be like depriving a cowboy of his horse? The usual excuse for the necessity of the car in this country seemed to be the vast distances but why doesn't anyone talk about a good cross-country railway network for the bulk of the tourist traffic, with electric-powered public transport connecting stations to the national parks? So let the tourists *walk* or *bicycle* within the parks – isn't that what the preservation of nature is all about – keeping it unspoilt and only accessible to those who truly appreciate it for its natural state and therefore would make an effort to get there in order to enjoy it? The way tourism in national parks is now being practised in the US, tourists might as well stay at home and look at a set of slides with accompanying CDs playing nature music.

*

We met Tod and his girlfriend on our last night in the park – they had cycled all the way up from Moab just to see us. This time Nop and I cooked, and the five of us had a wonderful evening together before Tod and his girlfriend cycled back (in the dark) to Moab. Fortunately for them there was a full moon.

The next day, Nop and I set off again, having said goodbye to David for the second time, and headed north for Salt Lake City some 250 miles away. We managed to cover this distance in only three days, cycling a new record of 101 miles on the third day. That day we were climbing to Soldier Summit – elevation 7,500 feet – when David passed us in his camper again. He gave us grapes to energize us for the climb up to the top (which wasn't half as bad as he had insisted it would be – never take the word of someone driving!) where we rewarded ourselves with coffee at a roadside cafe. It was then a rare treat of tail winds the rest of the way down into Salt Lake valley.

We found a hospitality home – the Hanson's home – in the suburb of Sandy. We had actually contacted them a few weeks earlier to let them know we were heading their way and also because we needed a mailing address. What a relief it was to be able to wash off the layers of accumulated dust, dried perspiration, sun-screen lotion and dried insect repellent under a hot shower and sleep between crisp clean sheets. Ahh . . . . the comforts of a house!

*

The next day we cycled into the city (*noise* pollution!) to the Immigration Office where we were asked to fill in some forms. Then the immigration officer asked us at which address we would like the visas to be sent. We had come all the way up to Salt Lake City just to fill in some bloody forms which could have been mailed to us!

But since we *had* come all the way to Salt Lake City we decided we might as well see the sights. We cycled to *the* Mormon temple in the centre of town. There were a lot of tourists walking around, but also a lot of suspicious-looking characters walking around in dark suits and sunglasses, whispering into walkie-talkies . . . or was it my imagination?

The temple itself was unimpressive, at least from a European point of view, but we had to give the Mormons credit for having hauled all that granite by ox cart hundreds of miles across the country in order to build their precious church in this city.

We found spare generators for our stove and went back to the Hanson's who, after dinner, took us for a drive to Salt Lake which was, at the time, flooding as a result of the melting snow in the surrounding mountains. They also drove us up to the foothills on the outskirts of town where we had a good view of the city lights in the evening. But the few

147

days in the city already made me long to cycle in the countryside again and we decided to leave the next day despite the comforts of their wonderful home.

*

It was quite a steep climb up to Timpanogos Cave National Monument, 27 miles east of the city in the Wasatch Mountains. We decided to join a ranger-guided tour through Timpanogos Cave.

The cave was actually a series of limestone caverns which were created when pressure built up and pushed the rocks along the Wasatch Fault and created the Wasatch Mountain Range. Faults were created within the mountains where the walls ground against each other and pulverized the stone. The porous pulverized material was later washed away by the American Fork River which, once its level dropped, allowed air to enter open spaces, thus creating the caverns. Water continued to make its way into the caverns through the faults creating the beautiful stalactites. These caverns also contained a lot of helictites which were tangled masses of colourful stony deposits.

As we squeezed through a narrow fault, the ranger stopped in the middle of it and said, 'Well folks, this is where I am required to tell you that the Park Service is not responsible if an earthquake occurs . . . .'

*

Someone told us that Alpine Loop summit was at 9,000 feet. It was, in any case, a steep climb to the top. Just before the top we had to cycle through a river of water which was flowing uncontrollably over the road. Now we could see why Salt Lake had flooded.

It started to drizzle as we descended to the Sundance ski resort where we made a short stop for coffee. The girl attending the souvenir shop proudly pointed out that the famous Robert Redford *himself* came to *this* very resort to ski

148

every year, *yes m'am!*

As we neared Heber City lightning started to flash so we took cover at a nearby farm. We had asked a woman on the farm if we could wait under the roof of the garage till the storm blew over. She didn't seem to like the idea very much so she stood near us, looking at us suspiciously all the while we were there.

She was so eager to see us go that after a short while she said, 'Well, the storm seems to be lettin' up.' But when we didn't move she tried, 'Even the birds are singing!' Really, did she have to be so obvious?

At a church some of its members told us we could pitch our tent next to the ex-bishop's house, so we did. The ex-bishop, however, didn't seem too enthusiastic about finding us there, but later he relaxed somewhat as we talked about our travels (tell someone you've cycled 6,300 miles and their ears can't help but prick up). In the evening some children dropped by our tent and gave us some home-baked cookies.

*

On June 11th we arrived at Dinosaur National Monument after two rather gloomy days of cloud, rain and even hail. But now it was hot again as we took a look around the town of Vernal before entering the park. It seemed as if everything in town was geared towards the image of dinosaurs: there was a Dinosaur Motel, a Dinosaur Cafe, a Dinosaur Museum . . . .

We found Split Mountain campground where we pitched our tent and shared the site with uninvited gnats and mosquitoes. But later in the afternoon we heard the unmistakable voice of our companion ('Wooooopooopooo!'), Randy.

After we had split up at Cortez, Randy told us he had gone on to the Rockies where (for the fun of it) he had cycled up the highest road (about 14,100 feet) in the country. It was good to see him again.

149

The next day we went to the quarry to see the fossil remains of dinosaurs – petrified skeletal remains preserved in the sedimental layers of the mountains; the public could observe paleontologists still painstakingly working on the excavation.

*

We followed Highway 44 and camped by Lake Steinaker where we had to pay, but the refreshing swim in the lake was definitely worth $5. The next day was a tough climb to Flaming Gorge starting with steep switchbacks, followed by a long ascent. But just when we thought we had had the worst climb and were finally descending, we had to climb again! It *was* a beautiful area, I had to admit, but the climb was so tiring I hardly enjoyed the view and I couldn't even see Nop and Randy any more – the buggers were so far ahead of me. But finally, I caught up with them in the town of Manila where we met two (drunk) cyclists, Adam and Tom.

Out of town the five of us found some land by a river where we camped together. We were immediately attacked by mosquitoes as we pitched our tents, and it wasn't until the tents were up and my mosquito coils were burning that they left us in peace.

The following day I woke up with a splitting headache – the strain of the previous day must have hit me (we had managed to cover 66 miles despite all the climbing) and was irritable the whole day. At one point, as I sat by the road waiting for the men to return from the 'restroom', some dust got into my eyes and as I rubbed them one of my contact lenses fell out. Just what I needed . . . ! The three of us squatted there for half an hour cursing the midday heat of the desert looking for my damn contact lens. Randy finally found it.

*

Having camped on the bank of the Green River (after obtaining permission from the local Sheriff) we were now back on the main road. We came across a place called Little America – not a bad name for a place with an enormous gas station, a fast food joint and a motel – where, being a truck stop, truck drivers could take free showers. We pretended to be truck drivers and were given towels and soap. The men shared one big room with many showers and I was given a key to a motel room to shower in private. What a treat! Moreover, the restaurant next door was promoting soft ice cream for twenty-five cents – Nop and Randy gorged on three in a row.

The tiny town of Opal was no more than a general store, a railroad and a couple of blocks of houses. We took a look at the unused old freight buildings next to the railway line and decided it was a good enough place to spend the night. The town was such a peculiar place that we took some aerials of it. For once the conditions were ideal for our kite except that the mosquitoes feasted on our exposed legs as we tried to stand still in order to keep the kite steady.

It was great not to have to pitch our tent for once and the building we had settled in was so big we could spread out all our things in spacious luxury. The town was so small that all was quiet as soon as it became dark and we turned in early.

But around midnight a train rolled in from nowhere, shaking the building we were sleeping in with tremendous noise. Then another train came by, then another and another until they kept coming non-stop. And they didn't just ride by. No, they stopped in the middle of Opal, right *next* to us and started connecting and disconnecting carriages! This was done by a noisy locomotive and every time a carriage got connected there was a large 'boom' and the earth shook with earthquake force. We had ended up sleeping in what turned out to be a central station for freight trains!

*

Horrible as our memories of Opal are, I have always wondered where the town had got its name from and the answer came to me quite coincidentally a few years later as I watched a documentary about the American Southwest on television. Suddenly I saw the very Opal we had camped in, which I recognised immediately. The documentary explained that the name 'Opal' derived from a greeting used by cowboys who, during annual cattle drives, drove large numbers of cattle to this particular railroad station to load them on the trains for the cities. It was here that they reunited with their comrades whom they hadn't seen for a year. When the loading of the cattle was done it was customary for the cowboys to part from each other with the words, 'See you next year O'pal!'

*

The road was quite level the next day and the ride was pretty easy but the lack of sleep the previous night (an understatement) had put all three of us into foul moods. By the time we reached Bear Lake, which was a nice uncommercialised lake, and pitched our tent, we started to get on each others' nerves. We went for a swim, but it didn't help. I was being my usual flirtatious self with Randy, which was never serious, when Nop got angry and took off on his own for a walk. Then Randy took off in the other direction and I was left alone in the tent bewildered by what was happening to us. What did I do? Was Nop jealous? Did Randy feel left out?

Fortunately the bad feelings didn't last; Nop and I talked about it that evening, and although he was still grumpy, he admitted that he had indeed been jealous. (In a way it was nice to know that he *could* be jealous at times – he had never once shown it before. But after that I tried to be more considerate).

We had only pitched our inner tents thinking that it would stay dry but at about four in the morning it started to rain; we all had to get out of bed to pitch the outer tents as well.

Two consecutive nights of restless sleep made us decide to stay at Bear Lake one more night, this time on someone's land on the western side. We just lazed around, enjoying the view, swam in the lake and did some reading.

Bear Lake was on the border between Utah and Idaho – after Idaho we would finally be leaving the Great Basin Desert which saddened us but we knew it was getting too hot to remain in the desert any longer and the voracious gnats were beginning to get on our nerves. At least it was a consolation to know that we would (hopefully) be back in the desert the following winter.

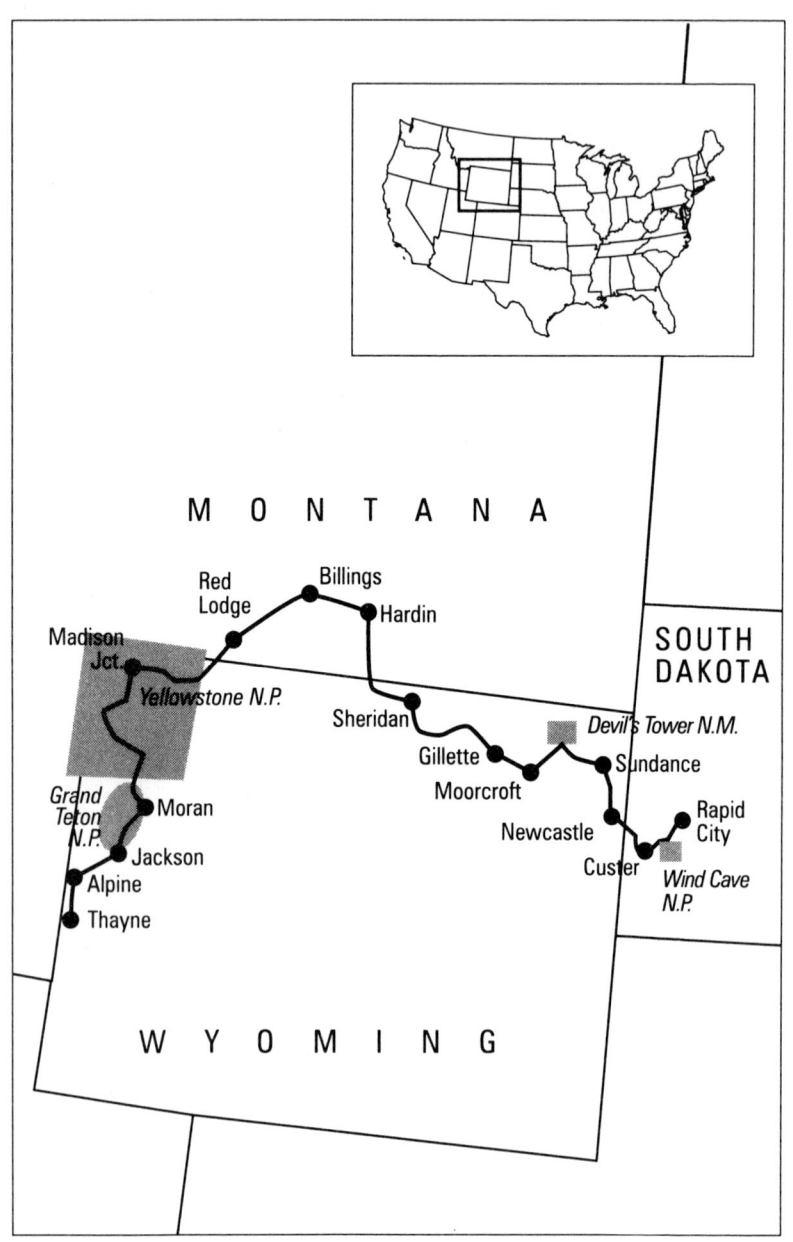

Endless horizons in Organ Pipe Cactus National Monument, Arizona

Aerial photograph of the town of Opal, Wyoming

Rock slide on the Pacific Coast Highway, California

Campsite for the night: golden canyon walls along the Pecos River, Texas

Author and month-long companion, Randy, cycling out of Monument Valley, Arizona

Adam and his dog 'Toe-cutter' in Sentinel, Arizona

Two ancient pecan trees growing out of the Bowman's home, Texas

Snowbirds of Oleander Acres RV Park, Texas

'Buckskin' of Ucross, Wyoming

Nop flying his Genki in Death Valley National Monument, California

The 25 cent ferry ride to Staten Island, New York

Undulating hills of Napa Valley, California

Signs like these had little effect on the drivers of Texas

Giant saguaro cactus of Arizona

A scenic break along the Blue Ridge Parkway

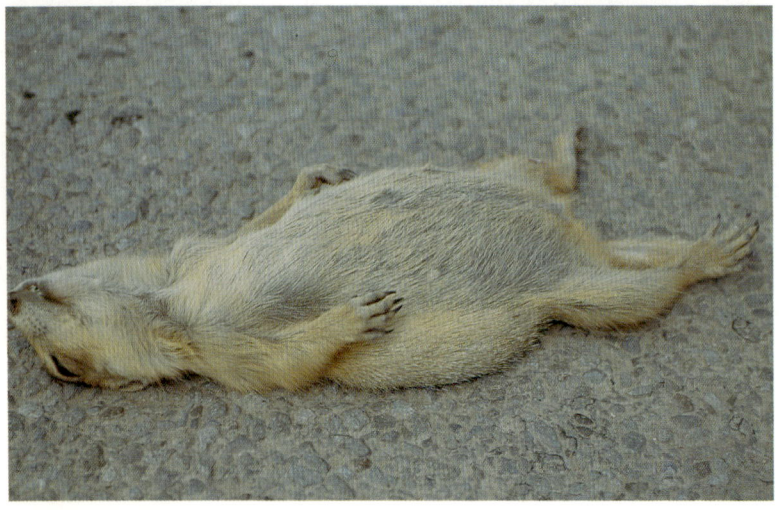

One of the countless roadside victims we came across

ABOVE THE CLOUD LINE

We could already see the Grand Teton Range – an awe-inspiring skyline of rugged snow-capped peaks some 9,000 feet high which made us terribly excited. We hadn't seen mountains like this since we left Yosemite and just the sight of them made me apprehensive about the climbs to come but I also knew they would be well worth the effort.

Randy knew the Heeps, an elderly couple who wintered in Phoenix but lived in the town of Thayne during the summer. Thayne was more or less situated in the foothills of the Teton Mountains.

The Heeps kindly let us pitch our tents in their back yard and make use of their shower and kitchen so that evening we cooked up one of our tent specials for all of us and chatted with the Heeps about our trip. Although they were retired the Heeps were professional breeders of racing horses which they ran in the horse races of Phoenix during the winter months. After dinner we were given a little tour of their place and were shown some of the graceful creatures which grazed on the land right behind their house.

*

In the morning we passed a cheese factory, which also had a restaurant, and we treated ourselves to a large breakfast in preparation for the climbs to come.

Highway 89 became very scenic once we passed the town of Alpine – we climbed a gorge along a rushing river where several people were rafting down in large rubber boats. Three women cyclists raced past us without a single 'hello' – we weren't used to such rudeness from fellow cyclists since all long-distance cyclists greet each other on the road. I concluded that they were probably out for the weekend or for a work-out. A breed apart, in other words.

Jackson was an ugly tourist trap, so we went on into Grand Teton National Park and shared a camp site with two guys from Chicago at a campground next to Jenny Lake. We had covered 79 miles that day and were quite tired from all the climbing but we were also enraptured with the scenery around us.

Jenny Lake, situated at an elevation of about 6,600 feet was surrounded by a coniferous forest along its shores and had, as a backdrop, the towering snow-capped mountains we had seen all day. The lake had apparently been formed some 9,000 years ago by a glacier from Cascade Canyon but the geological history of the Teton region itself was some nine million years old. A crack had appeared in the earth and formed the Teton Fault which began to swing upwards, creating the mountain range on one end and Jackson Hole on the other. It was only in the last 200,000 years that several glacial periods sent ice and water through the mountains, carving the U-shaped canyons and sculpturing the landscape which surrounded us.

*

It was very cold that night and a myriad of stars glistened above the dark skyline of the mountain range. We had forgotten how cold it could be in the mountains!

We were just making some popcorn in our tent when Randy came in after having phoned his girlfriend back in Phoenix. He had been missing her quite a bit and I thought he would have been glad to have heard her voice again but he was fuming.

'Fucking bitch!' he mumbled.

'What happened?' I asked, surprised at his anger.

156

'She said she had gone out with someone else!'

Randy's girlfriend had actually resented the fact that Randy had gone on this trip – he had wanted her to come along but she had refused. Now she was apparently getting back at him in this vengeful way. We really felt sorry for Randy.

We tried to cheer him up by diverting his attention to some popcorn and conversation with our new neighbours but it didn't help. He remained quiet and gloomy the rest of the evening which was a depressing sight since we weren't used to seeing him so down.

*

We hiked about 13 miles up the Cascade Canyon Trail only to discover that it wasn't passable because of snow. But it didn't really matter that we couldn't go on – the scenery we had hiked through was fabulous enough. The recent melting of the snow had caused the river to overflow and as a consequence many young trees had been uprooted and were being washed down the mountain. The torrent of water was a turbulent scene, making us appreciate and respect the forces of nature. Yet by contrast, the river's surroundings were tranquil with beautiful flowers and singing birds reassuring us that spring was imminent.

*

We decided to leave early the next morning so that we could avoid paying for the camp site again (it cost $7). Randy managed to get us up at 5.30 a.m. so we were on the road by 7.00, shivering from the chilly mountain air.

The weather was bright and clear as we continued on the beautiful road to Yellowstone where a proliferation of wild flowers was in full bloom. As I stopped to photograph some of them by the side of the road the first camper to pass us that morning stopped and the driver who stuck his head out of the window, turned out to be ... David Cooper! (It was the

157

fourth time we met him on our trip!)

As the hours passed more and more cars appeared on the road obviously heading for either Yellowstone, the Grand Tetons or both, as we were. We were annoyed with the intrusion but it couldn't be helped – it was already the 22nd of June and the summer vacation was just beginning. In fact half the US would soon be on the move but at least we had reached the Rockies before the Fourth of July crowd.

At a place called Signal Mountain we found a lodge overlooking Jackson Lake where we had coffee and doughnuts. And at Colter Bay Village we visited a museum which had a wonderful collection of utilitarian Indian artifacts. We also saw a film about the coyote.

We did our shopping, had lunch, then proceeded on to Flagg Ranch where we met a girl called Stephanie who was a rafting guide in the summer and a ski guide in the winter. Randy, having already forgotten about the unhappy telephone call the previous evening with his girlfriend, immediately fell in love with her as he did with most girls he met along the way (I had to conclude therefore that his relationship with his girlfriend couldn't have been *that* serious after all).

As we were about to go on we met a ranger who tipped us about an ex-campground called Huckleberry Hot Spring located right before the Park's entrance where he said we could camp for free.

It turned out to be a wonderful isolated place with a shallow river flowing past a little hot spring. We pitched our tents right next to the spring on some overgrown grass and gloated at our luck in having such an idyllic place to ourselves. However, we weren't that lucky for long . . . a little while later some men arrived in a car – stone drunk and still drinking (it was only three in the afternoon) – and started shouting at the top of their voices. Every time they finished a bottle of beer they flung it into the air and let it drop onto the untouched wilderness. I was so angry at their behaviour I went to collect their bottles and dumped them through their car window onto the back seats and, silly as the action now seems, jotted down their licence plate number. But this unexpected behaviour from a total stranger seemed to sober them up somewhat and with slurred apologies they got into their car full of bottles and drove off.

In the cooler hours of the evening we finally managed to take a dip in the springs without getting scorched although it was still too hot to sit in them for long. Feeling clean and refreshed we had planned to get a good night's sleep but towards midnight another group of people arrived – this time a bunch of teenagers doing seasonal work in the park – who came to take a dip in the springs as well. We ended up joining them since we couldn't sleep with all the chatting going on right next to our tent.

At about three in the morning we were awakened by yet another gang of drunks but this time Randy managed to persuade them to leave so that we could finally get some sleep.

So much for the 'secret' spot!

In the morning we found a wallet, some underwear and a watch left behind by the drunks. We should have just left them there but instead we dropped them off (minus the underwear) at the nearest ranger station.

*

Yellowstone made me think of a giant fuming monster which was about to explode – hot springs, thermal pools and geysers constantly let off ominous clouds of steam and the air stunk of sulphur. Yet the park also offered dense forests, open meadows, deep canyons, wild cascading rivers, omnipresent mountains, and silent lakes. It was certainly a region of many contrasts.

We followed the eastern route through the park, stopping several times alongside Yellowstone Lake. The lake was so perfectly tranquil that it reflected the snow-capped Absaroka Mountain Range on the surface of the water like a mirror image.

We took walks along a number of thermal pools which

159

smelled terrible but were weirdly beautiful with their unreal colours. We also passed fumaroles which hissed and gurgled, forewarning us of impending bursts of steam. A rather desolate landscape of dead tree trunks sticking out of a murky ground reminded me of what the aftermath of a nuclear war could look like. There was also a canyon known as the Grand Canyon of Yellowstone which had yellowish walls and a large waterfall we could spot in the distance.

Yellowstone is the epitome of earth's violent powers – only three to five miles under the surface of this park lies the magma which is the source of heat in this thermal region. A combination of this heat and water (in the form of rain and snow) – which seeps through the ground where it is heated – produces the hot springs, geysers and fumaroles we were seeing. We were told that only Iceland, New Zealand and Kamchatka of Siberia have similar features to Yellowstone National Park although the latter is the largest of them all.

Norris campground had, to our delight, Hiker and Biker sites and we made a camp fire in the evening to celebrate our reaching the park. But Randy was not to be cheered up that evening – he had phoned his girlfriend again and came back to tell us that they had broken up for good. Perhaps it was just as well . . . .

*

We moved to the Madison Junction Campground the next day and while Randy and Nop went to the town of West Yellowstone to do some bicycle repair work I set up camp. Four cyclists from the East Coast – Eric, Seth, Bob and Joe – and another cyclist, Tim, from Louisiana also set camp on the same campground. When we were all settled we went to a nearby hot spring someone had heard about. This one was a shallow but wide hot spring with a very reasonable temperature. As I drowsily lay listening to the guys getting into a philosophical discussion I suddenly saw a face looking down at me – it was Bill, the cyclist from Minnesota

160

who had shared our camp site at Bryce Canyon! It took me a full minute before I recognized him – he now had a beard and a dark tan.

That evening all of us cyclists at the campground got together at Bill's site where we made a big camp fire and swapped travel tales. There was also a Dutch girl sharing Bill's site; she told us she had travelled a while with Gerrie and Inneke, the sisters in the VW van we had also met at Bryce Canyon.

The world was beginning to seem very small indeed!

*

Bill, Tim, Randy, Nop and I made a small tour of the park together the next day. We stopped at Old Faithful, the most famous of the geysers in Yellowstone, but the large crowds turned us off so we went on to Lone Star Geyser – a smaller geyser three miles away which one could only get to on foot or by bike. It goes without saying that we had the whole place to ourselves.

The geyser goes off every three hours but, as if to welcome us, it went off just as we arrived. It gurgled slowly at first, then it gradually started to spurt water and steam out of its silvery cone; first low, then higher and higher, culminating with a powerful fountain several metres high in the air. We had a lazy picnic under one of the trees near the geyser, enjoying the food and the surroundings until the geyser erupted again three hours later. Only then did we go back to Old Faithful to have a look at its eruption which was announced by loudspeakers and large display clocks. The crowds sat around on benches like schoolchildren to watch it go off. Well, what can I say . . . .

We had all gone wandering off on our own at Old Faithful when Nop and I saw Tim lying on a bench with his arms over his eyes. We thought he had a headache (he hadn't been feeling too well when we left in the morning) and when we got to him we saw that his eyelid was badly gashed.

'What happened to your eye?' I asked anxiously.

161

'Oh . . . I was lying here resting when my bike fell over me and the brake poked my eye.' It was a nasty cut and it was bleeding.

'I think you should have it checked by a doctor,' Nop suggested. 'It's a pretty deep cut.'

Tim hadn't realised how bad it was. We told him to stay where he was and we went looking for a clinic which we found in the vicinity. Fortunately a doctor was in so we took Tim to him.

'Well, it looks like you're going to need stitches,' the doctor said.

When the doctor was about to inject the eye with an anaesthetic I decided to leave the room.

When Tim came out he had no less than six stitches above his eye. Luckily a ranger offered to take him back to the campground in a truck.

As we were cycling back to the campground, we suddenly saw a cyclist who looked awfully familiar . . . of course, it was Stefan, the German cyclist we had met in the Grand Canyon! Speak of the devil, I thought! Just yesterday some of the cyclists had been talking about Stefan ('Met the weird German cyclist yet?' they had asked). Stefan didn't know it but every cyclist seemed to know about *him*.

'Ste-fan!' we called as we caught up with him.

He seemed to be as glad to see us as we were to see him. We told him where we were camping, so he joined us, bringing us up to date about his adventures since we last saw him. He was still mumbling about how hot the 'dezert' had been and how glad he was now that he had reached the cooler mountains.

*

It rained in the morning the next day as we made pancakes for our fellow-cyclists; we felt like the salvation army as they lined up in front of our tent to receive their share. Actually we did take pity on some of them – Bill practically lived on canned food, others lived off pure junk food. Stefan was ready to try something other than his usual 'bucketful' of muesli. There was even a cyclist who didn't carry a tent and had ended up spending the night in one of the restrooms of the park only to wake up with a mild case of hypothermia!

It was the last breakfast we shared with Randy – he was leaving that day with another cyclist called Matt, from California, who was also heading for Glacier National Park in Canada. It was hard to part with our cycling companion; we had been a trio for so long now. But between bear hugs we promised to meet again when we headed west in the winter. We were certain to pass Phoenix then.

*

Yellowstone isn't only famous as a thermal basin, but also for its wildlife. We passed moose and deer (who were quite oblivious to the tourists, I must add) and even some bison. The latter were shedding their woolly winter fur and looking rather shabby. They were otherwise very impressive creatures – most of us humans chose to watch these great beasts at a safe distance. At one point we came across a huge bull obstinately sitting in front of the men's restroom, calmly chewing some grass and enjoying the fear he evoked in the men who didn't dare pass him. They all went to the women's restroom instead. But the men's fear was understandable; bison were known to gore people who annoyed or provoked them.

*

New cyclists arrived at the campground (which we used as our base for a few days while we explored the park); one of the cyclists, called Steve Marcus, told me he had also lived in Japan as a student. That was enough for us to start a conversation about Japan and the respective universities we had gone to and to jabber in a mixture of Japanese and English, a student habit neither of us had lost since we

163

graduated. It was surprising to meet someone like him under such circumstances – it was also a welcoming change. Sometimes I forgot all about Asia while cycling in the States – in a way it was like I was living a western life while denying my Asian past – a chronic syndrome found in most 'rootless beings' like myself. Meeting Steve somehow revived a part of me which had been dormant for months.

Steve was cycling with his sister, Lynn, a girl called Sally and another guy, David. They were heading for the East Coast after Yellowstone – the same direction as ourselves.

*

Stefan was terribly excited because the world cup football (soccer) games were going to be shown live on TV that evening. Germany was obviously in the game so he was all of a sudden very patriotic.

'I am going to buy me some nice cold beer tonight and vatch it on the TV in one of the hotel lounges!' he said gleefully, confident that his countrymen would win.

We cycled together to Mammoth Hot Springs, 44 miles north of Madison Junction. It was a nice ride, the last part rolling up and down like a roller coaster. When we got to the campground we got into an argument with a volunteer at the entrance about a camp site we wanted to share with Steve's group who had arrived earlier since we all took up very little room.

After half an hour she finally gave is, saying, 'I am only going to make an exception this *one* time, you understand?' You would think we were asking her to let us get away with some serious crime!

Nop and I went to see the Mammoth Hot Springs – a huge cascade of boiling water over limestone terraces – while Stefan went hunting for his beer in preparation for the game that evening. At the Visitor's Centre we were again tipped about a local hot spring which was supposedly at the base of the campground. We visited the spring at sunset with Stefan and Steve's gang of four. It was the nicest and prettiest of the hot springs we had come across; a pool of hot water poured in little waterfalls down a rocky wall and someone had placed large stones in a circle to contain the hot water and protect the bathers from the icy river which ran right past the pool. When the water got too hot one merely had to shift one's body to the edge of the pool where a narrow stream of the river water flowed in and cooled the water. We all sat happily in this ideal pool under a clear sky of sparkling stars for quite a long time, not wanting to leave the warmth of the water. Outside the pool it was getting unbearably cold.

*

We parted from Stefan the next day and cycled with a new temporary companion – Allen, who was from Washington. It was interesting how solo cyclists easily joined us on rides, whether it be for a day or a week. Cycling solo must be awfully lonely sometimes, especially when cycling through stretches of wilderness where one passes little or no habitation.

Allen was in his late forties or early fifties (I couldn't tell) and had an enormous moustache. He told us he worked with handicapped children and that he himself suffered from epilepsy, although we didn't notice. We could see that children were easily attracted to him – wherever he went, whenever he saw a child he took out some balloons from his pannier (he seemed to have an endless supply of them) and within seconds turned them into animals of all shapes which he then presented to the bewildered child.

He had served as a soldier in the Special Forces during the Vietnam War until he was wounded for a second time in the legs. He told us that although the wounds still bother him when he hikes, he could cycle without any pain (as we were to find out when he went over the Beartooth Pass – a climb of more than 11,000 feet – and *back* just for fun).

We cycled together towards the notorious pass. Allen was far too fast for my tempo and anyway Nop was longing for us to cycle alone again (it had nothing to do with Allen; Nop was just tired of constantly being with other people) so Allen went on ahead of us to conquer the pass first.

The climb to Beartooth Pass wasn't an easy one. It took us two full days and there was a constant eight to ten per cent gradient for about 20 miles which drained my energy. But finally, after breathing with difficulty up the last long switchbacks we reached the top in time to meet Allen who had climbed back up from the other end; incredibly enough, we actually saw people skiing *below* us.

The view from the top was breathtaking – we were glad we had taken our time because the weather was magnificently clear now and we had a bird's eye view of the grandiose peaks of the Rockies and other mountain ranges in the distance as well as the weather-beaten, treeless landscape polka dotted with deep blue lakes we had just left behind. This was to be the highest point on our trip: 11,497 feet.

'Too bad there isn't a small cafe up here,' I was saying disappointedly to Nop after we parted from Allen who was heading back for Yellowstone.

'Yeah . . . .' he agreed with a sigh as we remained seated, taking in the view.

Then, just as we were about to leave the viewpoint a couple stepped out of a car and the woman came up to us and said, 'Would you two like some hot coffee? I've got some in a thermos so it's still nice and hot . . . .'

*

It was a 22-mile descent to Red Lodge, Montana, and boy did we take our time to enjoy the switchbacks down! The view was quite different on this side of the mountain –here the imposing mountains had extremely rugged and pointed peaks, and at first the valley we descended into looked tiny. We could now see how high we had actually climbed.

Red Lodge was a pleasant little town. We did our shopping and laundry and at the laundromat we met a guy called Bill who later said he had obtained permission from the pastor of the local church for us to camp on the church grounds! Bill also tipped us about a shower building in town.

When we arrived at the building and were about to pay the attendant he simply smiled and said: 'I was expecting you. No need to pay – compliments from the town.' We were beginning to like Red Lodge.

We spent the rest of the day roaming around town and reading in our tent. As we were having dinner, friends of Bill – Jim and Suzanne – came by and invited us to their house for coffee and cake. They lived quite high up the valley in a pretty wooden house which they had renovated themselves. We joined a group of people from town and watched the sun set behind the mountains as we sat chatting on the porch. These darkening mountains had a way of humbling people and I, for one, felt totally mesmerised by their close presence. I didn't feel like we had conquered these mountains just because we had cycled over them; it was simply an incredible sense of satisfaction in having crossed them relying on our *own* physical power.

The following day we went to see how much Rodeo tickets were – it was the 2nd of July and there was supposed to be a big rodeo on the 4th (we had no idea what a rodeo was like and felt we simply *couldn't* leave the States without having witnessed one, much as I disapproved of the sport), but we were disappointed to find that the tickets cost close to $8 per person – a price too high for our meagre budget. There was a parade going on in town so we watched it for a while and then visited the Chamber of Commerce where we hoped to get a map of Montana.

When the woman behind the desk heard us asking for a map for our trip she suddenly said: 'Oh! Are you the ones on the bikes? We've been looking all over the place for you!'

'Really?' I asked, wondering why.

'Yes. You see, we wanted to give you free tickets for the rodeo show tonight. Hold on a minute and let me get them for you! Oh, I'm *so glad* you finally showed up . . . .'

These tickets, too, were with compliments from the hospitable town.

167

In the afternoon, a local newspaper reporter came by to interview us and at 5.30 we climbed a hill behind town to get to the rodeo. We were the only ones who went on foot.

The rodeo was quite an exciting event, although I winced at the manner in which the bulls and horses were strapped. But who was I to change an American tradition, I kept reminding myself.

The event was half show and half contest; cowgirls raced across the arena on swift horses to see who could swing around some barrels and get back first; cowboys dashed after nervous calves, catching them skilfully in one quick motion with their ropes; cowboys rode angry bulls and horses. Even children participated in the show – they came into the arena dressed like cowboys with oversized hats riding sheep instead of horses; the sheep inevitably threw them off leaving them bawling on the ground as the audience rolled with laughter.

*

The city of Billings (apparently the largest city in Montana) was located 3,000 feet lower than Red Lodge and it was such a gradual descent that we practically cycled downhill the entire 70 miles.

The scenery was now turning into ranch land again as we began our trek across the Great Plains – the large land mass between the Rockies and the Appalachian Mountain Range on the east end of the continent.

As we got to Billings the road became congested which came somewhat as a shock to us after months of empty roads between and inside National Parks. But in town we found a nice bike shop called 'Spoke Shop' where I got myself a good pair of sunglasses and some spare tyres. The owner of the shop was kind enough to let us pitch our tent at the back of the shop which was in a little suburb. The only problem was that there was nowhere I could relieve myself in the evening – there were city lamps lining every street, all the land was private property and the local citizens were

168

letting out their dogs. In the end I had no alternative but to relieve myself in our own tent and discard the bag in a nearby garbage bin!

*

The landscape was grassy and dry and it was very hot as we cycled over undulating hills. We reached a junction where the general store was closed but where there was a phone booth. We made our monthly calls to our respective mothers and later had some lunch by the side of the road. It was while we were having lunch when we first noticed the grasshoppers – and I'm not talking about a few grass-hoppers hopping about but *millions* of them. We were witnessing *the* plague of the decade according to the local farmers. When we cycled on we tried to avoid riding over them but they were everywhere and I flinched every time I heard the disgusting sound as the grasshoppers were crushed under our wheels *en masse*.

It was the Fourth of July and we didn't want to be anywhere near firecrackers, so we sought out a church in the tiny town of Crow Agency. There wasn't anyone home so we pitched our tent by the wall of the church out of the ever-increasing wind and were glad we did so because towards the evening the wind picked up to gale force. A few firecrackers did go off in the distance in the evening despite the wind but nothing to keep us from sleeping.

As we packed and got ready to leave the next morning the pastor of the church, who had returned the previous evening but had kindly left us in peace, invited us for coffee and a second breakfast of pancakes. The pastor was a Hopi Indian, and his wife, Isabella, a Navajo. They were the first Indians we met personally and we were glad of the opportunity. The pastor explained that the town of Crow Agency was actually a part of the Crow Indian Reservation so we got to talking about reservations in general. I asked him why Indian Reservations were, on the whole, so dependent on the government and not very self-sufficient.

'Well, there are numerous reasons,' he answered. 'On the Crow Reservation, for example, it's mainly because of petty jealousies. When someone starts a business and shows success there is always someone who gets jealous and goes out of his way to ruin the business. There is a real lack of cooperation between the inhabitants of the reservations,' he explained.

He went on to say that another reason was discrimination, 'On the part of the whites as well as the Indians. They just can't seem to work together,' he said with a sigh.

Apparently unemployment was very high among the Indians on the Crow Reservation mainly because they couldn't get work in prosperous places like Billings and Hardin. 'Discrimination was the major factor,' he added.

We went on to Custer's Battlefield National Monument which was a bit of a tourist centre, and listened to an interesting, if a bit over-dramatised, account of Lt. Col. Custer's last battle with the Sioux and Cheyenne Indians (Custer's army was wiped out). The ranger glorified the deaths of the US army soldiers but I would have thought that it should have been the Indians he should have glorified; after all, how often in American history had the Indians won a battle against the whites? Not to mention the fact that we were now living in the twentieth century – I would have expected a ranger to talk more objectively about American history. Glorifying Custer's army on the very Indian reservation on which the monument was located, seemed to me like an insult to the Indian inhabitants.

After a small pass we found a free campground by a river in the town of Ranchester, where we met a cyclist, Joseph, from San Francisco. He told us he had just come over a pass from the west where he had witnessed the aftermath of a tornado which had recently passed through the area.

'It was really a scary sight. You could literally see the path the tornado had taken – all the trees had been uprooted along the way – it was like a bulldozer had made a clearing for a new road. Pretty awesome really.'

Hmmm... tornados. Another bloody thing to be afraid of.

I was beginning to think that it wasn't the crime rate people should be worried about in this country but the destructive forces of nature.

*

We followed a pleasant country road from Ranchester to Ucross – the undulating scenery reminded us very much of France.

We were planning to get to Spotted Horse that day, but when we passed the town of Ucross (population: twenty-five) an Indian dressed like a cowboy came running towards us from behind the Trading Post shouting, 'Stop! Wait!'

So we stopped to see what he wanted and he said, 'Could you guys come to the back of the house – I want to show your bikes to someone for a minute.'

We followed him and were introduced to 'Buckskin', a dignified-looking seventy-five-year old man with a white beard and two greying long braids smoking a pipe. He was also stone drunk.

Buckskin took a look at our bikes and insisted we be his guests for the night.

The Indian introduced himself as Rudy Studbrook and then introduced us to Buckskin's friend, Jim, who looked just like Buckskin (and just as old), and who was equally drunk. It appeared that (between the two lookalike grandpas) an entire bottle of whisky had been consumed that single day. There was also a couple – Jerry and Suzanne – and Suzanne's teenage daughter, Sharon. It was the strangest assortment of people I had ever seen.

In between slurry conversation we discovered that Buckskin used to be a world-renowned hunter and we were later guided around the trading post by Rudy who showed us all the animal trophies Buckskin had brought back from his hunting trips. The place looked like a museum – it contained piles of old photographs, stuffed animals, animal heads and their horns, hunting gear, skulls, paintings, hides and other assorted curios. The place was also a complete

171

mess and numerous Chihuahua dogs ran nervously around the house yapping at us whenever we moved. In the back yard there was a grey goat with long horns called Casey tied to an empty barrel.

We were told that Buckskin used to own most of the town but later sold the bar which was just across from his trading post. He was obviously retired now but on what he subsisted we had no idea. But one thing seemed to be clear – he didn't spend much money on food since he seemed to live mostly on whisky which he shared with his pal, Jim. Even Gerry and Suzanne couldn't help Buckskin there since he wouldn't even eat the food Suzanne had specially brought for him that day. Suzanne genuinely cared about these two old men and was obviously worried about them. Rudy was the only one permanently around to help Buckskin and Jim; Gerry and Suzanne, who tried to come as often as they could, said they would soon be moving to Arizona, because they couldn't find work in these parts. Buckskin seemed to resent her for this decision and claimed they were going to desert him. She was in an obvious dilemma as to what to do and felt very guilty.

Later in the afternoon Buckskin turned to me tearfully and said in a creaky voice, 'Suzanne is going to leave me. Won't *you* stay and take care of me instead? Please?'

Much as I sympathised with Suzanne's dilemma, I couldn't help but detect a slightly manipulative look in Buckskin's eyes and wondered whether he was actually shedding crocodile tears. Somehow I didn't pity him, and that made me hard. I told him I had my own obligations back home.

For the rest of the afternoon the gang continued drinking. At one point Gerry and Rudy started shooting their guns off, using the windows of an old unoccupied house next door as target practice. I didn't appreciate the gun-slinging nor the noise they created and we began to regret having to spend the night amidst these bored drunks. But we managed to take hot showers and Suzanne offered us some delicious home-made potato salad so we couldn't very well leave after the hospitality they had shown us.

The 'party' continued on into the evening when Rudy put music on and kept bugging me to go dancing with him in town. Really! I was in no mood to go dancing with a drunk let alone allow a drunk to *drive* me to town! I reminded him I was married and that seemed to quell his attraction to me. Finally, when the evening became quite unbearable, we excused ourselves and retired to our tent which we had pitched in the back yard next to Casey, the goat, our neighbour for the night.

*

Was I ever glad to leave the town of Ucross the next morning! I hadn't realised how the place had depressed me – it was almost frightening to think how we could get so immersed in other people's lives in such a short time.

The terrain became a bit dull – we cycled undulating prairie hills most of the day. In the afternoon dark threatening clouds began to form so we called it quits at a big farm where we were given permission to pitch our tent next to a barn.

The farm was run by a family of three generations and in the evening the children came up to us and politely asked us whether we would like to be guests to a firecracker show they were planning to put on for the entire family. Apparently the weather had been bad in these parts on July 4th so the kids had saved the firecrackers for a clear night.

The children were very sweet and went out of their way to get all the adults seated comfortably on chairs they had specially lined up for them. They really did their best to make a grand show out of the whole thing by carefully lighting various firecrackers one by one.

*

After doing some shopping in the town of Gillette, we headed for the Black Hills which bordered on Wyoming

173

and South Dakota. It was a pleasant ride through a narrow, rocky valley apart from a construction site where workers were widening the road.

At the small town of Carlile we pitched our tent on some farmland and were later joined by Steve's gang who had caught up with us.

The following morning Nop and I patiently waited for the four to get organised. We had to chuckle at the way it took them forever to break camp.

'Has anyone seen my shoe?'

'Where the hell's my pump?'

'Did you pack the food already?'

By the time we finally got going dark clouds were already gathering in the sky, threatening a serious thunderstorm. We managed to make it to a junction where the road led to Devil's Tower National Monument when lightning struck very close. We quickly took cover under some buildings and waited for the storm to blow over. Our companions cycled very fast – too fast for me, in fact, but also far too dangerously. I was shocked to see them draft *inches* behind cars while cycling full-speed downhill. No wonder they wore helmets!

We hiked around Devil's Tower – a rocky perpendicular mountain jutting 867 feet above the ground in the otherwise flat and bare landscape. The tower was formed by molten magma which pushed through overlying sedimentary rocks, cooling off; while doing so its wall contracted and fractured into columns. Over a period of several millions of years the sedimentary layers above it eroded, eventually exposing the colossal tower.

After a pretty but gruelling ride over hilly terrain we arrived in Sundance at sunset, which – thank goodness for the summer – was quite late, giving us ample time to cycle through the day. We found a KOA campground – fortunately it only cost $15 for the six of us and we could take hot showers.

It took the gang as much time to set up camp as it did for them to break camp and by the time we finally got dinner ready it was completely dark.

*

The summer had truly begun in the Great Plains – the mornings were almost always sunny and very hot and the afternoons were characterised by dark threatening clouds followed by the most terrifying thunderstorms I have ever experienced. It was the humidity, of course, which caused these storms at the end of the day and it was precisely these violent storms which could at any time and place produce the notorious tornadoes of this region. I wasn't too excited about the prospect of having to endure a month and a half of this cantankerous weather and I never felt more vulnerable than on these open plains in the middle of the summer . . . .

The past days clearly warned us that we had to start early if we wanted to get anywhere before the afternoon storms arrived so the next day we left earlier than the gang. Two days later, when they finally caught up with us again, we were cycling through the Black Hills which are, despite their name, more like mountains. Together we visited Jewel Cave National Monument where we went on a tour into the caves. During the tour David cracked such hilarious jokes that we were all left with stomach cramps from laughing and none of us could listen to the ranger seriously.

David, Nop and I were cycling ahead of the gang again when storm clouds loomed in front of us. When we entered the town of Custer we found some land to pitch our tents on. I went on my own to town to shop and came back with three more cyclists – Bill, Bill and Earl from Minnesota who were out on their first day of cycling and were as chaotic as Steve's gang – the camp site ended up looking like a hiker and biker campground with all our tents, cooking gear and bicycle tools strewn about.

*

Nop and I decided to make a detour to Wind Cave National

175

Park, south of Custer State Park, so we parted from Steve's gang for the last time. They were planning to participate in a cycling event across Iowa which was starting in a few weeks' time.

We continued cycling through mostly ranch land and at a tiny town called Pringle we stopped to watch a local festivity which included a live band playing country and western music. Every single person we saw was dressed in full cowboy attire – hats, buckles, jeans and boots – making us feel completely out of place with our discoloured T-shirts, baggy shorts and jogging shoes – not to mention the fact that we had come by bicycle and *not* by pick-up truck or horse.

Wind Cave was located under an untouched prairie wilderness. On the prairie we observed comic prairie dogs barking frantically to warn each other of our impending arrival, and we also saw some free-roaming buffalo. At the Visitor's Centre we joined a candlelight tour of the caves – a new experience for us and very exciting. The group was very small – less than ten people – and the ranger, Darren, said very little during the tour but made everyone laugh whenever he did make some kind of observation. We were told that the boxwork formations found on the walls of the caves were honeycomb-shaped formations of calcite (a crystalline form of calcium carbonate). Other formations to be seen were 'frostwork' and 'popcorn' formations, both aptly named for their shapes, as well as huge helictite 'bushes'. It was these formations which distinguished Wind Cave from other caves. In fact, stalactites and stalagmites found in other caves are rare here. Darren also explained that the name of the cave derived from the wind which blows into or out of its mouth, depending on atmospheric pressure.

'We'll now put out the candles so you can get an idea how dark total darkness *really* is,' Darren said during the middle of the tour.

So we all put out our candles and stood still in pitch darkness which was quite a disorientating and unnerving

176

experience.

After quite a long time Darren finally said, 'Now... if only I can find the matches ....'

Back at the Visitor's Centre, Darren showed us his pet bullsnake. It was a non-venomous, pretty snake a few feet long and for the first time in my life I actually touched a snake. Slimy as they may look I was surprised to find that snakes are actually very dry and cold to the touch. The snake didn't mind the attention he was getting; in fact he seemed to enjoy himself as he slithered between the feet of his audience, showing off his beautiful scaled back.

I have never seen any place quite so touristy as Mount Rushmore. The 'Shrine of Democracy' had actually looked quite impressive from a distance as we caught glimpses of it now and then while winding our way up and down the mountain road to the park. But the nearer we got to the place the more congested the road became with hundreds of campers and cars heading in the same direction. The only relief from this massive movement towards the park was the comical sight of some enormous campers literally getting stuck in the narrow tunnels along the way and causing a long traffic jam. They had probably ignored the signs posted in numerous places at the beginning of the road which warned about the narrow tunnels ahead. We, of course, just manoeuvred our way through the jam.

The heads of the four famed presidents of the United States – Washington, Jefferson, Lincoln and Roosevelt – were carved out of one of the granite walls of Mount Rushmore and the carving process had taken some 20 years before funds finally ran out and the project had to be abandoned. Nevertheless, the faces of the four presidents did look complete in my eyes.

At the Visitor's Centre we watched a film about mountain sculpturing which was quite interesting, but we were soon dying to get away from the place – the park was literally crawling with tourists from all over the world.

That night we ended up pitching our tent in the back yard of Art and Bev Niedan's home in Rapid City. Nop had, by chance, met Art at the local Safeway supermarket while shopping for groceries. The Niedans were a gentle, hospitable couple who, as we talked in the evening, told us they had two adopted part-Indian children who were already grown and out of the house. They proudly showed us pictures of them.

The following morning Bev made a huge American breakfast of scrambled eggs and toast before seeing us off. I couldn't help but think the Niedans must have been great parents.

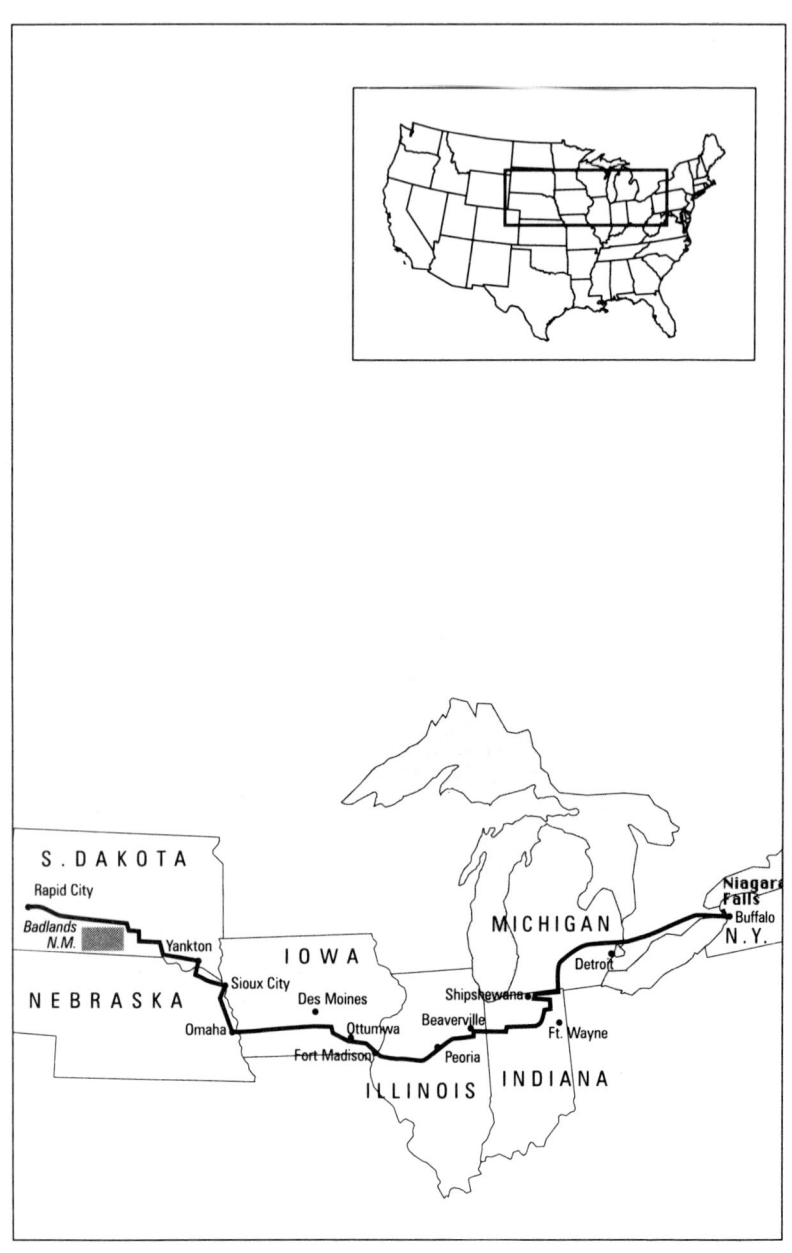

CORN AND BEANS
AND LIGHTNING STORMS

The only paved road to the Badlands National Park was Interstate 90, with an occasional frontage road running parallel to it. It was becoming unbearably humid in the heat of the plains and the days now consisted mostly of cycling from one town to another in search of cold drinks and shade.

We took a shade break in the town of Wasta and after a while I noticed a large, ominous formation of black clouds growing in the distance so we quickly left our shady spot and went on to the town of Wall. With the storm looming right behind us and lightning already flashing I cycled so fast even Nop couldn't keep up with me.

We made it to Wall right before the storm did and stopped at the first church we saw. A stern-looking Catholic priest reluctantly let us pitch our tent at the back of the church building. After a while he seemed to relax a bit – perhaps he realised we weren't bums after all and he even invited us in for some 7-Up and bananas ('Bananas contain lots of potassium, you know,' he lectured). As we started to chat he admitted that he had been a bit wary of us at first because he got so many people coming up to his church begging for money, gas and/or food.

We stayed in the church till the worst of the storm had blown over and then went into town.

Wall was literally situated in the middle of nowhere, yet it was a very successful tourist trap. In the 1930s, the wife of the local drugstore owner did some serious thinking about how to attract the increasing number of motorists crossing the plains to the insignificant town of Wall. She finally came up with a briiliant idea. She decided to advertise free iced water along the hot and dusty highway which went by Wall in the direction of Mount Rushmore and Yellowstone. It was an immediate success – tourists finally started to drop by the small town where they not only drank the free iced water but also spent their dollars on groceries, which was precisely her point. In this manner the drugstore grew from a small shop into a huge enterprise and now it practically owned the entire town. But one could still get iced water for free. . . .

*

Badlands was to be the last National Park we would be seeing for quite a while, so we didn't want to miss it.

The grassy hills of the extensive open plains surrounded us on all sides and it was hard to believe we were so near the Badlands – it wasn't till we got to the edge of a plateau that we actually saw the rocky desert of fanfold mountains, canyons, gorges and the cross-section of sedimental layers depicting geological history. It was definitely a strange break from the otherwise never-ending prairie land we had been cycling through.

We cycled down into the park – which was even hotter than the plains – till we reached the Visitor's Centre. We took a break there and sat in the shade of one of the buildings when a huge camper stopped near us. A couple came out of it and as they headed for the Visitor's Centre the man stopped to take a brief look at our bikes and us.

'Are you two travellin' on *ba-cycles*?' he asked with disbelief.

When we nodded that we indeed were, he said, 'But how on earth can you ever see anythin' if you go so slow?!'

*

182

The campground consisted of some grumpy, unfriendly people who were in no mood to share their camp site with us so we went out of the park to the small town of Interior where we found a deserted churchyard. We pitched our tent as I apprehensively watched a not-so-cute dark cloud growing bigger and bigger and coming nearer and nearer by the minute. And sure enough, by the time it got dark the storm hit us with all its force. It was the most terrifying storm we had ever experienced in our tent – I mean it was so violent that even Nop got scared.

The storm started with a wind which gained tremendous force and was followed by horrific booms of thunder with lightning striking so near to us there weren't even any intervals between the flashes and the strikes. It was the first time I really thought we were going to die then and there.

All through the first hours of the terrible storm Nop held onto the tent pole with all his might as the gale force winds tried to lift our tent off the ground – at one point the front of the tent lifted several feet before it came crashing down, breaking both front poles in the process. All I could think of was that the next flash of lightning might strike our centre pole and kill us instantly – I kept thinking, 'Will it be the next one?'

Finally, towards midnight the wind mercifully died down and the storm subsided, but early in the morning the winds picked up again but fortunately without the dreaded thunder and lightning. It was nevertheless disturbing and all in all we didn't get much sleep. It was certainly a terrible night that I will never forget. I also decided I *never* wanted to camp out in the open in the plains again without some kind of shelter in the vicinity we could run to in case such a storm hit us again. We decided, or rather I decided, that from now on we should look for churches (preferably ones with basements). These storms just weren't funny anymore.

Nop didn't argue with my decision since he knew how scared I had been.

'But,' he added, '*you* are going to be the one to ask at the churches from now on, OK?'

You bet I would!

*

'Were you two the ones flying the kite above the Badlands?' the ranger asked us at the exit of the park.

'Yes,' Nop answered matter-of-factly. I wondered whether we were going to be reprimanded for that.

The morning after the storm we had got up early and cycled through the rest of the park towards the north. When we found a nice viewpoint we tried somewhat unsuccessfully to take aerials of the rock formations.

'There is another ranger here,' the ranger went on, 'who also saw your kites and would like to ask you some questions about your kites and your aerial system if it's all right with you.' We then met the other ranger who explained his interest in our system.

'We found some archaeological sites in the park,' he said, 'probably an ancient Indian village. But in order to discern the outline of the village we need aerial photographs of the site. We usually have to use aeroplanes but they're awfully expensive. That's why I'm interested in your kite system,' he said.

So Nop explained the technical details of his system and then suggested we try taking some aerials of the area the ranger was talking about. So the ranger drove us to the site and in the hot late-morning hours Nop and I managed to get the kite up (despite poor wind conditions) and take a few aerials which we later sent to the park (unfortunately we never found out whether they were of any help or not). The ranger picked us up a few hours later and brought us back to the exit of the park. The first ranger we had talked to, who had introduced herself as Cathy Lynn, suggested we go on to Kadoka where she lived, and camp in her back yard that evening.

It was a good idea – we were exhausted from flying our kites, cycling in the heat and the terrible sleepless night we

184

had experienced the previous night.

Cathy lived with her nine-year-old son, Lance, who turned out to be an energetic, happy child who was very excited when he met us and saw our bikes. He got even more excited when Cathy told him about our kites. After a wonderful dinner of pizza which we ate in the cool shade of the local park across from Cathy's house, Nop first taught Lance how to make a simple sleigh kite and then I taught him some Origami basics. It took quite a lot of effort on Cathy's part to finally get Lance off to bed.

*

Much of the crops of the Great Plains were being harvested as we continued east. The exposed brown earth clashed with the uncut green grass and the huge yellow balls of hay which dotted the landscape. The symmetrical patterns of the land where the grass had recently been cut contrasted sharply with the gently undulating hills. It looked like a land of plenty. Occasionally we passed through small farming towns which usually consisted of a cluster of houses, a church, a general store and a water tower.

These water towers, which we could always spot in the far distance, were to me, the symbol of welcoming habitation, meaning water, shade, food and most important of all, shelter from the abominable storms. Almost every town park provided ideal camping spots – grassy fields with toilets, water and picnic sites.

We cycled through the towns of Kimball, Wagner, Whynot (why not?) and Homer, and in each town we were able to pitch our tent in a town park with no objection whatsoever from the local inhabitants.

When we crossed the Missouri River we knew we were officially in the East. We followed the river into Nebraska – our tenth state – and went on to Omaha. There the son of the Hansons (the couple we had stayed with in Salt Lake City), Barrett, was a student and was expecting us. It had been a long time since we had entered a city of such size and it came as a shock to us. It wasn't only because of the traffic congestion, but because the suburb we entered looked like a ghetto.

We had entered Omaha from the north on 22nd June after covering 90 miles, and it was getting dark as we looked for Barrett's home. We couldn't help noticing an increasing number of blacks after not having seen any since the lone hiker in the Grand Canyon. The dilapidated condition of the large old homes told us we were cycling through what Americans call the 'slums'. But the derogatory connotation of that label hardly seemed appropriate here – in the last gentle rays of the setting sun the place had a pleasant relaxed atmosphere about it. Entire families sat outside on their porches chatting and enjoying the cool afternoon air. A refreshingly village-like atmosphere found in a city. Almost everyone waved cheerfully to us and asked us where we came from.

'What the hell *are* those bikes?' and where we were heading. They seemed mostly interested in the fact that we came from Holland, *Europe.*

One man rolled down the window of his car as he passed us slowly and asked, 'Jus' how far've you come on those things, man?'

'Nine thousand miles,' I answered.

'Nan thousan' mailes . . . ? *Man!*' he exclaimed, rolled up his window and drove off.

Just before it got dark we finally found Barrett's flat – it was smack in the middle of this ghetto. He was a student at the University in Omaha, the campus of which was very close to where he lived. Because of the reputation of the neighbourhood we took his advice and put our bikes in his flat. We were glad to find a pile of mail waiting for us – it had been seven weeks since our last mail in Salt Lake City.

We stayed two nights at Barrett's flat which gave us a chance to catch up on letter-writing, send off our old books and used maps home as well as do some decent shopping.

*

186

Once out of Omaha it was back to rolling farmland again. At the end of the day, when we got to the town park of Griswold we could see a storm building up in the distance which made me jittery and nervous (a common trait I'd developed ever since the bad storm which hit us in the Badlands). The town park's picnic tables had a roof over them so at least we wouldn't get wet; if the worse came to the worst, I thought, we could always run to the rest rooms which were built of concrete.

As we sat at the picnic table – more or less waiting for the storm to hit – a guy in a pick-up truck stopped by and asked us if we wanted to take shelter at his house a few miles east off the main road.

But Nop said, 'No thanks!'

I could have wrung his neck!

The guy then said, 'Suit yourselves! I'm going to check on the chickens on a farm near here but I'll be back later in case you change your minds.'

The storm was just about to hit when he came back to the town park a couple of hours later. We were packed and ready to join him.

*

Kyle and his wife, Margie, and their children lived on a farm next to a dirt road off Highway 92. This was a picturesque region, predominantly farmland dotted occasionally with neat, white farmhouses, and large barns surrounded by rows of trees which provided shade and some form of shelter from the winds. Thanks to the rather large tracts of land between the homes, neighbours weren't too far away in case of need, yet also not too near, giving some form of isolation and privacy to the inhabitants.

The Bensons let us sleep in the house because of the storm, although it remained pretty much in the distance. But I had been right about these storms having the tendency to turn into tornadoes.

'Tornadoes hit almost every year,' Kyle told us the next

day as we shared breakfast with the family, 'they appear all of a sudden and you just hope they don't come your way.'

'What do you do if a tornado *does* come your way?' I asked.

'Nothing much you can do. A basement is the best place, of course, but if you're caught out in the open you should try getting into a ditch and lying flat.'

Kyle was interested in Nop's kites and asked us to stay another day so he could see them. So we flew them for him (for once in perfect wind conditions) and even took some aerials of the farm and its surroundings (the photographs turned out well as we found out half a year later).

*

As we got our stuff ready the next morning Margie embarrassed us somewhat by praying out loud for our safety and gave us, after a little lecture about God, the New Testament as a farewell present. What could we say? 'No, thank you – we're atheists'? She was too sincere and kind-hearted so we thanked her for her consideration and accepted her gift (which still stands on our bookshelf). When we were ready to go she drove us back to the main road in her pick-up truck.

Once again we headed east on Highway 92. We had left late that morning and only covered 45 miles when we got to the town of Stanzel. There we stopped to have a drink and chat with the 94-year-old owner of the gas station called Worth who was still going strong. He asked us many questions about our bikes and, as we chatted with him, a young farmer drove up in a tractor and joined in the conversation. We ended up sitting there for over an hour talking about farming conditions in the US. Later we were invited by Steve, the young farmer, to pitch our tent on his land a mile back.

Steve lived with his wife, Tina – who was heavily pregnant with their third child – and his two daughters in a sweet farmhouse a short distance from the road. This house was perched on a hill and surrounded by trees; there was also a barn with a horse in it called 'Joe' whom Steve said he was training. When Steve heard that neither of us knew much about horses let alone ride them he was simply flabbergasted. In these parts, as in many parts of the US, most people learn to ride a horse almost as soon as they learn how to walk. But I suppose he reacted as a Dutchman would upon hearing of someone who couldn't ride a bicycle.

After dinner Steve decided we couldn't possibly go on in life without at least learning the basics about riding a horse and immediately took it upon himself to give us our first lesson. His trainee horse, Joe, was very sweet and did exactly as Steve told him to. I never knew people could communicate with horses so well. Steve taught us how to steer the animal to the left and right, forward and backward, but most important for us: how to get on the enormous creature in the first place.

I had the uncanny feeling that Joe was afraid of Steve – as he was constantly being reprimanded – and I felt a bit sorry for him. After our intensive one-hour course I fed him some fresh grass I had gathered. He was so grateful and tame and seemed like a good listener as well. He just stood there patiently, listening to me chatter away . . . .

The next morning Tina fixed us the biggest and heaviest breakfast I have ever eaten: potato hash, scrambled eggs, bacon, toast, orange juice and coffee . . . we were told some ranchers and farmers even ate steaks for breakfast. Sometimes I found it hard to be a vegetarian in front of farmers from the Midwest. I usually tried to avoid the subject unless I was confronted with a meat dish as now. My explanation that I objected to the *mass-production* of meat and all the adverse effects it was having on the environment wasn't a form of logic Steve understood nor wanted to understand. But it wasn't only during the discussion concerning meat that I found Steve exasperatingly narrow-minded. In general, he seemed to base most of his opinions on what he heard and saw on that most vile of mass-media devices which ever existed – the television.

My suspicions about his ignorance and naivete was confirmed by the fact that I couldn't detect a single book, magazine or newspaper in the house and also by the fact that he was paranoid that one of his daughters would one day be kidnapped, raped, killed and never be heard of again if he didn't keep a constant eye on them. Television had brought terror into his own living room, in the middle of the peaceful Iowan countryside.

I was glad that the preconception *we* had had of the US at the start of our trip (also a result of television's influence) had totally disappeared and that we now saw the country through clearer eyes. In fact our journey had so far taught us that the United States actually consisted of two entirely different worlds. The first was that of the cities which were concentrated on the east and west coasts (and unfortunately *the* world constantly depicted on TV) and rural America – small-scale, provincial, unpopulated and very conservative. But also the *bulk* of the US, thank goodness.

After breakfast, Steve drove us out to the ranch he also worked on and in the afternoon, when we got back to the house, we saw that out tent had collapsed. The centre pole had broken as the tent dried and shrank in the heat. Fortunately, Nop managed to fix it with some spare aluminium Steve gave him.

For the rest of the afternoon we found ourselves not knowing what to do with ourselves – it was too hot and humid to stay in our tent, but bugs ate us alive if we sat outside. We were beginning to wish we hadn't stayed another day . . . .

*

The map of Iowa is very deceiving – the roads are marked with straight lines, giving the impression that the terrain is flat. In reality the road goes continuously up and down almost the entire way. However, we did finally have a day when the hills diminished somewhat as we cycled towards

190

the town of Knoxville. We were beginning to notice that a lot of the towns in this region had little squares in the centre of town, reminding us of towns in Europe.

In one such town we passed through, a man gaped at us from the side of the road and said, 'Hey, last time I saw you two was back in Why, Arizona!'

In the town of Harvey we found a church where the pastor turned out to be a woman. As we talked to her and explained our situation, she suddenly said: 'Are you from Nederland?'

Pastor Degreef was of Dutch descent – of course, we should have noticed her name on the sign in front of the church! In the Netherlands her name would actually have been two words – de Greef.

Tornado warnings were out on TV that night (weather forecast programmes are the *only* programmes on American television with some credibility, by the way) so Pastor Degreef suggested we stay in the church which had a basement.

'I'll join you if it gets real bad,' she added as we said goodnight.

This storm was pretty bad – all night the wind howled, shaking the church, and lightning kept me awake most of the night. But for once I wasn't afraid – we were lying right by the basement. Nop, of course, didn't even notice that there was a storm and slept like a log.

The ravages of the storm of the previous night were quite visible the following day – trees had been uprooted and thrown across the road and electricity poles had fallen and their wires ripped. Was I glad we had stayed in the church!

We stopped at a town called Oskaloosa, which had a bicycle shop. The owner, seeing we were on bicycles, thought we had been on the RAGBRAI – a huge bicycle event which had taken place a few days back – where thousands of bicyclists gather to ride across Iowa (this was the event Steve and his gang had been eager to participate in). We told him we had unfortunately missed it by a couple of days.

191

The bike shop owner then said excitedly, 'Well, there was this guy who came by here recently who had been on the RAGBRAI and guess where he had cycled all the way from? *Kansas!* Can you believe it – that's 900 miles from here!'

*

In the town of Fort Madison we were interviewed by a reporter from the paper *Democrat*. We were becoming a bit bored with all these interviews for local newspapers. The questions were all the same: 'Where are you from, where are you going, what are these bikes called, how many miles have you covered, where do you camp, what do you think of this state, or worse: what do you think of this town (had been there five minutes), how many miles do you cover in a day,' etc. . . etc. . . . .

A few miles after Fort Madison we crossed the Mississippi River and entered the state of Illinois. We should have never taken the route through the city of Peoria – we found ourselves fighting for every inch along the non-shouldered roads during Friday afternoon's rush hour. The congestion was terrible and the drivers downright rude and aggressive and I soon had a splitting headache from the traffic fumes. I called a hospitality home in town and for the second time we were rebuffed.

The guy who answered the phone merely said, 'Sorry, I was just leaving . . . .'

So, tired as we were, we decided in any case to get out of this hell-hole and find a spot on the outskirts of town. As we passed the town of Washington a guy stopped his car and asked us if we wanted to camp on his back yard – naturally we accepted his offer, and were given an address in Eureka, the next town. When we arrived at the house, another car stopped with a couple who also invited us to camp on their land. They seemed nicer than the first guy, but we had already arrived at the first guy's place so we had some drinks together and chatted for a while before they left.

We pitched our tent next to the house of Philip, our host,

beside a picnic table.He was very secretive about a woman in the house who he first claimed was his mother and then his landlady. We never did get to meet her. After we cooked up dinner Philip said we could take showers in the basement since 'the way was clear'. He was very strange in a creepy sort of way and we didn't feel very comfortable accepting his hospitality although nothing happened that night.

We had been given the address of the couple from the previous night (who lived further up the road) so we looked them up the next day.

'We were worried about you last night,' Mrs Arvin said as we sat eating delicious corn on the cob from her own garden.

'Why?' Nop asked.

'Well, that man seemed *so* strange!' she said with a shudder.

'Yes, he was a bit weird but he was OK. After all, he was kind enough to invite us . . . .'

The Arvins had quite a lot of land: a vegetable garden, a large lawn, numerous trees which graced the place, four horses, three cats, two dogs, two birds and *seven* children! There was only one word for the place – *gezellig* (Dutch for cosy or snug). Before we left, Mrs Arvin gave us a bag full of her vegetables.

That afternoon we managed to reach the town of Flanagan, where we camped at the town park. Late in the evening when we had already gone to sleep some kids came by and mischievously pulled some of our tent stakes out, hoping, I am sure, the tent would collapse on top of us. We probably would have slept through the minor incident except that one of the kids tripped over one of our tent ropes and fell on top of our tent for a brief moment before dashing away with the others. Although it scared the hell out of me the tent did hold.

*

We had wonderful tail winds as we continued on Highway 116. (Please note: the fact that I actually *mention* tail winds implies how rare they were!)

In the town of Saunemin, we stopped at a cafe (by now, an unbreakable habit of ours) but as we entered the woman of the cafe told us she was just about to close. We must have looked awfully disappointed (a cyclist's face can read: 'but the next cafe is 50 miles away') and she said, 'Oh . . . come on in!'

As we were having coffee and doughnuts relatives and friends of the elderly couple started to arrive for some kind of lunch party and we were soon invited to join in. Although it hadn't been our intention to have a two-and-half-hour break this is just what we did. The elderly couple who ran the cafe were the Timmkes, and the others consisted of their daughter, Mrs Timmkes's sister and husband. They were so friendly and hospitable that when it was time to go it was like parting from good friends and we all found ourselves hugging each other goodbye!

*

We followed country roads all day, passing tiny towns and occasionally chatting with people along the way. In the town of Rennselaer (not on the map) all the waitresses and customers of a bakery/cafe in front of which we had stopped, came out to talk to us.

The high cornfields we were passing were ready for harvest and all day we spotted farmers working hard in the hot sun. I kept thinking though, what a pity it was that all this good food – corn and beans – was mostly for animal feed and not for human consumption. A result, unfortunately, of the massive meat industry. We were even told there was an overproduction of animal feed! But even if it weren't for animal feed – why the monocrops? Didn't the farmers in the Plains ever hear of diversification? Flowers . . . for example. All this land and yet flowers had to be imported from . . . The Netherlands, of all places.

194

In the tiny town of Pulaski (not on the map either) – pronounced *pu -la -sky* – we stopped at a little wooden house for some water. A couple were sitting out on the porch, enjoying the cool afternoon, and as we filled our bottles we chatted with them. When we told them we would probably get to Star City that afternoon they (Lance and Beverly) suggested we stay at Beverly's parents' home. The town was halfway into Indiana. We accepted their offer and in doing so covered 73 miles that day.

The Keisers (Beverly's parents) were a wonderful couple, and later when Lance, Beverly and their children joined us for dinner (what was a 60 miles drive to dinner for them?!) we found ourselves amidst a warm family full of humour. I couldn't remember laughing so hard as I did with this wonderful family.

*

In the large town of Columbia City, we finally looked up one of the many couples who had given us their address in Oleander Acres RV Park in Texas, where we had been so warmly welcomed during the previous Christmas.

The Sundermans were a couple we had got to know quite well in Texas because they had taken us out for Mexican food, and Virginia had interviewed us for the park's *Snowbird's Paper.* We were happy to find them home, accompanied by Ethel, another Snowbird we had also met at Oleander Acres.

We spent the next four days at Glen and Virginia's home, reminiscing about Oleander Acres and bringing them up to date about our travels so far. We reorganised our things, caught up on mail and sorted out slides before sending them home. Between these 'domestic chores' Glen and Virginia took us out on drives and treated us to all our meals. During our stay, we also visited Glen's ninety-year-old mother who lived in a nearby home for the elderly and disabled: she had diabetes and had finally turned blind in the last stages of this illness. More recently she had even lost her legs. Yet despite her handicaps she still enjoyed books through book cassette tapes provided by the government and she eagerly listened to us as we told her about our trip. I really had to admire the way she still managed to maintain her dignity – we couldn't detect a single hint of despair or bitterness in her voice.

We were now entering Amish country. The Amish, a Christian sect that separated from the Mennonites in the US in the 18th century (the Mennonites were members of an Evangelical Christian sect with Anabaptist origins, founded in the Netherlands in the 16th century), live within their own isolated communities because they don't want to conform to the modernised world around them. Their homes have no electricity, they ride buggies driven by horses (and bicycles, which they allow), they still speak an old Germanic language and they continue to use their hands where machines have otherwise taken over in the modern world.

We immediately appreciated their way of life (minus the religious part) since they were so self-sufficient. They had neat pretty wooden houses (no electricity cables!) and large vegetable gardens. It was so pleasant to cycle through such peaceful, quiet neighbourhoods with only an occasional horse-drawn buggy passing us and the occupants waving at us. We liked the Amish for sticking to their own traditions and refusing to modernise. Having seen what the advent of modernisation had done to the rest of America, we were glad to see these people live in such harmony with their environment.

Surprisingly enough it was actually in this Amish region where we came upon one of the best bicycle shops we had ever seen in the entire country. Outside Shipshiwanee, on a dirt road through one of the Amish neighbourhoods, we found a bicycle shop run by an Amish family. We were helped by a woman who, along with her daughter, was dressed as all conservative Amish women do, in bonnet and long dress. They had *everything* – tyres of all sizes and shapes, spokes of varying lengths and thicknesses, thorn-proof inner tubes, and . . . and they even sold recumbents! Now, how complete can a bicycle shop be! No wonder the Amish waved so often to us – they were familiar with reclining bicycles!

*

On our first night after Columbia City we pitched our tent next to a small airport in the town of Kendallville and early the next morning we watched five colourful balloons take to the sky.

We felt we had finally crossed the Great Plains when we got to Michigan – here the terrain was somewhat rougher and wilder, although it was still farming country. Almost every day we were able to purchase cheap fresh vegetables from small stands alongside the road – usually there was nobody present and customers simply added up their own bill and placed the money in a little money box at the stand. It must have been a region where petty crime was unheard of.

When we cycled through the state of Michigan and told people we were from Holland, they almost always said, 'Holland, Michigan or Holland, Holland?'

At the town of Howell there was a large vegetable stand with a big assortment of fresh produce.

We gathered everything we wanted to purchase and were about to pay when the owner shook his head. 'No, go ahead, take it . . . and take one of these too,' he said, handing us an enormous Howell melon which we had difficulty balancing on top of all our gear.

*

We were getting near Detroit and could feel it. Drivers suddenly became rude and aggressive, and as we got onto Highway 59 at rush hour (we had forgotten what that was like), we literally felt like the drivers were out to kill us. The traffic got worse as we passed through Pontiac.

197

One driver had some kind of loudspeaker attached to the roof of his car and as he passed us he shouted: 'Get off the road you stupid . . .' and some other profanities we couldn't catch.

At least we found a nice second-hand bookstore in town with a friendly owner who recommended several good books to us. But other than the bookstore we didn't see a single friendly face the rest of the way. We should have known . . . wasn't Detroit *Car City No. 1*?

*

Crossing over to Ontario, Canada, was like crossing from hell into heaven. We were back on quiet country roads amidst bean and corn fields again. It was surprisingly flat, but it was still hot and humid and storms still threatened us in the afternoons.

We noticed that the English accent was definitely different here; people always seemed to end their questions with 'ey?'

For the first time on our trip, we were turned away from a church. This happened at a Baptist Church in Springfield (so-called because everyone has to drill their own well for water here). The minister, who appeared more like a mafia member rather than a minister, looked us up and down with obvious disdain and said we should camp at the town park and not on the church grounds. Later, as though he had changed his mind, he came up to our tent and offered us the use of the rest rooms in the church.

Just as we got settled for the night, a Mr Smith and his son, Max, from the neighbourhood came by and invited us to stay at their house instead. We had just pitched the tent, but I persuaded Nop we should take up the offer anyway. Mr Smith let us take showers before we went to bed and the next morning he personally made us a hearty breakfast of pancakes and eggs. It was Sunday so he was free to chat with us over breakfast.

Mr Smith had a tragic story to tell: he was divorced now –

198

his wife had remarried, was living in LA and had taken custody of Max's young brother, so the two boys were, sadly, separated. Apparently the divorce case had been quite terrible when his ex-wife took both sons away in the beginning – Mr Smith fought his way through court and ended up having to pay the exorbitant sum of $4,000 to get his older son, Max, back. It must have been a horrific time for the kids, but Max and his father were very close and Max was glad to live with him. Before we went on our way, Mr Smith collected a bunch of vegetables for us from his garden, and Max gave us a grand tour of their land – which combined numerous dogs, chickens and white doves. As we cycled on that day I reflected on this short encounter and felt like we had just popped in and out of someone's personal life, if only to lend a listening ear. Perhaps it is easier for some people to unload their problems on total strangers . . . .

*

It's funny how tourists all over the world like to flock to certain places *en masse*. Niagara Falls was the equivalent of what we had seen at Mount Rushmore National Monument. Thousands of people walked along the boulevard where the falls could be seen from a safe distance, with still and video cameras dangling on their pot bellies. We sat on the grass and stared at the crowds going by, amazed at how just a few hours ago we had been cycling through a quite countryside of corn and bean fields.

199

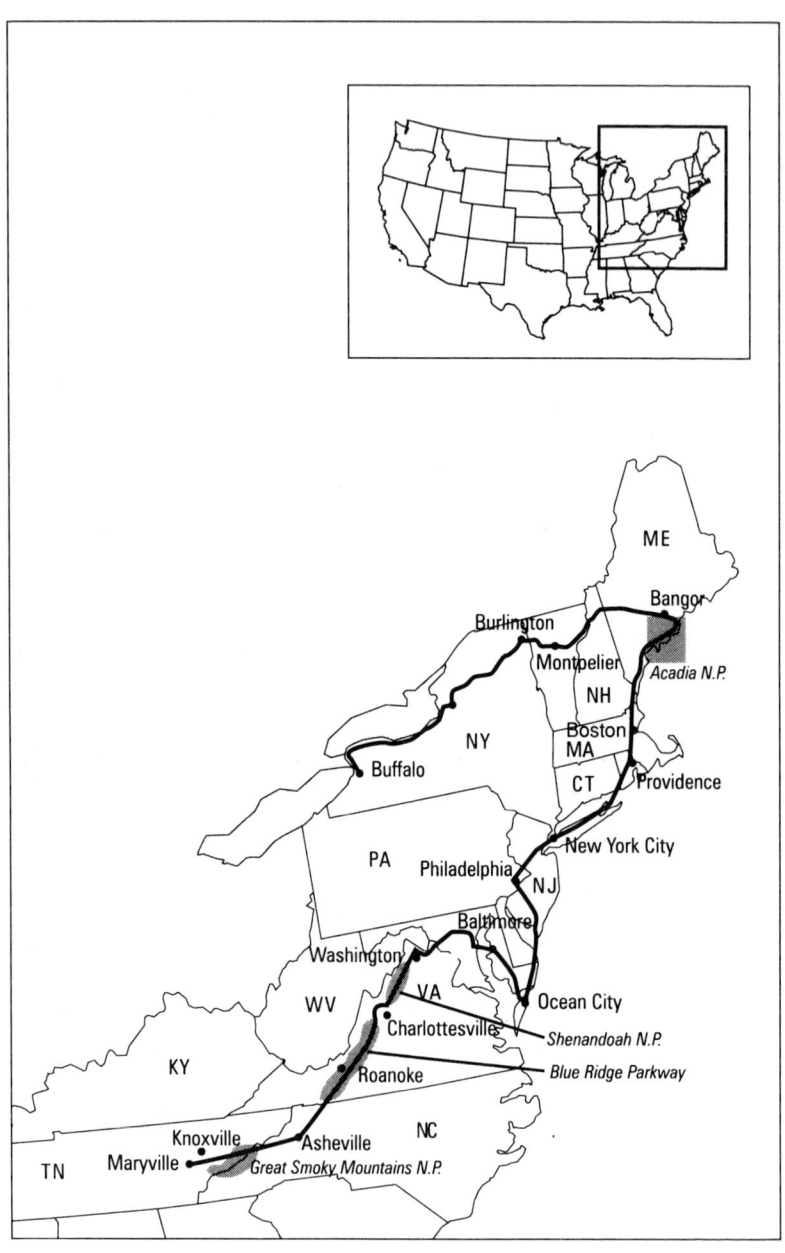

THE ATLANTIC

The immigration officer at Niagara Falls let us enter with our old visas (he didn't seem to consider Canada a foreign country). Unfortunately, this meant we would have to renew our visas in some big city. But not to worry, there were plenty of those along the east coast.

As we headed for the Sea Way Trail, which follows the southern shore line of Lake Ontario, we descended steeply under an overpass. The passageway was short but very dark. I was cycling ahead of Nop and when I came out the other end first I heard a loud bang behind me. I looked back and saw that Nop had got off his bike which now looked like a total wreck. He had cycled into a big pothole with sharp edges (which I hadn't seen either but had luckily missed). His rear tyre had exploded as it hit the pothole, irreparably denting his rear wheel. This was our first major breakdown.

'What do we do now?' I said. We both started laughing for some reason.

'I suppose I'll just have to get a new wheel,' Nop answered.

Just then we spotted a black cyclist in the distance who we called out to. When he came close to us Nop asked, 'Is there a bike shop around here?'

There was, he said, and gave us directions. It was too late to go to a bike shop now, so Nop asked him if there was a church we could camp next to. The guy looked at us as if we were crazy.

'Well,' Nop bluntly suggested, 'could we perhaps camp in

your back yard if you have one?'

We were having a hard time understanding what this guy was saying – he had an accent we never heard before and which sounded like mumbo jumbo to us. But somehow we realised that he wanted us to *pay* him if we wanted to camp at his place! Nop just said no and, to our surprise, the guy shrugged his shoulders and led us to his house anyway.

I had to load Nop's gear on my bike while Nop retrieved an abandoned shopping cart by the side of the road onto which he put his bike. Now his bike really looked like a piece of junk and he, a baggage man.

As he walked towards Cliff's house (the one word we understood clearly was his name), we passed some children playing in the neighbourhood who, when they spotted this strange entourage, followed us all the way to the house, bugging us with hundreds of questions about the bikes.

When we finally got to Cliff's back yard one of the boys said: 'You're going to camp out *here?*'

'Yep,' we answered cheerfully. It was a spacious grassy spot between several houses. It was fine as far as we were concerned.

'But this is a *really* bad neighbourhood,' the boy then said.

'Really?' I asked, 'Well, and where do *you* live?'

That seemed to have caught him by surprise. 'Well . . . I live here too, but . . . .'

So it was a predominantly black neighbourhood, true. But the houses looked OK, they were big and spacious villa-like houses with everyone sitting out on their porches chatting and singing and laughing. It was actually very cosy. As we pitched our tent in Cliff's back yard news of our visit seemed to get around and we could hear people saying, 'Man, they're from Holland, Europe man . . . travellin' on weird-lookin' ba-cycles!' But no one came to chat.

In the morning of the following day Nop went to the bike store to get a new wheel and spokes. Meanwhile, I stayed in the tent and later briefly met Cliff's wife, Denise, and their baby. Denise was also wary of me but perhaps she was just shy. Still later, as I was sitting in the tent reading, a man from an electricity company came by to check on some meters in our vicinity and was stunned to find me there, lying comfortably enjoying the free day. I explained what I was doing there (city people are *not* used to people camping in the city and I suppose I would react similarly if someone was camping in someone's yard in The Hague).

The electricity man then said, 'But this is a dangerous neighbourhood! How could you *camp* out here?'

'Nobody bothered us last night,' I said. And it was true. We had had a good night's sleep as a matter of fact.

'Well, *I'd* sure hate to camp out here!' he said, still shaking his head.

Was that what had been bothering Cliff and Denise too? That we would be attacked in their own back yard and that they might be held responsible if it had happened?

*

The shoreline of Lake Ontario was windy and quite chilly. For about 30 miles we followed an empty super-highway called the Lake Ontario State Parkway. This highway was meant to stretch as far as Niagara Falls. Construction was halted, however, when the governor who started it had to resign after state riots eroded his popularity. Nevertheless it meant a stretch of smooth and quiet road to ourselves.

We were cycling towards Manitou Beach when a cyclist we had passed caught up with us and invited us to camp in his yard. Bill worked for Kodak (as most people do in Rochester, which was where the headquarters of the company are located). He explained that Rochester *was* Kodak – 30,000 people were employed at the Kodak Park, which is seven miles long and one mile wide.

'A city within a city, you could say,' he added.

Bill and his wife, Bonnie – who also worked for Kodak – offered us a meal of fresh corn on the cob, potatoes, chicken (for Nop) and apple sauce which we ate in their back yard, while talking about Kodak. They advised us to take a tour of the park and visit the International Museum of Photography at George Eastman House.

We did so the following day, out of respect for the company which had provided us with all our film, but also out of plain curiosity. We left the Golden's home early the next day so we could be in time for the 9.15 tour of the park. The factory tour was a bit boring but the museum turned out to be fascinating for us amateur photographers. We learned that George Eastman, founder of the company, got into photography as he was planning a trip to the West Indies. He found the existing photographic equipment of the time to be too cumbersome and came up with the idea of creating a portable camera which anyone could use. He became so engrossed with this idea that he never did go on his trip to the West Indies, and instead founded the Eastman Kodak Company where he revolutionised photography.

His house, which is now the museum, still depicts the place as his home but it has been partly converted into galleries which explain the history of photography, and includes a large collection of antique cameras.

*

In the state of New York, we finally started to see cyclists again. We passed a couple from Quebec, but they hardly spoke any English and we didn't speak much French, so it was 'hi', 'where are you heading' and 'bye'.

The weather wasn't being very kind to us and we were getting sick of the winds along Lake Ontario. We couldn't wait to head east, but we had to wait until we reached Highway 177 further north. Otherwise we would have to go further south through the busiest part of the state which we wanted to avoid.

We had our lunch on a little ramp near a tackle and bait store.

When we were about to leave, the woman of the store came out and said, 'We usually don't allow people on that ramp – it's private property. You should've asked first.'

At Oswego we tried phoning a hospitality home but no one was in. We then tried a Catholic church, and no one was there either, so we pitched our tent next to it. It was terribly windy that night and the rustling leaves of the tree next to us kept us awake half the night.

The next day was another gloomy day with lots of headwinds as we got onto Highway 11. We passed the couple from Quebec again – they were sitting miserably on some grass by the roadside. The traffic picked up until we finally got onto Highway 177 and headed for the Adirondack Park. It was a small narrow road with little traffic winding through rolling hills. The Appalachians are old mountains, low and rounded and covered with forests; the elevations in the Adirondacks varied between 1,000 and 3,000 feet. After all the high mountain tops we had reached we didn't really consider such elevations as mountains.

As we stopped in the tiny town of East Rodman, a large bearded fellow came up to talk to us. He had an enormous black dog with him which looked like a St Bernard.

'It's a Newfoundland dog,' he said when I asked.

Rex Ennis was the man's name, and he invited us to stay at his guest house. His house was on top of a hill with a gorgeous view of the surrounding hills and the guest house was situated a little away from the house. From the outside Rex's house looked like any other wooden house we had come across, but the inside! Rex had decorated the interior with obvious taste and style. He had a library with books lining the walls from top to bottom and the carpeted room had several large comfortable chairs on which one could sit and read in luxurious comfort. One merely had to look up from one's book and glance out of the huge windows to enjoy the lovely surrounding scenery and daydream away. The three of us enjoyed a sunset that evening which had painted the sky a mixture of crimson and gold.

Rex used to be an engineer in Saudi Arabia, but together with his brother, now sold John Deere farming machinery. He had also planted a lot of trees on his land.

'It's better to plant something and get subsidised by the

government than to just have the land,' he explained. This was also famed maple syrup country, Rex told us, as he made some delicious pancakes which we ate with the tasty syrup.

'The syrup can only be extracted from the trees for about two weeks in the year, and it takes twenty gallons of the extracted sap to make a gallon of maple syrup,' he said.

Rex had built the guest house so that he could rent it out to soldiers from the military base nearby since there was a housing shortage. He certainly was very enterprising.

The guest house wasn't furnished yet, but we could take baths and use the floor to spread our sleeping bags on. It was wonderful to have a little place to ourselves.

*

We were very disappointed with the Adirondack Park. How could they call it a park when it is congested with cars and trucks and when just about every lake shore is closed off as private property? That they allow free enterprise into a place which should be a nature preserve is beyond me. We were really angry by the time we had covered 67 miles mostly consisting of private property and stopped in the town of Ray Brook to call a hospitality home.

The wife or girlfriend, or whoever she was, of the guy listed on the hospitality home list told us he was home but busy. I figured she didn't understand what a hospitality home list was and asked to speak to him anyway. She argued for ten minutes before she finally let us speak to him. The man admitted he was busy but said he didn't mind if we camped in his back yard and gave us directions to his house. I had argued on the phone for the sake of arguing because I was tired and furious at the woman and now, all of a sudden, I didn't feel like going to such an inhospitable hospitality home. When we looked for the house and couldn't find it I was almost relieved. We went on a bit further and camped in a forest instead.

Our first days on the East Coast were beginning to depress us – partly because of the weather and partly because of the traffic – both factors having so much to do with cycling mentality. That evening in our tent, Nop and I even started discussing an alternative route – going down to Florida and catching a ship to New Zealand, for example. We were beginning to feel we had already seen the best parts of the States and that the East Coast was a bit of an anticlimax.

'If we do go south and take a ship we'll never see the desert again Mip,' Nop said.

'I suppose not . . . .' It was a terribly sad thought.

'But what we can do is head west again after, say, Virginia. By then it'll be autumn and we should be able to get across the Rockies before winter again – I know we can do it,' Nop added encouragingly. 'After all, we crossed the Great Plains in a single month.'

He was right of course, and I knew he also wanted to experience the desert again. The mere thought of going back west was enough to sustain us through the East Coast.

At least the weather improved, although when we left the forest and headed for Lake Placid it was only 40° Fahrenheit in the morning.

Despite the fact that Lake Placid was a bit touristy (it had been the location for the Olympics in '32 and '80) and visitors had to actually *pay* to see one of the nearby waterfalls, it was a pretty town, with one of the most beautiful bicycle/ski shops I have ever seen. The shop was a large circular wooden structure on top of a hill with a wonderful display of bicycles, bicycle parts and accessories as well as everything related to skiing. I suppose it couldn't be helped that the majority of the bicyclists who came to the shop were, on the whole, local, fashion-conscious racer cyclists who chose to ignore us. Perhaps we looked a little out of place in the stylish store, but we were happy with their assortment of bicycle parts which we could finally stock up on. They even sold Carmex, the only lip cream, in my opinion, which works in the dry deserts.

We took a ferry over Lake Champlain into Vermont and were now officially in New England on the East Coast. It was a pretty ride through the Green Mountains of Vermont and the White Mountains of neighbouring New Hampshire as the mountain ranges are called. Both invited further exploration of their green forests, gushing rivers and glistening lakes. Alas, it was already the end of August and we had to keep the seasons in mind now. We did, however, decide to take a look at Acadia National Park, which was an island off the shores of Maine.

As we entered the state of Maine from the mid-west we found the scenery almost comparable in beauty to that of Yellowstone except that here there were no towering mountains or thermal basins. The map told us that we were just within the line separating the northern wilderness from the busier south. There were few roads in the north and it seemed like there was more water than land. How we wished we had the time to go further north, through the northern parts of Maine and into Canada, all the way up the last roads towards the North Pole! On the other hand, we were also content with the fact that we could enjoy what we had already reached in such nice weather.

We had stopped at a picnic-rest area where we met a woman cyclist travelling solo. Her name was Angelica – of Italian origin but an American national – who said she was heading for Vermont to pick apples before continuing north to Quebec. She told us she had been travelling off and on for the past six years, working along the way when she ran out of money. She had even done demolition work! She seemed like a fascinating strong-minded person and I was disappointed to hear we were going in opposite directions. I was sure I could have learned a lot from her had we cycled together for a while.

As we chatted at this picnic site, a reporter who had spotted us came to interview us. Angelica seemed to dislike reporters and told him not to put her name in the paper and not to include her in the picture. The reporter, however, turned out to be the best one we had met so far – he asked sensible and intelligent questions, and his comprehensive article about us in the *Bangor Times* the following morning made us famous for a couple of days. It certainly opened some doors for us while we were in Maine. We were very grateful to him for that. There was something about us being in a newspaper which softened people's attitudes towards us otherwise 'strange-lookin' people on even stranger-lookin' bikes'. People seemed to believe much of what appeared in the paper so when we were praised for our 'courage' and our 'adventurous spirit' and the thousands of miles we had cycled, people treated us like we were famous stars. And because we had been in the local paper, we could somehow be trusted. It's amazing what fame can do.

*

Acadia National Park was a bit of a disappointment – it didn't have the isolation and tranquillity of most of the parks we had seen. We were shocked to see traffic congestion as we crossed the bridge to Mount Desert Island on which Acadia National Park is located. We wondered why so many people were heading for the park (no national holiday or weekend) but later we were told that this had been private land before it was donated to the Park Service. So part of the island was, in fact, still privately owned. The congestion was due to people commuting from the island, where they lived, to the mainland, where they worked, and not due to tourists.

Fortunately, once we got onto the island the traffic dispersed and we found a perfect place to camp by the water. The next day we cycled part of what are called 'carriageways' in the park – paths designated for non-motorised traffic – and went to the Abbe Museum located on the east side of the island. From there we hiked up to the Door Mountain peak (1,058 feet) and were rewarded with a magnificent view of the island and finally . . . the Atlantic Ocean.

Looking out towards the blue expanse of water suddenly

made us feel homesick; we felt we were no longer so far from home.

*

We wanted to take a tour of the harbour on a boat the following day, so we cycled on to Gorham Mountain Trailhead – a gorgeous stretch of coastline along the one-way road – but had a difficult time finding a place to camp in Northeast Harbour. Every inch of the place was private property, so we ended up sneaking between three large estates and camping on a grassy spot hoping no one would notice us. We didn't dare light our lamp and we whispered to each other all night like fugitives on the run.

We took the historic cruise of Islesford Island – the smaller of the two Cranberry Islands – which was well worth the $7 we had to pay. We saw seals and ospreys and visited a museum on the island itself. The whole tour lasted three hours, and we were happy with the sea air, the nice weather and the diversion this tour offered us.

After the tour, we dropped by the Chamber of Commerce to ask about campgrounds (didn't feel like playing the 'fugitive' a second night) and the woman who helped us, a certain Mrs Myers, recognised us from the newspaper and invited us to stay at her guest house in Somesville instead, which was on the western side of Mount Desert Island.

When we saw the guest house, we couldn't believe our luck – it was a beautiful little dream cottage near her house overlooking Somes Sound Bay through a forest of pine trees. We were quite surprised that Mrs Myers just let us go ahead and use the place, she had only known us for about ten minutes! (Now this is what I meant about the advantage of appearing in a local newspaper.)

We later met Mr Myers, director of the Research Animal Resource Centre of Cornell University Medical College in New York City. Although he worked in Manhattan, Mr Myers considered Mount Desert Island his true home to which he flew back every other week. Mrs Myers sometimes

210

flew to New York and joined her husband in their apartment there, especially when there were special events going on in the city. It sounded like an interesting yet complicated life of constantly flying back and forth ... but this home of theirs in Maine was certainly a beautiful place to come back to after Manhattan.

The Myers were exceptionally nice to us and even invited us to stay in their apartment if we ever got to New York City. We had actually not even considered going to the city (couldn't very well camp in Central Park), but now that we were invited to stay in an apartment we changed our minds and I found myself thinking, 'I know it's crazy, but what the hell . . . New York City here we come!'

*

Highway 1 along the East Coast wasn't bad – it had a nice paved shoulder up to the town of Ellesworth where we stopped at a local bike shop, and on the way to the town of Bucksport we found a huge covered flea market where we bought some books.

The scenery after that along the coast became very pleasant and the day ended wonderfully on an ideal camp site off the road near the town of Stockton Springs. The view in front of us was water, some lobster boats and a sunset which later got shrouded in mist.

But Highway 1 of the East Coast couldn't compare to that of the West Coast. It soon became busy, athough we sometimes had shoulders to relax on. We hated the noise and smell of the constant traffic – it spoiled whatever nice view we were cycling through. Some of the towns and small cities we passed were quite pretty – Bath and Portland, for example – but the traffic got so bad after that, and continued to be so all the way to New Hampshire that we finally gave up and headed inland instead.

We got to a little town called Greenland where we decided to ask someone if we could camp in their back yard. We came to a house where the owner first interrogated us for ten

211

whole minutes before saying no, and then we were turned away from a church by a smiling priest who said we would have to get permission from the Chairman of the Church's Board of Directors! But just when we were cursing the East Coast as a long piece of shit (between ourselves, of course), a *kind* man came up to us of his own accord and led us to a secluded forest where we could pitch our tent in peace. He even gave us some wine to go with our evening meal! Sometimes I didn't know *what* to think of this country.

To our delight, Highway 111 was less congested. As we headed to Massachusetts – this hopping from one state to the next was becoming quite ridiculous – we passed a park called 'American Stonehenge'. The entrance fee was $4 and we didn't go in – Nop had doubts about its authenticity. I think he was right, after all it was strange enough that it was privately owned and was, moreover, owned by someone who called himself Mr Stone!

It became hilly once we hit Massachusetts, and we stopped at a house where some young people let us pitch our tent in a field with some horses. Later, the mother came by to greet us and invited us to come and have breakfast the following morning.

Mrs Brigham said she had started a dating service business after she herself found out how hard it was to find a partner at her age – she was in her fifties.

'There are so many people in their fifties who are very lonely – they just can't seem to find a companion at that age,' she said, 'and that's how I came up with the idea of a dating service. And it works!'

She was a very self-assured and frank person, and we found ourselves talking to her for a good part of the morning even after we had finished a hearty breakfast of pancakes she had prepared for us. We finally wished her luck with her new business and said goodbye.

*

On 12th September we crossed four state lines in a single

212

day: Massachusetts, Rhode Island, Connecticut and New York. We were actually passing through farmland again. Highway 201 between the towns of Voluntown and Old Mystic was particularly scenic.

Unfortunately, all this ended when we got to New London at rush hour and had to cross a bridge with no less than *eight* lanes – it took us approximately half an hour just to cross the exit way (where cars were getting off the highway) in order to get onto the right hand side of the main road again!

We had to each pay $9.50 for the ferry ride to Long Island, *plus* $2.50 each for our bikes which we paid grudgingly since we couldn't very well swim across. The only pretty part of Long Island was its northeastern tip – the nearer we got to Manhattan the worse the traffic got and the worse my hub sounded. The ball bearings were so worn out that the hub-gears weren't functioning any more.

We passed an upper-class section of the island near King's Park where all we saw were golf courses, enormous houses, riding clubs and exclusive yachting clubs along the seashore. All traffic came to a standstill at Queensborough Bridge which connects Long Island across the East River to Manhattan. We managed to squeeze in between the cars to get to the bike path on the left side of the bridge and finally, with an increasingly croaking hub, we crossed the river and entered the concrete jungle called Manhattan.

We arrived in Manhattan on a Sunday. When we got off our bikes on the bridge to take a look at the view, Nop said, 'Look, Michèle! There's a bicycle race going on!'

We looked down at the city streets and saw a line of cyclists racing through the streets between the towering skyscrapers – from the loudspeakers we could discern that it was a professional race and even Greg Lemond (winner of the Tour de France) was in it! Thanks to this race the road was closed off to traffic so we easily cycled to Mr Myers's apartment which was situated on 63rd Street.

The doorman looked at us with surprise, but soon Mr Myers was down to greet us and help us put our bikes in a storage room – in New York we were going to *walk* for a

213

change.

What can I say about Manhattan that hasn't been said before? I can only add that it is a very good example of man's absurd extremities. Visit New York City and you will leave it with the feeling that man is doomed after all. I hated the place the moment I set foot in it, but at the same time I was strangely fascinated by it.

I had to admit the city had some merits: it was the one place in the entire United States where people actually *walk*; by walking I mean walking to work, walking to the stores, walking to school etc. . . . This was because the traffic was jammed every minute of the day so that walking was the only logical alternative (although you could say the same about LA but you won't catch a Los Angelite dead walking). I also had to give the city credit for its concentration of museums, art galleries, exhibition halls and theatres of course. But three days of this concrete and glass jungle was more than enough although we were grateful towards the Myers for having granted us the opportunity to experience the monstrosity from the comforts of their apartment. Mr Myers agreed that Manhattan was definitely a strange place.

On our last night in the city, he took us up to the highest floor of Cornell University Hospital and from one of the windows said, 'Take a look at that' and we had to agree that whatever our feelings towards the city were, the view of millions of lights glittering up towards the dark sky was enough to leave us speechless.

*

The ferry ride across to Staten Island cost a mere twenty-five cents and took only a few minutes. Once across we were immediately back to low buildings and residential areas.

As we cycled along the eastern part of the island, a car passed us and a guy threw a beer bottle at us which went crashing right between our two bikes – a nice dramatic exit from New York City.

Crossing to New Jersey over the bridge on the southwestern end of Staten Island was a terrible hair-raising experience. The first part of the bridge had a narrow pedestrian path alongside it, but at the top of the bridge, where cars had no way of seeing us, let alone expect to see us, the pedestrian path disappeared completely and we had to hang onto our lives as trucks and cars stampeded by us, miraculously missing us by inches. By the time we got off the bridge both of us were shaking from the frightful experience.

*

An ex-classmate of mine, Martin, from Leiden University, had a scholarship at Princeton University, so we went looking for him when we got to the town late in the afternoon. We found him in the dorms for foreign students where he let us camp on his floor.

At night we went to a student party where Martin and I gossiped. We talked about Leiden and his studies in Princeton where he had a four-year scholarship for his PhD in Chinese studies. He was pleased with how his studies were progressing and was enjoying it so much that he wasn't sure he wanted to return to the Netherlands at all. Like many bright people from Europe, he was tempted to remain in the US where there are so many more opportunities for people like himself.

We had been invited to the home of Professor and Mrs Mote for breakfast the following morning. Professor Mote is an old friend of my mother and we were welcomed into a beautiful Japanese-style house where we gorged on a hearty American breakfast. It was wonderful to talk about subjects such as pottery (Mrs Mote makes and fires her own) and Princeton University and other interesting subjects over *breakfast*. By the time we said goodbye we still had the entire day to cycle 70 miles through the Pine Barrens – an odd empty region with rows of low pine tree-bushes – to the Bass River State Forest near New Gretna. There we camped in a

215

forest. It was wonderful to be back in our tent amidst *trees* again.

We followed Highway 9 all the way to the tip of Cape May the next day, and it was congested almost to the very tip of the Cape. Fortunately there was a shoulder most of the way, but all this traffic was really beginning to depress us. The East Coast was just too overpopulated and congested for us and we longed for the empty stretches of the Southwest and the deserts.

It was too late to take the ferry, so we went to the Cape May Canal (the entire beach had signs forbidding camping with 'Fine $250') where we spotted several senior citizens fishing together. They were kind and interested in our bikes but also a bit on their guard, as if they didn't trust us (I mean ... did we look *so* bad?) However, to the horror of the others, one woman – a Mrs Wilson – invited us to spend the night at her house so we followed her car a few blocks inland and the others followed us making sure Mrs Wilson would be safe with us. I wondered where the simple trust and belief in other human beings of these elderly people had gone. Was life near the large cities so full of danger that they suspected every stranger of murder, rape and theft, or were they watching too much television? I suspected they did. It was sad to witness such paranoia in otherwise kind and gentle people, but could I blame them? I only had to look back on the first few weeks of *our* journey and how insecure and afraid I had been to understand how all of us are so easily brainwashed by the media into believing that society is basically evil. Rotten humans certainly exist, but they don't outnumber the good.

We took showers and then ate some pizza with Mrs Wilson while watching a baseball game on television with her. She was very sweet and told us she loved baseball – she explained the game in detail to us. The three of us had to laugh when her thoughtful neighbours called now and then to make sure she was still alive.

After one such phone call Mrs Wilson came back to us and said with a chuckle, 'Know what she wanted to know?

216

Whether you two were married and whether you took a shower together or separately! Well, I reassured her you were married and that you took showers in turn,' she said.

Even later, one of her friends went so far as to drop by to make sure Mrs Wilson was OK. If this wasn't 'Neighbourhood Watch' what could I call it?

*

There was a kite festival the coming weekend in Ocean City, Maryland, and we were eager to get to it, but first we had to follow the coast of Delaware to get to Maryland. It was an easy, flat stretch and it was warm again.

Ocean City was a touristy beach resort with shops lining the seashore in the form of a boulevard. The kite festival was in full swing by the time we arrived, with hundreds of kites flying in the perfect soft summer breeze. The shop 'Kite Loft' had organised the festival and on the beach we met an old friend, Jon Buckhard, who had come down from Potomac for the festival with his girlfriend, Sheila. It was good to see a familiar face again and we spent a relaxing day talking about travel as well as kites – Nop was especially excited about the various new designs he spotted in the sky. It had been so long since he had made his last kite and he missed his hobby.

In the evening there was an informal kite flier's buffet-style dinner party at the shop to which we were invited. We didn't know anyone except Jon, but the atmosphere was relaxed and we were happy we had made it to the event. When it got dark many people went out to fly kites with lights. The owner of the shop let us sleep in a van that night – we were surprised it was so quiet and ended up sleeping well.

The next day was Sunday, the second day of the kite festival. We walked the boulevard and had breakfast of refill-coffee and doughnuts and when we got back to the shop we met Mel and Valerie Govig, also kite friends of ours who had often come to the kite festival in our home town,

Scheveningen. Valerie was the editor of the kite magazine *Kite Lines* in Baltimore and she and Mel invited us to drop by on the way to Jon's place in Potomac. Suddenly we had a long list of addresses of friends we could visit... a wonderful feeling since the East Coast had depressed us so much. Now we could count on occasional breaks from the ever-present traffic and enjoy good company along the way.

*

It was quite hot for 22nd September as we left Ocean City and headed northwest first on Highway 18 and then on Highway 404. It was partly forest and partly farmland there and pleasantly pretty. Much of the corn fields had already been harvested, but what was still standing was dry and brown and the fields of beans were of a bright golden colour. We even passed pumpkin fields and once in a while stands which had colourful displays of the glowing pumpkins of all imaginable sizes along the road. One such stand had a sign which said: 'All you can carry for $1.75'.

We stopped next to a forest because we both needed to relieve ourselves badly. There, as I found myself in an inconspicuous spot and was about to squat, Nop said, 'Er... Michèle . . . I *think* you should try some other spot . . .'

'Why? What? *What is it?*' I demanded.

'Well . . . don't panic now, but there's a black snake right under you . . .' he said. Nop could no longer contain his laughter.

Of course I panicked (which in my case means I just froze where I was) and with my pants still half down I asked Nop again, 'Well *where* is the thing?'

'Just move slowly back and then go to your right,' Nop said, still giggling.

It was only after I had moved that I noticed that the poor snake had been frozen too, and didn't move until we were well out of sight.

*

218

We had camped in many places with diverse scenery around us before, but this was the first time we had camped next to a mausoleum. We were in the vicinity of the Chesapeake Bay and had found a side road which led to the mausoleum. A local later told us that it had been erected by a farmer who had lost his only daughter a few years back.

*

The bridge was some three miles long across Chesapeake Bay. We hitched a ride on an open pick-up truck which had stopped for us at the beginning of the bridge – no more hair-raising bridge-crossing for us, thank you.

We took a look at the inner harbour of Baltimore which had been transformed from a dump into a pleasant boulevard and from there we proceeded on to Mel and Valerie's home. At the time, it was part-home and part-editorial office for the magazine *Kite Lines*. We arrived in time to see the layout of the upcoming issue being completed.

That evening Mel and Valerie took us out for dinner at a little restaurant called 'Puffins' where we talked about our trip and about kites. We had been out of touch with the kite world for quite a long time now and we gulped down all the latest news along with some Grolsch beer which Mel found at a local liquor store. I promised Valerie I would write an article for her about our kite aerial photography when we got back home.

*

We felt like we were cycling from one friend's home to another. The following afternoon we reached Jon's house in Potomac, which was quite near to Washington DC.

It had been a hilly day and we had taken the smaller country roads but towards rush hour when we were on Highway 28, we unfortunately got caught up in the suicidal driving techniques of yuppie commuters ('work in DC but

219

live on a farm' idealists).

Jon lived in a beautiful house right next to a forest. He had a 'kite studio' downstairs, where he designed and made his beautiful kites. The studio looked right into the forest.

'Sometimes deer come right up to the glass doors,' he told us as we looked around with obvious envy.

I couldn't think of a better setting for creativity to take its course. It was the perfect studio for any artist.

We felt very fortunate to be able to spend a few days in these ideal surroundings, using Jon's house as a base to go to Washington DC and visit the Air and Space museum in the Smithsonian Institute. On one of the evenings after dinner, Jon and Sheila took us to the Vietnam War Memorial in the centre of the city where we walked along the large marble wall which listed the names of the dead and missing soldiers in countless rows. There was also a life-size bronze scuplture depicting two American soldiers helping a third wounded soldier – it was very touching and, I felt, summed up the stupidity and tragedy of the war (and all wars) very well.

*

After 12,000 miles and thousands of revolutions my hub finally gave way completely. We were in the small town of Leesburg when it happened. Fortunately we found a bicycle shop where Nop could get a brand new hub. As Nop was fixing the bike in front of a supermarket, a guy came up to talk to us and introduced himself as Peter Aanspach. As his name denotes, he was Dutch although he told us he had lived in the States for the past fifteen years. One subject led to another and soon Peter invited us to camp on his land which he said was only four miles away – it turned out to be eight miles so it was dark by the time we had cycled the last few miles to his place, but we were glad we had made it anyway. Like many cityites on the East Coast, Peter and his family lived on one of the numerous ex-farms which had been converted into roomy homes for people who worked in the city but didn't want to live there. This meant having to commute ten to thirty miles by car in order to 'have your cake and eat it as well'. This obviously explained the congestion on the country roads during the rush hour. Peter told us he commuted by car to Washington DC *every day.*

We joined Peter and his wife, Brenda, and their children for a barbecue in their garden as we discussed commuting in America in detail. We weren't surprised to hear that he had started a carphone company and that business was thriving.

Brenda, on the other hand, worked for a video company in Leesburg – the town we had just cycled from. She said her job was demanding and that they were both under quite a lot of stress. What with two kids to support and full-time demanding jobs to fulfil, I could see why they would be under so much stress .... On the other hand, aren't these all choices that people make themselves? I sometimes wondered why people put themselves through so much trouble: taking on demanding jobs, buying so-called 'ideal homes' with enormous mortgages, having children and then turning to us and saying, 'Gee, I wish I could do what *you're* doing'!

*

The hills were beginning to turn into little mountains as we followed the country roads in the general direction of Charlottesville – we passed fields with horses, forests and little valleys with streams and . . . it was *quiet.* It was misty and quite cool, reminding us that autumn was in the air.

We stopped at a 7-11 store in a small town (of which I can't recall the name) for some drinks when we briefly met a man who introduced himself as Colonel Vaughin. He told us he had often been to the Middle East as well as to the Pacific for his work.

When I asked him what his function in the military was, he nonchalantly answered, 'Oh . . . I install missiles.'

*

Nancy and Per lived on a farm near the town of Barboursville. Nancy was an old roommate of mine from Japan and was now working for General Electric, while Per, her Danish husband, was professor of Economics at the University of Virginia. We took a two-week break at their home before embarking on the Blue Ridge Parkway and then the long trek across to the West Coast.

These occasional long breaks at friends' or relatives' homes were vital to us not only as breaks for physical relaxation but also for mental relaxation. (Being under an obligation can cause mental strain, especially when staying with strangers during a journey). With friends and relatives we could be our real selves – our true, often sarcastic, radical and eccentric selves – which we couldn't always be in front of strangers. Being a foreigner in a foreign country places the traveller on his or her guard because whether he or she likes it or not, local people tend to base their opinions on countries through the few individuals of those countries they meet. So the traveller is burdened with the thought that he or she is a guest in the country, silly as the concept may sound (especially when you consider the fact that all national boundaries are man-made).

Even in the US we discovered that people could be extremely sensitive and conservative. They were sometimes religious to an uncomfortable extent and other times they were overly suspicious of strangers like us. So much of their behaviour towards us depended on how we acted and reacted towards them that we had to be cautious. Perhaps my father's having been a diplomat had had an everlasting effect on me or perhaps my upbringing in Asia (where I was always so conspicuous as a foreigner) made me naturally careful as to how I behaved towards strangers. It definitely had its meritorious side but after a while I did get fed up with having to be so deferential and respectful towards everyone we met . . . it was just too tiring.

Fortunately for us, Nancy, Per and Per's niece, Sonja, who

was from Sweden and was living with them for a year, patiently put up with us, our eccentricities and moods for two long weeks. Being stationary for a while also gave us the chance to reorganise our gear and catch up on mail as well as remind ourselves of who we were, where we were and what it is we were doing. Well, I never did find the answer to the last question, but the mental therapy did us a lot of good and we even managed to help out with the domestic chores and the painting of the house while we were there. But when the September mornings started to get very chilly we knew it was time to get on with our journey.

With hugs and promises to write we left Nancy, Per and Sonja, the four horses, dog and cat on their land and headed straight for Shenandoah National Park.

*

We had only taken a two-week break, yet we felt completely out of shape as we struggled up to Swift Run Gap (2,365 feet), of Shenandoah National Park. We were finally in the Blue Ridge Mountains of the Appalachian Range which stretches from Pennsylvania to the state of Georgia.

The Blue Ridge Parkway is a wonderful road which follows the skyline peaks and gaps of the Blue Ridge Mountains all the way to the Smokey Mountains in Tennessee. There are few commercialised towns along this parkway, no commuters, no trucks – an ideal route for the cyclist. But it must also be said that it is one of the most strenuous routes a cyclist can take. After all, 375 miles of peak – gap – peak cycling can be quite exasperating and tiring. Moreover, to do any shopping one has to go down 2,000 feet into one of the valleys east or west of the mountain range and climb all the way back up to the parkway with a *full* load of food. But this was certainly better than having to contend with traffic . . . .

On our first day up in the mountains Nop had trouble with his knees because of the sudden strain; we took it easy the first few days so we could get ourselves back into shape

223

again. We only covered 39 miles the day we left Barboursville, and camped at Loft Mount Campground which demanded $7, which we didn't pay, of course. Campers paid the fee by enclosing the designated amount in little yellow envelopes and placing these in mailbox-like containers at the entrance to the campgrounds. I felt bad about not paying at all and usually enclosed half the amount with a note explaining we were cyclists – not drivers of thirty-foot campers – and therefore didn't find it necessary to pay the full fare. If the money was for the maintenance of the park, then surely bicyclists were only promoting a *non*-polluting mode of transportation while cycling quietly through the park without disturbing nature. As far as we were concerned the roads could have been single lane; maintenance would almost be nil if only people would cycle or walk.

The campgound was devoid of people except for one other camper, a guy called Kent. He made a living as a professional photographer earning most of his money by photographing wedding ceremonies.

It was very cold that night. I was glad we had the mohair blanket my mother had sent us upon my request. It weighed close to nothing but made a big difference in warmth when placed between our sleeping bag and inner sheet.

*

From the moment we got onto the Blue Ridge Parkway we were not to cycle a single level stretch until we got to the state of Tennessee. Nop's knee was still bothering him so we stopped at every other viewpoint to rest and enjoy the view, which was always breathtaking in this park. The autumn foliage for which the Blue Ridge Mountains were famous for was simply magnificent.

Although we were back in black bear country, they were unlikely to bother us since they must have had plenty to eat by now. Nevertheless we once again had to hang up our food away from the tent every evening. The days were also getting

224

shorter again and sometimes it didn't warm up till well after noon so our cycling hours were also diminishing. But we enjoyed camping early again – it meant the evenings in our tent were long enough to finally read our books at length and for me to take my time to write in my diary. I, in particular, looked forward to the evenings after a hard day of pedalling up and down the innumerable peaks and gaps of the park. After dinner we usually sat cosily by our lamp and drank hot chocolate while we wrote or read. Sometimes we would leave the stove on very low so as to keep the tent comfortably warm. A full stomach, a warm tent, good company and a cup of hot chocolate. How simple our needs were.

But I did have a problem – getting myself out of our warm sleeping bag in the morning to relieve myself. Nop, having been born with the skin of an elephant, would simply jump out of the sleeping bag and go outside wearing only his underwear, relieve himself and come bouncing back saying, 'Boy, it's cold!' But me . . . I usually waited till the very last moment when I couldn't stand it any longer, dash out with all my clothes on (getting my cold clothes on was my first problem) and dash back into the tent as fast as I could. I think my record was fifteen seconds!

*

We went off the Parkway and stopped in the town of Bedford for coffee and pecan pie at an ugly fast-food joint. Then we followed Highway 122 to the town of Rocky Mount. Down in the valley, the hills were less strenuous and were mainly used for pasture. Before we got to Rocky Mount we visited the Booker T. Washington National Monument which was dedicated to the black leader by that name who was a Martin Luther King figure of the late 19th century. Born a slave on a small plantation, he was declared free at the age of nine after the Civil War. In the years that followed he managed to educate himself, then he became a school president in Alabama and finally, in 1895, he became the

225

acknowledged leader of his race.

In the town of Rocky Mount we took showers at a police station – we had gone in to ask about a camping spot (new tactic) and the officers in charge said we could take showers there if we wanted to. We were later directed to a grassy spot next to a community centre where we could put up our tent.

A dog was chained next to the centre day and night. I felt terribly sorry for it, especially since it was so cold at night that we had to scrape ice off our tent the following morning. Someone finally came in the morning to feed the dog so I reproachfully asked him why he left the poor dog alone and chained all the time.

The man answered, 'I work for the community centre here but I live in jail where I can't keep him.' I didn't pursue the matter and had no idea what he meant about 'living' in jail.

The next day was slightly warmer as we climbed back up the Parkway. We were sitting on the grass at a viewpoint away from our bikes when we heard a group of elderly people discussing our bicycles.

'Look at 'em ba-cycles,' one man was saying, 'they don' seem to have any handlebars!'

A woman then said, 'Oh, I'm sure they took 'em off so the bikes won't get stolen. Isn't that smart?'

At the viewpoint at Groundhog Mount a couple came up to us and asked where we were from. When we said Holland the woman then proceeded to scold us, 'Well, we were in Holland *just* this summer and our car was broken into and *everything* was stolen in Amsterdam. Hmmmmf!'

What could we say: please don't generalise about the Dutch people? We defended ourselves by saying we came from The Hague and not from Amsterdam. I suppose it helped because she then gave us some coke and fruit by way of an apology.

*

The road now followed some gradual slopes of open grazing lands which were fenced in by attractive crisscrossed wooden fences instead of the usual horrid barbed wire. We stopped at a little town called Meadow's Dan which had a part-crafts-store-part-bakery where we had coffee and some delicious apple cake. The woman who owned the shop introduced herself as Rain and seeing we were on bicycles told us she had also travelled around the States for two and a half years. We swapped travel tales as we had our coffee and before we left she kindly gave us some home-made bread for the road.

We passed beautiful scenery consisting of meadows, forests and panaoramic views of the lower valleys.

At one viewpoint a couple stopped and said, 'Hey! We read about you in the *Bangor Times!*' and gave us some cans of soft drinks.

On the same day, at a different viewpoint another couple stopped to talk to us. When they heard we were from Holland the woman became very excited, saying she had recently been in Holland and that she *loved* it (we should have introduced her to the previous couple who had had everything stolen in Amsterdam). This woman was so impressed we were from Holland that she started to take out all the food they had in their car and give it to us. But since we protested that we couldn't carry all of it, she gave us what would fit into our panniers, including one of the most delicious cakes I had ever eaten in my life. The woman called it a 'friendship cake' and said it took a good 30 days to make. I didn't ask for the recipe.

*

We were tent-bound at Crabtree Meadow campground, about 190 miles into North Carolina, because of heavy rain. We didn't have any more books to read so we went up to a camper van near us and the couple gave us a pile of magazines. On the third day the rain stopped but this time there was dense fog. We went on anyway, and cycled through the fog up to Craggy Gardens – a long climb up to 5,497 feet – where it was very cold. The fog lifted the following morning and the sun came out staying with us for the next three days as we cycled up and down more peaks and gaps. Everywhere we looked now there seemed to be only mountains, and when we neared the Cherokee Indian Reservation, which was in a valley between the Blue Ridge Mountains and the Smokey Mountains, we could easily see why the Smokey Mountains had got their name: hazy mist-like clouds seemed to shroud the lower valleys perpetually, exposing only the tips of the peaks of the mountains.

The Smokey Mountains were the last real mountains we would see until we hit the tail of the Rockies in New Mexico again. With this encouraging thought, the climb up to 5,700 feet was exhilarating. But the nearer we got to the park entrance, the more tourists and cars there were. It couldn't be helped, I suppose, since this park was another one of the most visited national parks in the entire country. But despite the number of tourists it was well worth visiting. The park is said to be a wildlands sanctuary of temperate deciduous forests abounding in wild flowers and migrating birds between late Arpil and early May. Having arrived on the 29th of October we missed the wild flowers and birds but it was certainly the ideal time to enjoy hiking through the autumn foliage.

When we got to Elkmont Campground in the valley floor of the park we met a couple called Bud and Maurie Hoekstra (and their dog, Nikki), who let us share their camp site with them. We immediately got along and decided to hike together up Mount Le Conte the next day. Bud was a freelance writer and Maurie had worked as a librarian so books were a popular subject between us. Bud even took notes about our journey and used an entire roll of film on us. He also had plans to write about their journey.

The following day we made the promised hike together. It was a climb of about four and a half miles, mostly gradual, and the trail was virtually empty.

It was a cloudy day, but as we continued Bud suddenly

said, 'Look,' pointing to a little round break in the sky from where the sun's rays shone through like a spotlight, brightening up a single area of forest on the mountains across the valley. It lasted but a few minutes and the sun didn't appear again for the rest of the day, but it had been a most magical moment. When we got to the top of Mount Le Conte we were disappointed to find the view completely engulfed in fog – at 6,593 feet all we could see was each other!

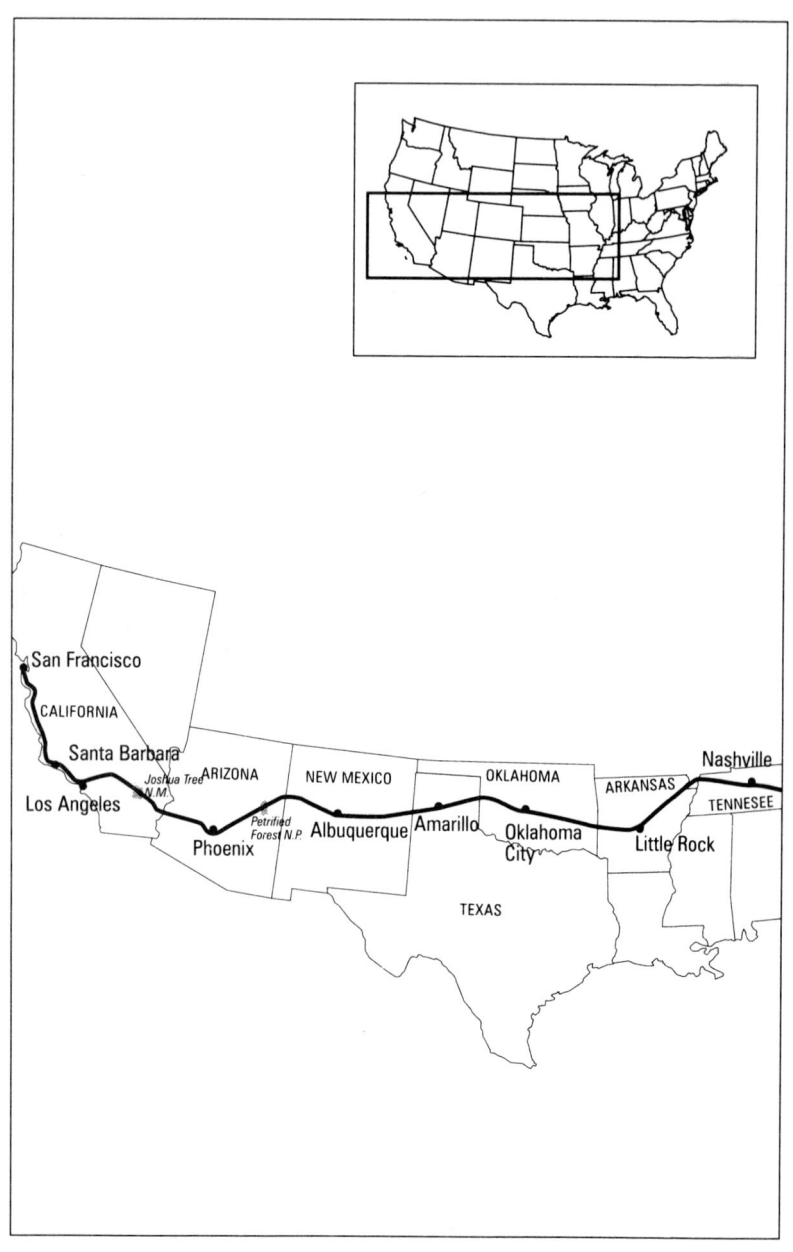

THE RACE AGAINST WINTER

After 630 miles of gruelling cycling along the ridges of the Appalachian Highlands, we finally found ourselves in an easy, rolling terrain of low hills and plateaus. The traffic got quite bad once we left Smokey Mountains National Park, but here and there was a wide shoulder which helped restrain our tempers. We were cycling south of Knoxville, in the general direction of Nashville, and there were few roads in the east-west direction between the two cities. But at a town called Crab Orchard the road split into Highway 70 and Interstate 40 and fortunately most people took the latter.

We camped off the main road near a place called Dowelltown where we found some pastureland full of cows. We somehow managed to pitch our tent between the numerous heaps of cow dung.

From Dowelltown we passed some scenic mountains but the abominable amount of litter along the way was truly a disgrace to the state of Tennessee. The garbage ranged from empty cans to disposable diapers and we passed countless rusting automobiles which were left to rot in people's back yards, next to garages in 'car cemeteries', or simply by the side of the road. And to top it off, the occasional towns we passed reflected the general attitude of the local population – they were untidy and treeless and the concrete parking lots were the ridiculous size of football fields. I wondered whether it was simply lack of pride on the part of the inhabitants of these parts or whether they were just born indifferent to their own surroundings and didn't have the capacity to tell the difference between beautiful scenery and a junkyard.

Traffic picked up as soon as we hit the outskirts of Nashville, but we managed to get to my friend's home in one piece. Debbie was an old high school classmate of mine from our days in Korea. I hadn't seen her since we graduated from Seoul American High School back in . . . 1976? Had it been so long ago?

I was glad to find Debbie unchanged except for the southern drawl I couldn't remember her having. She was working morning shifts at the main post office so we were first greeted by her sister, Lisa, who shared the apartment with her. Lisa, whom I had also not seen for donkey's years, had grown into a tall pretty girl and was working in the evenings as a backstage assistant for entertainment shows held on cruise boats which went up and down the Tennessee River.

We had a relaxing two days as Debbie and I reminisced about Korea and on one of the evenings we visited Debbie's parents who were now retired. It was an interesting experience to meet Debbie's father again who had been an imposing Lieutenant Colonel of the 8th Army in our school days, and whom I had always feared and found rather unapproachable as a teenager. I now found myself laughing and talking with him with total ease over home-baked pecan pie, ice cream and coffee.

That particular evening I was reminded of just how much older we had all grown over the years – the realisation brought about a certain sadness in me which was hard to shake off in the next few days but I was nevertheless glad that our trip was re-securing old relationships which may have otherwise eventually faded into oblivion. I have always felt that the journey, no matter how rich it was in itself, could never have been as fulfilling had we not had these opportunities to catch up on the life stories of some of my long lost friends.

*

The western outskirts of Nashville were as bad as the eastern ones had been; here even the residential areas were messy and even the occasional forests were used as dump yards for garbage. Fortunately, once we got near the town of Bellsburg we found a pretty area next to Cumberland River which belonged to the army and had a free camping spot.

The weather didn't improve much as we continued west, and neither did the heavily congested roads. We spotted many eastern box turtles desperately trying to cross the busy roads at a fraction of a mile an hour – more than half of them inevitably got driven over and squashed. We stopped to save one such turtle which was going so slowly that it was only a matter of time – not chance – before it would get hit. When we picked it up it retracted its face and legs and refused to show itself again until well after we had taken it safely to the other side of the road and left it in peace.

We had only covered 33 miles when it started to rain; we decided to call it a day and pitched our tent in a flat forest off the road near the town of Tennessee. Towards midnight the rain started to fall in torrents forcing Nop to dig a trench around our tent to divert the flow of water. But the rain remained heavy, and we soon found our sleeping bags and everything else in our tent drenched – a stream was literally flowing under our thermal mattresses! There was not much we could do till dawn, so we waited till it got light and then miserably packed up in the rain.

It was still raining when we got to the town of Wavery, only 17 miles away, where we found a warm laundromat to dry our drenched clothes and sleeping bags. Thank goodness for coin laundries! It was still raining when we finally got all our things dry. We were tired from the sleepless night we had had so, for the first time on our trip, we decided to stay at a motel. We felt utterly guilty as we paid a horrendous $24 in exchange for an ugly room consisting of a bed, television, chair and table, and a leaky bathroom. But, however ugly the room, there had been tornado warnings out and I, for one, was very glad to be indoors and dry for once.

The next day was a Sunday and the sun finally showed

233

itself. There was less traffic and, again, we spotted many turtles along the way. One had a different design from the box-turtles we had been seeing – it literally had a tic-tac-toe game board pattern on its underside – the only difference was that the turtle's 'game board' only had circles in the square compartments.

We were now entering quite flat terrain as we neared the border between Tennessee, Missouri and Arkansas on Highway 104. At the town of Dyersburg we dropped by a police station to ask if we were allowed on the Interstate which was the only crossing over the Mississippi River.

The policeman looked at us with surprise and said, 'Ba-cycles aren't allowed on Interstates?'

*

In the first town of Missouri, Caruthersville, we took a break near a liquor store where we witnessed a young man arguing with the owner of the store.

'I can't believe this,' the young man muttered to himself as he left the store in disgust.

When he saw us looking at him he came over and started to chat with us. We soon found out why the store owner refused to sell him beer.

'I happened to forget to bring my ID,' the guy said.

'Do you have to show ID to buy beer?' we asked, surprised.

'You do if you look underage. But they *know* I'm over twenty-one – I live here and have been to this store before and they damn well know I'm a married man and a father. They just do this to hassle me. Real jerks!'

I offered to buy the beer for him since I certainly didn't need to show any ID at twenty-eight. The guy was grateful for our help and once we gave him the beer he immediately invited us to camp next to his trailer in a trailer park nearby.

Terry told us he was twenty-two and that he had got married at the age of nineteen. His wife was fifteen at the

234

time and they now had a three-month-old baby. Terry introduced us to his wife and his mother-in-law when we got to his trailer – we had to shout our names above the full volume of the television set. No one thought of turning the volume down for one moment while we chatted. Leaving a television set on while conversing is something I could never get used to nor understand in this country. I mean you either look at the thing or you don't. But in so many homes we had been invited to the television was perpetually on like a lamp although no one ever seemed to watch the thing seriously.

That evening we made the mistake of pitching our tent at the rear end of the trailer where we thought we would be out of the wind. Well, we *were* out of the wind, but not out of earshot of Terry and his wife's bedroom (trailers having thin walls) – we not only could hear the perpetual drone of the television set but also a horrible domestic quarrel which involved a lot of yelling and screaming, not to mention the sound of the baby who began to whine as a result of all the noise.

*

There were towns with the names of Holland and Netherlands in the state of Arkansas, and why not, it was the flattest-looking terrain we had seen since leaving home. It was also getting very cold with northeasterly winds blowing constantly into our faces. We passed numerous bean and cotton fields and later were even surprised to see rice fields as we cycled along Highway 18.

In the town of Manila we were invited into a Baptist church by a group of women who gave us loads of cookies and coffee, and we were later interviewed by a local reporter.

When we asked the women if they thought we could pitch our tent next to the church, they said, 'Oh, I'm sure Brother Piercy wouldn't mind.'

So we left a note at the Piercy's house and pitched our

tent.

Later, Mrs Piercy came by our tent and demanded to know what we were doing there; apparently she hadn't seen our note so we had to explain again, and finally she left us in peace although she still wasn't convinced. At 7.15 a.m. the following day, we were awoken by Brother Piercy who invited us, or rather, demanded we be present for breakfast. It was freezing, but we got up and duly had breakfast with them, still having to convince them we weren't vagabonds. We had the uncomfortable feeling we had been invited to breakfast because it was their Christian duty to do so and also because they wanted to make sure we got up and got going.

*

On 13th November I wrote in my diary: 'Sunny but COLD, COLD, COLD – cycled all day in -7°C(19°F)!'

By sundown we reached the town of Bald Knob and we again asked at a church whether we could pitch our tent next to the church out of the wind. The pastor of the Central Baptist Church, Pastor Bax, looked at us as though we were crazy and offered to put us up in a motel instead because it was so cold. We declined, saying our tent was warm enough. But probably worrying we would freeze to death if we camped out he persuaded us to stay in a building where bible classes were held instead. Perhaps it wasn't such a bad idea after all – that night temperatures dropped to minus 15° Centigrade (5° Fahrenheit).

Despite having been able to sleep indoors, we had a very uncomfortable night. Nop seemed to have touched poison ivy while building the trench in the rain the other night and now I was beginning to itch as well. But the more we scratched, the itchier we got. The following day was still cold and cloudy but at least the wind had died down. We were back to gently rolling hills but the towns were still ugly and the gloomy weather didn't help cheer us up. But when we stopped by the road and went into a forest to relieve

236

ourselves, amidst the dull brown vegetation we saw a beautiful bright red cardinal perched on a branch of a low bush. The sight of the bird brightened up our moods.

As we neared the town of Beebe it started to hail.

'I'm dying for a pizza,' Nop said and the moment he uttered these words we spotted a Pizza Hut.

We normally only went into small local cafes where we could have cheap refill coffee and doughnuts, but today we treated ourselves to pizza because it was so cold and we had to wait for the hail to let up anyway. When we finally got the courage to go back out into the miserable cold we decided to call it a day and find a place to camp. We couldn't believe the assortment of Baptist churches in these parts – we passed a First Baptist Church, a Central Baptist Church, a United Baptist Church and a Missionary Baptist Church. I wondered whether there was some kind of war going on among the Baptists . . . .

There was nobody home at the church in El Paso but some people from the neighbourhood said it was probably OK to camp. But as we started to pitch our tent a different man from the neighbourhood came up to tell us we couldn't camp.

Nop got pissed off and started arguing with him, but I managed to persuade Nop it wasn't worth arguing with a brick wall and we found a spot in the town park instead. To round off our unpleasant experience in El Paso, some drunken idiots in a car came close to running us over in our tent in the evening, just to scare us. We decided it was best to keep the tent and our mouths shut and ignore them because they had no knowing whether we were monstrous men with loaded guns awaiting them or just innocent Dutch cyclists who didn't believe in carrying guns on a bicycle journey.

They kept up the provocation by driving around the tent and shouting at the tops of their voices, but when they got no reaction from us they finally got bored and said a final 'fuckin' ba-cyclists' before leaving. They came back once more that night, but after that we were left in peace.

The terrain *and* the weather improved somewhat the

following day, but the towns remained unattractive; the town of Conway, where we had some coffee and doughnuts, resembled an open-air museum of fast-food joints. Dull buildings lined the main road of town for nearly two miles with a row of electricity poles enhancing the ugliness.

We could now see the Ouchita Mountains to our left as we followed Highway 10. At Fourche Junction was had to *buy* water because the well water had been contaminated by someone who had dumped dead chickens into it recently. There was a campground by Nimrod Lake and it was closed but we pitched our tent anyway and no one bothered us. We had the entire place to ourselves and it was wonderfully quiet.

The litter alongside the road (especially concentrated at rest areas) was still horrendous, but our spirits were lightened as we entered the Ouchita Mountains and were surrounded by evergreen forests. Being Sunday there was very little traffic on the road. Once again we noticed many churches – we counted 37 on that day alone.

At a road junction I made a collect call to my brother in Japan – my mother told me she would be visiting, so I thought I'd talk to both of them in one go. He was home.

'Hi, Michèle speaking.'

'Michèle? Where the hell are you?' my brother asked in astonishment.

'Somewhere you definitely won't find on a map, that's where.'

'Where?'

'Somewhere in Arkansas.'

'Where?'

'Somewhere in the middle of the States. We're heading west for California again.'

There was a pause and I heard him laugh. I knew he was thinking we were absolutely nuts.

'Will you be coming to Japan?' he then asked.

'We'll try. I hope so.'

He laughed again.

'Good. We'll see you then. Mama wants to talk to you,' he

said.

'OK. Bye.'

I then talked to my mother and my little niece, Anne. They sounded so close, yet I never felt so far away . . . .

That evening we camped in a cemetery in the town of Washburn. It was a bit spooky with the mist coming in, but later we heard what we had been waiting for all this time – the howls and barks of coyotes and their pups. To us, we were now officially back in the Southwest.

As if to boost our spirits, the sun came out and it finally warmed up again. We even had tail winds as we entered Oklahoma – our 32nd state. After this state, we would pass through Texas, New Mexico, Arizona and finally California for the second time.

Nop's right hand was completely swollen from the poison ivy he had touched and looked like a baseball glove. He could hardly bend his fingers so when he got a flat tyre later in the day I had to patch it for him. This poison ivy was so persistent (or Nop was overly allergic to it) that it literally took weeks before the swelling was down completely and the rash had finally disappeared. But for now he just had to restrain himself from scratching and spreading it even further.

As we headed west the roads improved, with large shoulders for us to cycle on, but the gradual hills were becoming steeper and we knew we were nearing the high desert again. Even the names of towns were changing – we passed more and more towns with Indian names: Wewoka, Seminole, Shawnee, Tecumsen . . . . We skirted Oklahoma City, dropping by a town next to the university which had a bike store. There we stocked up on some spare tyres to prepare for the thorns we were bound to come across again.

Once we got to Tuttle on Highway 37 the congestion of the city disappeared and we stopped at a cafe to have coffee. We decided to order banana pudding which was on the menu. When the waitress came by to take our order we had to restrain ourselves from comparing our order to her physique – she was so obese it was a wonder she could walk at all. In fact, 'walk' is the wrong word. She more or less wobbled. We had seen so many obese people over the past months that I mention her physique here not as a personal criticism but because it was so symptomatic of the prevalent dietary habits in this country.

I later asked her if there was a bookstore in town.

She looked at me as though I was an imbecile. '*Here? A bookstore?*' she answered. 'You must be kidding . . . .'

Why should I be kidding, I thought, we had been to many secondhand bookstores in small towns – it was the one thing I loved most about them.

'But there *is* a local newspaper.' she said proudly.

Red Rock Canyon belied its designation as a state park – it was much too close to a city to remain wild and natural. But the park did offer showers and it only cost $3 so we didn't mind. At night we heard more coyotes barking, and in the morning we awoke to a conglomeration of singing birds above our tent.

*

How *wonderful* it was to be back in Texas – the first state we had entered almost a year before. Could time have flown by so fast? We had now been on the road for almost a year and it had become a way of life for us. To think of how insecure I had felt those first few days in Texas as we timidly looked for places to camp. Now we mostly pitched our tent wherever we pleased and I no longer worried too much about angry cowboys driving us off their land.

Only a few days back we had camped on some land and were caught for the very first time; but after I diplomatically explained to the owner who we were and what we were doing he just said, 'Oh, OK. Have a nice evening!' and drove off.

We were now cycling across what was called the 'Pan Handle' of Texas, the northernmost part of the state which protrudes as a square into the state of Oklahoma. The wide open spaces once again spread out in front of us with distances between towns growing larger. We cycled mostly through grazing land and as we passed tumbleweeds and sotol plants along the roads, we noticed more and more feed lots and cattle. We camped on some abandoned land in Pampa. Later a sheriff drove by and said it was OK – it was his land, he said.

There was some smelly oil refineries nearby and I don't know if they were the cause of it, but the following morning I woke up with a splitting headache which fortunately lessened as the day went by. The area around Pampa had been quite ugly – not only because of the refineries but also because of the feed factories.

I saw two red foxes for the first time on our trip – they were chasing each other playfully across the road and disappeared into a field when we came closer. Later we saw a poor rabbit being chased by four huge dogs. It looked as though the owner of the dogs had released the rabbit on purpose in order to train the dogs. It was a rather cowardly and despicable sight.

*

As if the high desert were the geographical boundary between Texas and New Mexico, we all of a sudden found ourselves at the familiar landscapes of mesas, buttes and cholla cacti! At this point, unless we detoured, there was no other road in New Mexico to take except Interstate 40. We decided on the latter, occasionally finding a frontage road we could take to get away from the trucks.

Near the town of Santa Rosa we found such a road, but after five miles it ended up as a dead end!

'Couldn't the dead end sign have been placed at the *beginning* of the damn road?' we cursed.

We were very pissed off and because we didn't want to have to backtrack five miles we finally pushed our bikes over some fields and fences and back onto the interstate.

I hated interstates – there was just no way to shut out the

droning sounds of the engines of the trucks and to breathe fresh air with all those exhaust fumes constantly blasting into our faces. Moreover, I always felt filthy after a day of cycling on an interstate. Officially bicycles weren't allowed on the interstates in New Mexico, but we had no choice.

The second day on it was worse than the first – it was terribly windy and the shoulder was narrower. Every time a truck passed us we had to hang onto our bikes or we would have been blown onto the road by a combination of vacuum caused by the passing trucks and the terrible headwinds which followed. There weren't even any towns we could go into to get away from the interstate for the night. We had to pitch our tent beside some trailers at a rest stop called 'Flying Ranch' which consisted of a gas station and a 'Dairy Queen'. We could hardly sleep with the noise from the interstate and the winds which continued to howl throughout the night.

The following morning was no better – in fact, the wind was so bad that as we sat having breakfast at the depressing Dairy Queen, we could see empty cans being lifted off the ground and into the air and flung about as if they were feathers. There was no way we could cycle to Albuquerque, which was 60 miles away, in these wind conditions on the dangerous interstate. But we certainly didn't want to spend another night in this horrid spot. So, after much discussion, we finally decided to hitch a ride to Albuquerque where there were alternative roads to take, although it went against our principle of going under our own steam. But just this once we decided to swallow our pride and not risk our lives....

It was all very well to say we would hitch a ride, but ... who could take us *and* our bikes? But it was no problem whatsoever – the usual crowd had gathered around our bikes outside and we ended up chatting with a nice truck driver whom we simply asked.

'Well, let me see if I've got some space left,' he said, and opened up his truck. It was filled almost to the brim with glass sheets but he said, 'Well, I suppose we can squeeze them in at the end here,' and indeed they fitted, just.

242

'Where are you heading?'

'We want to get off the Interstate at Albuquerque since we can get onto secondary roads there.'

'OK,' he said. 'Jump on in!'

It took a while for us to get used to the colossal machine – we just couldn't believe how high up we were and how tiny all the cars (and I mean American cars) we passed looked. For the first time I realised how miniscule we must look on our bicycles (if the drivers could see us at all, that is) and why so many truck drivers were such bullies on the road. With such machines, they must feel that they own the entire road network in the US.

The driver of this truck, however, was no such bully. In fact he didn't even come near to my stereotype image of US truck drivers (pot-bellied, tattooed, ignorant macho-type brutes with pictures of *Playboy* girls taped onto their rear-view mirrors). John was a lean middle-aged guy from Mississippi and knew more about geology and natural history than Nop and I put together. So, to our surprise, our unhappy decision to hitch a ride turned out to be a very pleasant experience. As we crossed the desert landscape John shared his knowledge about the geological history of the high desert with us. He too marvelled at this part of the country and loved it for its stark beauty. We later presented him with the book *Desert Solitaire* for the same reason David Cooper had presented it to us – here was finally someone who we knew would appreciate it.

When we reached Albuquerque John drove his truck into a parking lot of a shopping mall where we had lunch together. Then, because we needed some spare parts, he insisted on driving us to a bike store. We had to admit that his skills in driving the monster even through the narrowest roads of town was quite admirable.

At one junction I said, 'I hope you fit into *that* road.'

'Don't worry, if it doesn't fit I'll *make* a road!' he said merrily.

John didn't have to unload his truck in Albuquerque till the following morning. Since we enjoyed each other's company so much, he suggested he drive us up to Isleta Pueblo campground south of the city on an Indian Reservation where we had planned to camp, and join us for the evening. So, much to the surprise of the campground attendant, we entered the campground with John's enormous truck and pitched our tent snuggly next to it. It was an ideal wind breaker.

In the evening, as we chatted over dinner in our tent, John told us some interesting stories about the life of truck drivers in the States which we would probably have never heard had we not met him.

He started to tell us that a unique breed of prostitutes visited rest areas along the interstates where trucks were usually parked for the night.

'These prostitutes are specialised in truck drivers,' he said, 'and they're called 'ladies of the night', 'lot lizards', 'beavers' or 'coin-operated beavers'.'

'How do they approach the drivers?' I asked.

'Well, they knock on the window and ask if you want company for the night.'

'I suppose you've been approached as well?'

'Oh ... all the time. But once when I was asleep I heard this knocking on my door. Thinking it was just another lady of the night I said, 'Go away,' and then I heard, 'Open up! *State Police!*'

John also told us about the drug problem among the truck drivers. He said that some drivers had to drive immense distances at a stretch and were consequently under a lot of stress so they took all sorts of drugs to keep going. Drivers who took Crack were called 'Cracker Heads' and those who took uppers were called 'Road Aspirins'. If that were the case, then we had undoubtedly been witness to numerous Cracker Heads and Road Aspirins – those truck drivers which were always so keen on killing us instantly!

The world of the truck driver so fascinated us that we asked him for more stories.

'OK .... Did you know that when a truck driver has to take a leak he says: "Gotta check the tyres"?'

244

And: 'Most trucks are twelve feet high so all electricity wires, tree branches and bridges along the main roads are required to be at least fourteen feet above the ground. But one time – and this I heard from another truck driver – a truck went through town and pulled down all the Christmas decorations on the main road!'

John went on with these episodes until it was time to go to bed. He was afraid he would oversleep if he stayed in the campground so we exchanged addresses and said goodbye and sadly saw him rumbling off towards Albuquerque. Crossing paths in our lives with people like John and then having to part so soon after was sometimes unbearably hard, perhaps because the chance of meeting again was too slight.

*

However pleasant the ride on the Interstate had been in John's company, we were nevertheless glad to be back on a smaller road again. The wind had finally died down and it was sunny again. We followed the empty Highway 6 into the desert which was beautiful and quiet, and once again we enjoyed the scenery of mesas, buttes and rock formations – it was the best scenery we had seen since leaving the Smokey Mountains back in Tennessee.

There was very little traffic on the road which meant that we could hear a truck coming up behind us. After all the stories we heard from John I immediately thought of Road Aspirins, but when we saw the truck slow down, pass us and finally stop we knew it was him. John stuck his head out of the window and grinned.

'I just had to see you two again,' he said sweetly.

He had experienced the same feeling of emptiness as we had when we parted last night and since he was through with unloading he decided to catch up with us and meet one last time. So we loaded our bikes onto his empty truck and went into the next little town, Laguna, to have a last cup of coffee with him. We ended up chatting till sundown!

When John finally decided to leave he became very emotional and said, 'My life will never be the same again. From now on, every time I see a road like this, I'll remember you two and think of how great it'll be to cycle.' This time we parted with bear hugs.

Since it was already getting dark we went up to a pretty whitewashed adobe church on the Indian reservation (where the town was located) and asked the pastor if we could pitch our tent in the church grounds, but he said no, using the strange argument that it was Indian land as an excuse for his refusal. So we pushed our bikes to some abandoned land on top of a nearby hill and pitched our tent next to a little shack which protected us from the north. At least here we had a nice view of the town of Laguna which consisted of the white church we had stopped at and several adobe buildings. The pleasant town was surrounded by beautiful mesas. This particular view made me think that although it was true that the native American Indians had been deprived of their original lands, they sometimes certainly got what was, in my opinion, the best views in the country.

The following day was even warm enough to wear shorts again, although we kept our sweatshirts on. We followed old Highway 66 which ran parallel to Interstate 40. But we didn't realise until after the town of San Fidel that the road continued on the *other* side of the Interstate and so we ended up on a dead end road again. Once again, we had to push our bikes through the same rough desert terrain and go under and over fences only to get back to the damn Interstate until the next exit. This was one of the most frustrating stretches we cycled and we now regretted not having detoured south at Amarillo back in Texas. But of course, that would have meant we would have missed our encounter with John, the truck driver.

We were about ten miles east of the town of Thoreau when a pick-up truck with two drunken Indians drove next to us for several miles, oblivious to the fact that they were holding up traffic behind them.

'Where're you headin'?' the guy next to the driver asked.

'Thoreau,' I said, hoping the answer would satisfy him and make them move on. But they weren't in any hurry.

'Where?' he asked again.

'*Thoreau,*' I said again.

'Oh . . . you mean *Threw*! . . .'

'Why are you on bikes, man?' he then asked.

I really didn't feel like philosophising with this guy while struggling up a hill so I kept my answers simple. 'Because then you see more.'

'Man, I can't understand why anyone would wanna go by bike!'

That made me defensive.

'Haven't you ever travelled at all?' I asked snobbishly. It didn't affect him one bit.

'Na . . . I've been here all ma life,' he said indifferently.

After staring at us and shaking their heads for an unbearably long time they finally turned around and went back to wherever they had come from.

Thoreau – or *Threw* – was at about 7,000 feet. We found a field near a church to pitch our tent. That evening I finished reading the book *Walk West* by Peter Jenkins, and said to Nop, 'Imagine *walking* across this country . . . I bet those two saw a lot more litter than we did!'

'And a lot more of everything else. Walking is probably even better than cycling . . . you can get off the road.'

'But you have to carry the entire load on your back.'

'Well, I'm sure they didn't carry stacks of books, a stove, a lamp and litres of water like we do,' Nop said.

And he was right. Bicycles did have the advantage of gears, making it possible to carry a considerable load. Still, I had to admire their perseverance.

*

It was five miles to the Continental Divide at 7,275 feet. We stopped to have a ten cents coffee at a gaudy Indian store which had been advertised for the last several miles. We still had to follow the Interstate since there were no other roads to take, but here huge billboard signs with ads saying: 'Indian handicrafts – 3 miles ahead!' 'Next Exit MacDonald's!' 'Coffee for 10 cents!' etc. etc., marred the otherwise beautiful view of mesas and buttes in the distance. Just before the town of Gallup we were shocked to see a chemical plant standing in front of some beautiful red rock formations and the town of Gallup itself was one ugly line of fast-food joints. Even the inhabitants and visitors were of the 'fast life'. We witnessed lazy drivers pulling up to MacDonald's in their cars, getting their junk food through their windows and eating the food in a parking lot!

If we totally ignored Interstate 40 (the open wound of the body called New Mexico), the scenery after Gallup was very impressive, with occasional canyon alcoves we could spot in the distance. Before the border of Arizona, we saw an advertisement saying $5 campgrounds. We went up to it and found one such alcove whose ground was being dug up for 'archaeological purposes'. The place was dotted with hideous trailers which seemed to contain permanent residents seeking quick money from passing tourists rather than serious archaeologists. There was an Indian tepee in the campground and they said we could camp in it so we pitched our inner tent inside it because there was a constant draught. The tepee was so big we even had a go at making a fire in it to see if the smoke would rise (as it indeed did) although the smell of smoke remained with us for several days after that.

*

This was our second time in Arizona and we were excited about getting to Phoenix where we would see Randy again – our month-long cycling companion. John, the truck driver, had recommended Petrified Forest National Park to us, so we decided to visit it since it was also on the way to Phoenix.

248

We finally left Interstate 40 once and for all as we headed for the park. We went to the Visitor's Centre where they told us there were no campgrounds and that we would have to get a permit to camp in the wild instead, so we did. But it was already getting dark by the time we got to Kachina Point where we found a steep trail heading down into the valley floor. Near the trail head there were a few empty adobe buildings by the road.

'Why don't we just pitch the tent behind one of those buildings and hike down tomorrow,' Nop suggested. 'That way we won't have to drag all our stuff down.'

'Good idea,' I agreed. We were pretty tired and didn't feel like having to go down the trail twice just to get all our gear down and it was also getting dark. But as we started to pitch our tent behind one of the buildings, an unsympathetic-looking female ranger in a car spotted us and proceeded to tell us we couldn't camp there.

'But there's no one here,' I argued, 'and anyway, we would otherwise have to haul all . . . .'

'You either leave *now* or go down the trail!' she ordered.

We could immediately tell she was a militant and gave up trying to reason with her.

We packed up our stuff and went down the trail in the dark instead. I sincerely hoped she got a medal for reprimanding us criminals.

We camped on a dry wash because we couldn't find the trail in the dark any more – I worried most of the night that it would rain and that we would end up drowning in a flash flood – Nop, as usual, slept in utmost peace.

The sun was out briefly the next morning as we sat on one of the rounded hills enjoying coffee in the midst of the tranquillity of the park. As we looked around us it was hard to imagine that this eerie, yet beautiful moon-like landscape had actually been an immense forest some 200 million years ago. As some of the trees fell, they were buried in stream deposits of mud and volcanic ash which kept them from rotting since the ash contained very little oxygen. Then, water containing silica penetrated the cells of the wood and finally when the water evaporated the silica remained and turned into quartz. The land then sank below sea level but was later lifted back up above sea level, exposing the petrified trees as we saw them – huge tree trunks made of stone.

It was a pity the sun disappeared as we cycled the length of the park – it would have been a beautiful ride in full sunshine. Instead it was cold and windy as we cycled up to the various viewpoints. At Blue Mesa we took some aerials of the rock formations and the broken chunks of petrified trees on the valley floor. But we froze our fingers in the process and became frustrated when our camera began to act strangely, perhaps as a result of all the rain we had had.

By the time we left the park it was getting dark. Fortunately we found a campground right outside the park. The ground was a bit sandy and it later turned into mud when it started to rain. Nop had to go outside repeatedly to put the stakes back into the soft ground.

The rain let up in the morning so we decided to move on, but as we were packing it started to rain again and everything got wet in the process. We were getting sick of this dull weather. Where on earth *did* the Arizona sun go? It kept raining as we made a go for the town of Holbrook, but at least it wasn't too cold. On the way, Nop got a puncture – he found three holes in his inner tube. We hadn't been able to obtain our usual trustworthy thorn-proof inner tubes for a while so we had had to do with 'Mr Tuffy' instead which we now found to be worthless.

In the town of Holbrook we took shelter at the 'Quick Stop' and drank loads of refill coffee as we watched a Christmas parade. People were running about doing their Christmas shopping (mind you, it was only December 6th!) and no one paid any attention to our miserable state. We were feeling sorry for ourselves that day, depressed from the consistent bad weather and tired from weeks of racing against winter and were, for once, hoping someone would

250

invite us to stay in their warm home with a fireplace, hot chocolate, hot showers and clean beds.

The only person who came up to us was an elderly lady who asked, 'Are you two travelling?' When we said we indeed were, she looked at us affectionately and said, 'Oh! Bless your souls!' and walked away.

Er . . . thanks.

We then tried the Episcopalian church where we found a couple who kindly phoned the pastor for us to get permission to camp on his land; although the pastor didn't mind he thought we would probably be driven off by the police. So we then went to the police station where the officers in charge, after hearing our story, gave us their word that they wouldn't drive us off the church grounds in the middle of the night. Having got that straight (what trouble to go through just to get a good night's sleep!) we were about to go back to the church when we met the couple who had phoned the pastor for us. They had felt bad about us having to camp in the cold rain and invited us to their home instead.

Glenn and Judy Naylor lived in a beautiful house on top of a hill which overlooked the town. The interior was done with taste; they even had what they called a 'sun room' which had large double-glass windows with a wonderful view of the desert.

Judy worked as a secretary at the local Junior High School and Glenn at a power plant which had huge cylindrical chimneys we could see from the house.

'During lunch break at work I often climb to the top of those chimneys to throw down paper aeroplanes,' Glenn told us, not without some mischief in his eyes. 'It's great fun to see how far they go from that height!' Nop and Glenn were now obviously friends for life.

Glenn and Judy had had children when they were very young – Judy was only thirty-six but had a son who was already at college and a daughter at high school.

Our dream of hot chocolate, warm showers and clean beds really came true that night. We were given their son's bedroom to sleep in and we were like two immensely content children. Leading an outdoor life certainly had its merits – one of them being learning to be eternally grateful for the indoors!

*

Although there were dark clouds in the distance, Holbrook was bathed in sunshine. After a hearty breakfast with the Naylors we headed for Heber which was located 1,500 feet higher on the slopes of the Mogollon Mesa – a plateau reaching about 7,700 feet at its highest point. We had been mistaken about the dark clouds – they weren't dispersing at all but growing and as we climbed up from Holbrook it first started to rain, and then as we reached the plateau it started to snow! There was no place to take cover and it was freezing. I felt so miserable I cried as we cycled through the cold. I sometimes hated the hardships on our journey, and I especially hated it when Nop went nonchalantly on, way ahead of me as usual. I thought, what kind of husband was he, not even looking back once to see if I was all right? And just as I was about to get off the bike and sulk by the side of the road, leaving Nop to go on wherever he pleased without me, the snow stopped, the mist literally lifted before us and the sun burst through the clouds and created a magnificent rainbow across the sky. I was so totally struck by the incredible scene that at once I forgot about the misery of a few moments back and started to laugh. It was one of the most absurd experiences I ever had.

*

The following day we climbed to the Mogollon Rim – the plateau at 7,700 feet was densely forested and we saw a number of people chopping down their own Christmas trees.

At the town of Forest Lakes – which consisted of, as far as we could see, a single store – we had coffee by a big stove in

252

front of which we warmed ourselves before the icy descent into Payson. It was so cold and I didn't have any gloves so I ended up putting socks over my hands as we descended steeply down the mountain rim in dense fog. Barely able to wiggle our fingers, we arrived at Kohl's Ranch which was a pretty wooden hotel with a restaurant. This time we splurged on a complete meal of catfish, soup, bread, fries and coffee.

While we were having this delicious meal the waitress had called the local paper in Payson who, in turn, asked us if we minded dropping by the newspaper office once we got there. Hoping that it would lead to a place to spend the night we agreed, and after two hours of cycling through steeply undulating terrain we arrived at the office for the interview. A woman called Carolyn Cox of the *Mogollon Advisor* interviewed us for about an hour. By the time she was finished it was dark, but she showed no signs of inviting us to spend the night at her place or even camp next to the office.

When we asked her finally where she thought we might be able to pitch our tent for the night, she took a map out and gave us directions to an abandoned place outside of town. We were angry at ourselves for having agreed to such a late interview without even requesting a camping spot as a condition, but we were even angrier at the reporter for not even considering our plight. We ended up having to cycle in the dark to the place she designated and having to pitch our tent in the moonlight. It didn't even turn out to be a nice place to camp!

*

We were surprised to find ourselves surrounded by mountains as we descended into the Tonto Basin, but were even more surprised when we climbed out of the Basin and over the Mazatzal Mountain Range. Here we entered a rocky valley surrounded by mountains dotted with thousands of saguaro cacti – those wonderful towering

253

giants we hadn't seen since four seasons back. The view was so totally unexpected, especially since it contrasted so sharply with the evergreen forests we had cycled through only an hour before, that it truly caught us by surprise. We literally stopped and looked at the scene before us with gaping mouths.

And I'm not exaggerating when I say we saw saguaros *everywhere*. They lined the ridges of the steep rocky mountains, resembling a pin-cushion, as well as dotting the entire valley. There were also huge bushes of prickly pear cacti.

We now knew we couldn't be far from Phoenix. We were excited about reaching Randy's place, but we also didn't want to spoil the day by having to cycle through Phoenix at night, so we camped out again, this time in the warmth of these lower elevations, surrounded by the wonderful saguaros.

*

A toxic orange smog hangs over the desert city of Phoenix all year round forcing the inhabitants of this monstrous sprawled-out city to inhale the awful air. Occasionally there is an exceptionally strong wind which can somehow find its way between the mountains and into the valley where it temporarily cleans out the filthy air. We were to learn that when the smog was really bad, the media would send out warning messages to the public such as 'We advise those with respiratory problems to remain indoors today'. How anyone can want to inflict such bodily damage on him- or herself by voluntarily settling in such a place was beyond me.

Randy was living a student life in one of the thousands of trailer parks scattered around the city which accommodate the sudden influx of snowbirds in the winter months. He was still studying at the local university at the time and did odd jobs to keep going. Of course, he hadn't changed one bit. He was the same as when we left him in Yellowstone –

254

crazy.

For two and a half weeks we stayed with him in his trailer; first we tried looking for work, which we didn't succeed in finding, and then we ended up taking long walks through the car-infested city. *No* one walked in Phoenix; in this city it was as if the word 'legs' didn't exist. But that didn't deter us. Walking, we had found out, was the best way to see any city and it kept our muscles in shape. But we had to admit that after ten days we got rather fed up with the city and so Nop and I loaded a few neccessities on our bikes and went to camp out by Saguaro Lake in the desert again. When we got back to Phoenix right before Christmas, Randy was free from school and work so he and his girlfriend (the one he had broken up with for the umpteenth time and was back with the umpteenth time) joined us for a three-day hike through the Superstition Mountains. We had never done real overnight hikes before and we loved it! How wonderful it was not to have to depend on paved roads and to be able to choose spots with the best views as camp sites! It was certainly the best way to spend Christmas – away from all the over-commercialisation and nonsensical sentimentality. It was also a great way to end our stay with Randy whom we would have to part from the very last time.

The break in Phoenix had done us a lot of good but we were also glad to leave the smoggy car- and human-infested city behind us and cycle through the quiet desert again. We had wonderful sunny warm weather during the last two days of the year, and on New Year's Eve, surrounded by the Harquahala Mountains on one side and the Harcuvar Mountains on the other, we pitched our tent in the town's park of Wendon among some Spanish Bayonets and enjoyed the sight of a jackrabbit and roadrunner before the sun set. At midnight, as we kissed each other and wished each other 'Happy New Year' a single fire cracker went off in the distance and then all was still. This had to be one of the most memorable New Year's Eves we ever had . . . .

We woke up to the sounds of birds *in* our tent. Nop slowly unzipped the inner compartment (our 'bedroom'), and to our delight we found several plump little wrens taking peeks under our tent and occasionally daring to come in and dash across and out again. It was as though they were playing hide-and-seek with each other (or with us, for that matter) – definitely a New Year's Day show to remember.

Nothing was open all day – not a single roadside cafe nor general store in any town – as we cycled through creosite and mesquite desert terrain. When we reached a junction, we simply decided it was a good enough place, sat down and ate what we had which wasn't very much – some muesli cereal and bread. As we were having this lunch a van drove up the road we had come and stopped in front of us. A Dutch couple of Indonesian descent stepped out and kindly gave us some coke and oranges – they said they had noticed our Dutch flags.

'Why don't you come and stay with us?' the woman said.

'Where do you live?' Nop asked.

'In Lake Havasu City,' she said. We took a look at our map – it was 31 miles to the north.

'It's a bit too far for us at this point. We've already covered 60 miles,' Nop answered. 'And anyway, we're heading west. Thanks for the invitation anyway.'

'Don't tell me you're taking *that* road?' the man asked, pointing to Highway 62.

'What's wrong with that road?'

'There's absolutely *nothing* there! It's all desert!' the woman exclaimed in horror.

'That's precisely why we're taking it . . .' Nop responded, smiling.

*

Ah . . . the Mojave Desert: the overwhelming stillness, the open space, the rugged mountain ranges, the dominating creosite, the lake-like salt flats in the distance turning pink as the sun sets . . . sometimes it was frightening to realise we were out there all alone in the total silence of the rough,

256

unpredictable, relentless and yet oh so beautiful desert . . . .
Our hearts were already beginning to sink at the thought
that we would soon be leaving this part of America we had
come to respect and love with a passion. The thought was
almost unbearable and I occasionally wondered why we
should go on when we had discovered one of the most
beautiful places on earth. Was it curiosity for the unknown
paths we had yet to pedal? A longing for more adventure?
The possibility of discovering equally or even more
beautiful places? The desire to return home eventually?
Who knows what the answer was? Perhaps it was a bit of all
these things.

*

For the second time on our trip through the US we visited
Joshua Tree National Park; this time we entered by way of
Twentynine Palms from the north, and instead of roasting in
the sun as we did the first time, we now had to contend with
cold headwinds as we climbed up to Ryan campground
(primitive sites) with enough bottles of water to last us a
couple of days.

It was still terribly windy the following day as well, and
clouds raced across the sky at great speed. But despite the
wind, we decided to hike up Ryan Mountain to get a better
view of the park. At certain corners on the trail we literally
had to hug the mountain so that we wouldn't be blown away.
We met no one along the way and were therefore surprised
to find a solitary backpacker who was making use of a large
rock as a windbreak and enjoying his lunch on top of the
mountain in solitude.

'Sorry for disturbing your peace,' I apologised when we
reached where he was sitting.

'That's OK,' he said cheerfully.

Although none of us realised it at the time, this unexpected
encounter was to be the beginning of a deep friendship
between Marten and us which would last to this very day.
Marten Berkman turned out to be a Dutch-Canadian from

Montreal whose passion was to hike. He worked for a Canadian airline and made good use of his flying privileges to fly to distant places in his free time and explore them further on foot, by bicycle or by canoe. This was certainly someone we had to get to know better so we invited him to join us on our camp site when he was ready to come down.

Marten had been hiking the park for five days now and hadn't eaten any warm food all that time since most of his luggage had to consist of water. We made a big pan of *nasi goreng* (fried rice) – one of our 'tent specialities' – and cosily swapped travel stories with him that evening in our tent. It seemed as though Marten had seen so much more of the world than we had. Name any desert, rainforest, alpine region, arctic region, continent or country – he had been there. But he didn't just globe-trot, he actually explored the regions he went to on foot and he almost always went alone – an admirable feat considering the extremely isolated regions he went to. Although I personally find travelling solo to isolated places a rather frightening idea (not because of human obstacles one might be confronted with along the way, but the danger of injuring oneself or getting sick and not being able to find help), I also understand completely that to truly see the world one should do it alone and I therefore envied Marten's courage. Having met Marten on top of Mount Ryan was one of those things that none of us could have anticipated. It had been pure chance, yet this is how our long-lasting friendship began and how Marten eventually took up the difficult task of editing this book for me.

It was precisely these kind of experiences and their consequences which made travel so interesting and addictive no matter how stressful, tiring or even disappointing it sometimes could be

We had nothing but headwinds for the next few days and were happy to find shelter at a cafe in the town of Lucerne Valley on Highway 247 on our second day out of Joshua Tree National Park. A man who introduced himself as Stanley

Shaw started talking to us in the cafe and asked the usual questions about our bikes and our trip. He then asked us if we wanted to stay the night at his place which was only a few miles off the road. We accepted, not wanting to go back into the awful wind again.

Stanley and his wife lived in a rather chaotic but otherwise comfortable house surrounded by innumerable dogs, cats and several old cars rusting in the yard. We were given showers and dinner by this kindly couple and later Mrs Shaw told us some gruesome stories about several murders which had been committed in the vicinity, something we certainly didn't expect to hear about in such a small place.

'A friend of mine was once threatened by a psychopath – a total stranger, mind you – and in self-defence, my friend shot the guy dead. After some investigation, the dead man was found to be a criminal with a whole list of charges against him!' he said.

'What happened to your friend?' I asked.

'My friend? He was never convicted, nor did he ever go to trial. Another time,' he went on, 'there was a couple living near here who went away for a few days leaving the house and their dogs in the care of a young man. Well, this young man completely neglected the dogs, you know, didn't give 'em any water even! The poor things were half dead with thirst when the couple got back. The husband got real angry at the young man they had hired but then the young man got into a raging fit and shot the couple dead!'

His stories got more gruesome by the minute. 'Another friend of mine was murdered for a Cadillac he owned, can you imagine?'

'Did they get the murderer?' Nop asked.

'Well, when my friend was murdered and it came on TV, the police report's description of the Cadillac was actually wrong so I called them up and gave them a proper description. As it turned out, the murderer later murdered *another* person, someone who was out fishing alone, just because he wanted to switch cars so the police would lose his trail. But when he went up to the pick-up truck with the keys he had taken from the man he had murdered he discovered the truck was stick-shift. The guy didn't know how to drive a stick-shift and while he was struggling with the pick-up truck a cop, who had spotted the stolen Cadillac nearby (with the proper description I had given), found and arrested him.'

Perhaps these stories would become the seeds of a new American folklore?!

*

We were now back in familiar territory – we were crossing the Angeles National Forest and heading for LA. This time we got to see the real *smog* rather than fog. How could we miss it – we just about coughed the whole way down into Hollywood.

We spent a few days at our friend Greyland's flat again to rest and reorganise our things before the last dash to San Francisco. We actually did some walking while we were in LA this time; once to Little Tokyo (a twelve-mile hike) and once to Ellen and Fred's home in Glendale (a 13 mile hike). We were surprised to hear that Ellen and Fred now had seven people working for them in their business – last year they had only two – which was an amazing jump for such a small company.

'Having personnel can give you a lot of headaches though,' Ellen complained as we had lunch near her office.

But we could tell that, besides the new headaches, Fred and Ellen were proud of having finally broken even in their business and could now look forward to reaping the fruits of all their efforts in the past. And the next time I was to hear from her was when Ellen was six months pregnant with their first child after they had moved to a much larger house in Tarzana.

*

How strange it was to retrace our steps up the West Coast – it was the same and yet it was different. One advantage of following a familiar road was to know beforehand where we could camp. On the first day, for example, we camped on the exact same beach as we had the previous year, and the following day we camped in a state park, assured of the fact that it would have Hiker and Biker sites. We suddenly felt travel-wise.

At the McGrath State Beach Park near Port Hueneme we met a drifter called Bryce who described himself as a modern hobo. He dragged a golf bag with all his belongings in it and told us he 'travelled' sometimes on foot and sometimes by hitching rides. He claimed to have been on the road for eight years now.

We also met a cyclist called Frank who had been on the move for the past year, roaming around California looking for work. I had thought that we beat most people by living on $5 a day each, but these guys were *real* experts. For example, they both told us that it was easy to get fresh food from supermarkets for free.

'How?' I asked, thinking he meant stealing.

'Supermarkets throw away an unbelievable amount of fresh vegetables and fruit *daily*,' Bryce said, 'and they dump cans and other containers with food if they're dented or merely a day older than specified.'

Much as I admired them for their thriftiness, I just couldn't picture myself rummaging through Safeway's garbage pile.

We found our way easily to Simon's house in Isla Vista again. We hadn't told him we were coming yet he wasn't in the least surprised to see us. When he saw us he simply smiled his boyish Californian grin.

We brought Simon up to date about our travels as he cooked his famous burritos for us and we chatted with Derril, whom Simon had also invited for dinner, and who owned a bike store in town where Simon sometimes worked. It goes without saying that the conversation centred around the pros and cons of recumbents and travelling by bicycle.

We said our last goodbyes to Simon the next day and headed in the warm sun for Solvang to visit Ron and Sue who had been on a motorcycle trip when we met them in Zion and Bryce Canyon National Parks. It was great to see them again and exchange experiences of our respective trips which we talked about over what was called Smørgasbord (Danish buffet) in the predominantly Danish town of Solvang.

Ron had called the local paper about us before he went to work the next morning so we were interviewed after a deluxe breakfast of eggs, muffins, fruit and coffee. Sue had even made us various food bags for the road which made it harder to say goodbye again when we had just been reunited!

The flu we had both caught in LA now seemed to weaken us and Nop was feeling particularly miserable as we got to Montana de Oro State Park. So we decided to take it easy for a couple of days to give ourselves some time to recover before we hit the steep roads of the coast again.

We noticed there were many racoons in the park – funny plump creatures with big rings around their eyes – and we saw some of them go up to people who were picnicking and beg for food like dogs. They appeared quite tame and unafraid of people. We forgot all about them until late in the evening when we had already gone to sleep. One of them came into our tent and dragged one of our backpacks (which contained our camera equipment) out. Nop had to go after him in the dark and later came back to tell me that he had survived a vicious attack by a whole group of racoons when he tried to retrieve the backpack. They had become very aggressive and had growled as if they were ready to bite any minute. He literally had to fend them off with a stick in order to get to the backpack!

The racoons stole our bread and our cereal as well so we put every single thing in our inner tent. Or at least we thought we had put everything away. When we heard another racoon enter our tent, and a few minutes later heard a slurping sound, we knew it had stolen our precious milk as well.

Where there had been the huge landslide which we had had to scramble over the previous year the road was now clear and the mountain wall patched up.

At the campground in Plascott Creek along the coast, we met three cyclists from Long Island whom we shared some wine with after dinner. One of them, Jeff, told us he had been on the road off and on for the past six years through the US, Europe and the Middle East. But despite his international experiences, I was glad to hear that he was as terrified of lightning as I was. Here was someone I could finally relate to with regard to storms and he and I ended up spending a good part of the evening gleefully exchanging frightening details of our respective experiences, not unlike two children telling each other horror stories before bedtime.

Moss Landing was in front of a little inlet of water and for the last time we pitched our tent on American soil. We couldn't have picked a better spot. Just as the sun was setting, some seals came into the inlet and frolicked in the water right in front of our eyes. And even well after the sun had set we could still hear them splashing and spraying water only a few feet away from us.

*

In between the towns of Freedom and Corralitos on the G12, we dropped by the Easy Racer company, which sells recumbents, and met the owner, Martin and his partner, Nathan. They took their time to show us around and Nop of course talked about designs with them, glad to finally talk to experts like himself. As we headed out of Santa Cruz later in the evening a cyclist rode past us and suddenly slowed down to look at us. Finally, he stopped and smiled. It took us a while to recognise him – it was Matt, the cyclist who had left with Randy from Yellowstone to cycle to Canada (at the time he had had a crewcut but now his hair was almost shoulder length!)

He invited us to his home so we spent the night in his flat near the sea. After a delicious vegetarian dinner, Matt showed us slides of his trip. It was so funny to see slides of him and Randy – sometimes the bicyclist's world seemed so small.

*

With mixed emotions we finally arrived in Portola Valley on 27th January 1987 – our last stop in the United States of America. We had cycled a total of 16,000 miles in fourteen months . . . .

While cycling up the West Coast, we had considered going up to Oregon and Washington, but for the second time decided against it because it was too early in the year. Nop's mind was already on Asia anyway, so we spent the next month at my sister's home reorganising our things and preparing ourselves (mostly mentally) for Asia. A bulk of our savings had to be sent to us so we could pay for a world ticket that would eventually get us back to Europe.

San Francisco was one of those cities with the best travel agencies and best rates for airline ticket deals – we found such an agency in town and managed to purchase a ticket that would take us to Japan, Bangkok and finally Athens. I was adamant about cycling through Japan, Korea and Southeast Asia because I had lived in all three regions and wanted to see them again, by bicycle. And Athens seemed to be the most logical southeastern point of Western Europe where we could proceed back home over the Alps before real winter set in.

For a month we relaxed our muscles and enjoyed the company of family again. We also discovered what it was like to take care of such a household when Karen and Mark had to go to New York and later to New Orleans. We were suddenly confronted with having to drive kids to school, to swimming lessons, French lessons, friends and having to shop and cook for four voracious, growing kids and two bouviers as well as having to take care of all household matters. The responsibility was quite terrifying and I had to admire my sister for her patience and perseverance in being able to put up with such a hectic and demanding life. After all, she even managed to work as a Mensendieck therapist.

But despite all the chores we were confronted with, we did manage to discover a bicycle shop called 'Just Recumbents' owned by Marc Duisenburg in Palo Alto and were so thrilled with the find, that one day we cycled down to the shop to talk to the owner and try out all the various recumbents he sold. Marc then told us about Steve Roberts and Maggie Victor who had also travelled extensively by recumbents. They happened to be in San Francisco at the time and were giving a talk that evening. So we went to the talk and were surprised to find two ultra-modern high-tech recumbents. We had once read an article about Steve in *The Times,* and had learned that he was a freelance journalist and carried a computer with him, but we had never expected to actually meet him and see recumbents equipped with no less than *five* computer systems generated by a solar-cell panel, a security system, electronic compass, a CB radio and a list of other technological things I didn't quite understand. Steve was undoubtedly a computer whiz. He had actually started out alone with his 'office' bike, sending home messages, articles and parts of his future book (*Computing Across America*) by connecting his computer to a payphone and transmitting the information to his office in Ohio. He later met Maggie along the way and they now travelled together. They were directly connected with a CB radio so they could communicate while on the road.

We listened to their talk with interest, especially when it came to their travelling experiences. They were so similar to our experiences in so many ways that we decided we had to talk to this couple before we left the States. So, after the talk, we invited Steve and Maggie as well as Marc and his wife, Marsha, for dinner the next day – which was also our last day in the US.

Naturally, all we could talk about was recumbents and

travel by recumbents. It was one of the most wonderful experiences to talk with people who *really* understood.

When Steve and Maggie saw our bikes – devoid of any kind of electronic equipment – Steve said, 'I can't believe you guys actually travel without even a CB radio!'

And I thought to myself, yeah, I suppose we do travel light . . . .

APPENDIX I

List of Equipment and Tools

Clothing:
    2-3 T-shirts per person
    2-3 pairs of socks per person
    3-4 underwear per person
    1 pair of shorts per person
    1 pair of lightweight pants per person
    1 woollen turtleneck tight-fitting sweater per person
    1 sweatshirt per person
    1 set of raingear per person
    one ski hat (for me)
    plastic bags to place clothes in

Kitchen:
    Coleman stove plus spare generator
    special bottle for storing gasoline
    1 deep non-stick pan with lid
    1 shallow non-stick pan
    wooden spoon
    2 sets of chopsticks, spoons, knives, forks and small
        spoons
    1 large cooking knife
    1 small plastic cutting board
    2 large plastic plates
    2 large plastic bowls
    matches, lighter, candles, small flashlight
    sponge (for washing dishes), drying towel

can opener
extra ziplock bags for food

Regular food supplies:
    cans of tuna, corn and peas
    pasta, rice and bread
    spices, coffee, creamer, cocoa, tea
    peanut butter, cheese, jelly
    granola bars, chocolate
    popcorn

Toilet articles:
    toothbrush and toothpaste
    floss
    hair brush
    contact lens case plus cleaning solution (used water to
      store contacts)
    general cream
    soap
    small deodorant stick
    tampons
    toilet paper
    shampoo and conditioner
    tweezers and nail cutter
    sunscreen lotion
    sewing kit

Medicine:
    aspirin
    Norit (charcoal tablets against diarrhoea)
    band aids
    antiseptic cream
    insect repellent
    Carmex (to prevent chapped lips) – the best make we
      found

Miscellaneous:
    short wave radio, batteries
    books
    notebook for diary
    pens
    maps
    address book
    cameras in waterproof plastic container and slide film
        in ziplock bag
    plastic bag to put the above in
    sunglasses
    visors

Camping Equipment:
    2 joining sleeping bags (cotton with down filling)
    garbage bag to cover sleeping bags
    inner sheet
    mohair blanket
    2 thermo rest mattresses (joined with a strip of
    velcro)
    home-made inner and outer tent
    tent stakes
    Coleman lamp, spare mantels, spare generator

Bicycle Equipment and Tools:
    2 large 4-part Rhode Gear panniers per bike (zippers
        tend to wear out after a year)
    2 speedometers
    2 2-litre water bottles per bike
    2 small water bottles per bike
    1 bike pump
    1 spare small inner tube (thornproof)
    1 spare small outer tyre
    1 spare large inner tube (thornproof)
    1 spare large outer tyre
    spare spokes plus spoke wrench
    chain connector

screwdriver
adjustable spanner
pliers
bicycle oil plus ball-bearing grease
glue plus patches for tent and mattresses
tyre repair kit
scissors
pocket knife
spare brake plus brake pads
spare derrailler
duct tape
spare screws, nuts and bolts
spares for derrailler
spare ball-bearings

APPENDIX II

Some Tips for First-Timers Planning a Long-Distance Trip around the US

Camping

National Parks: if you're on a tight budget or on a long trip (in which case you'll also be on a tight budget) hang up a note at the visitor's centre or at the front of the campground (where payment slips are usually located) inviting other campers to share your site and split the costs. Most sites at national park campgrounds are large enough for several 1-2 person tents. This is also a good way to meet other bicyclists and backpackers.

The US is littered with 'No Trespassing' signs, but most of them can be ignored. In the fourteen months that we camped out we were never driven off any land. However, we did adhere to simple rules of our own: we entered private property late in the day (about a half-hour before it got dark), we camped well away from the entrance and road, we never built a campfire, and we packed up everything, including all garbage. We always tried to leave the place as we had found it *or cleaner.*
If it's winter and very cold or if you're in tornado-prone areas or if you're too near a large town to feel comfortable to camp out in the open, churches are a good place to turn to. Most pastors and ministers won't turn cyclists away and will let you camp in the grounds or let you sleep in the

271

church. We were often invited in for food, showers, the use of the cellar (in case of bad storms) or simply for a chat. Just don't take advantage of this hospitality or you'll give bicyclists a bad name.

In the Great Plains region almost every small town has a town park, often with running water, toilets and picnic tables. We were never told that camping was prohibited on these grounds and no one ever told us to leave.

Other useful places to camp are cemeteries (quiet!), school playgrounds (on weekends), golf courses and abandoned lots in small towns.

In case you get caught in a large town and can't find an inconspicuous place to camp, drop by the local police station and ask them for their advice. At least you'll be told where you *can* camp and won't be bothered by them. One station even allowed us to take showers before indicating a place to us.

Try to avoid camping in towns bigger than, say, population 3,000. It's hard to find an isolated spot and being conspicuous invites mischievous kids who like to pull out tent stakes just when you fall asleep or drunken teenagers who arrive uninvited at your tent step for some midnight conversation. It can also get noisy with cruising cars, especially on Friday nights.

Take along large plastic bottles (we each had two 2-litre bottles attached to the front of our bicycles plus two water bottles next to our seats) and fill them up at a gas station about half an hour before you go looking for a place to camp. We used this water for cooking, washing dishes, brushing teeth, washing faces and hands, and for drinking.

Thermorests are probably the most comfortable

all-terrain, all-season mattresses available. We never got cold even during the winter months, and we never got sore backs from protruding rocks or tree stumps. The only problem we had with these mattresses was when they got punctures (by thorns, etc.) – patching them up was very difficult and we have yet to come up with a 100% remedy. (Tell *us* if you find the magic recipe!)

If you are a member of Bikecentennial you can ask for a Bicyclist's Hospitality Home List. This lists fellow bicyclists in almost all fifty states who are supposedly willing (with prior notice) to put you up or let you pitch your tent in their yard when you come by. Wonderful as the idea may sound, at the end of our journey we had mixed feelings about the people listed. Many were indeed wonderful and went out of their way to make us feel at home, but we also got quite a few cold responses from others even though we always phoned ahead. I had the feeling that many on the list were weekend cyclists or racers; in other words, cyclists who don't understand the first thing about long-distance travel. In my eyes *no* cyclist who had made an extensive trip would turn away a fellow traveller in need of shelter or companionship. I didn't get this impression from this list of people. By all means take the list with you but don't count on automatic hospitality from the people listed. It's better to keep other options open.

Food and Drink

We took a Coleman stove on our journey using unleaded petrol instead of white petrol because it was much easier to find. We did have to take a spare generator though – with unleaded petrol the generator tends to get clogged after about three to four months of intensive use.

If you're on a tight budget, make all your own meals.

Standard food for us was: cereal for breakfast, sandwiches for lunch and a warm cooked meal (vegetables with pasta or rice etc.) for dinner. In between we ate fruit, granola bars and chocolate. We rarely ate out and managed to live on $10 per day for the both of us. The only luxuries we allowed ourselves were coffee and doughnuts in the morning after about the first ten to fifteen miles. This ritual gave us something to look forward to in the mornings – it gave us an excuse to get out of the heat or cold, it recharged our energy, and there was always the chance that we would learn something from the locals or meet someone interesting.

In larger towns we usually stocked up on basic food supplies which would last for three to four days and supplemented this with fresh produce along the way. In the Great Plains during the summer there are many roadside stands piled with locally grown vegetables and fruit. Many are unattended with a little box where you should insert the money.

Clothing

Take only what you think you will need during the first few months. Almost every small town has a coin laundry and in larger towns you can always look out for garage sales where you can replace tattered T-shirts and worn out shorts at a very cheap price. But don't forget that even in the summer, mountainous regions can get very cold so always keep an all-climate wardrobe.

During cold weather wear layers – large sweaters and down jackets are of no use when cycling and only add bulk and weight to your luggage. On cold days our clothing was: T-shirt, turtleneck (tight-fitting) cashmere sweater, sweatshirt, wind-proof rain jacket, ski cap, polyester bicycle pants. Nowadays fleece jumpers are a wonderful substitute for sweatshirts.

Socks make good mittens when it snows or if you have to descend mountains in very cold weather. (Thermal socks retain their warmth even when they get wet so if you're going to cycle or hike in very cold and wet weather take them along.)

Winter

Take along a petrol lamp. The days are short and the nights long, and even a tired cyclist doesn't require fifteen hours of sleep. We found ourselves looking forward to long evenings of reading, popping corn, writing and drinking hot chocolate during the winter months, thanks to the Coleman petrol lamp we took along. Also with the lamp we used unleaded petrol and had to take a spare generator.

Although our cotton sleeping bags were stuffed with down and were perfect most of the time we did tend to get cold in the winter months. We solved this problem by placing a mohair blanket between the inner sheet and the sleeping bag. Mohair weighs next to nothing and is very warm – we found that it doubled up as a snug blanket for our backs when we sat around a campfire.

Miscellaneous

Insurance: it's important to be insured properly when taking off on a long bicycling trip in the US. Foreigners should be reminded that doctors and hospitals can be pretty pricey in this country and that you may not be treated if you aren't properly insured. In the Netherlands we found an insurance company called ZilverenKruis which has connections with the Blue Cross of Canada.

They insured us initially for six months but extended the policy every six months with no hassles.

Money: we carried traveller's cheques (which you can use in supermarkets and even get change from when your bill is less than the amount on the cheque), but credit cards would do just as well.

Visa: as citizens of the Netherlands we initially got a six-month visa (you have to prove that you have the money to support yourself during your stay – copy your bank statement and take it to the Consulate). We extended our visa every six months at larger cities (Salt Lake City and Washington DC) – likewise we made copies of our traveller's cheques to prove that we could still support ourselves.

Spares: we had a hard time finding spare tyres in some parts of the US (Texas etc.). It may be a good idea to keep a list of bicycle shops along the way and carry enough spares when you get to cowboy country where everyone prefers riding either on a horse or in a pick-up truck. Bicycles are considered 'kid's stuff' in these areas so although small tyres (good for recumbents' front wheels) are readily available, larger tyres can be a problem.

Thorns: we used 'thorn-proof inner tubes' which were excellent against the thorns in the deserts. Make sure you replace your outer tyres before they wear out completely or the thorns will penetrate both tyre and inner tube (these tubes are virtually impossible to patch up). These tubes can be bought at bicycle stores or at K-Mart.

APPENDIX III

National Parks and Monuments in the USA

Alabama
  Russel Cave Nat. Monument, Rte 1, Box 175, Bridgeport, AL 35740
Alaska
  Denali Nat. Park and Preserve, PO Box 9, Mckinley Park, AK 99755
  Glacier Bay Nat. Park and Preserve, PO Box 140, Gustavus, AK 99826
  Katmai Nat. Park and Preserve, PO Box 7, King Salmon, AK 99613
  Kenai Fjords Nat. Park, PO Box 1727, Seward, AK 99664
  Lake Clark Nat. Park and Preserve, 4230 University Dr., Suite 311, Anchorage, AK 99513
  Wrangell-St Elias Nat. Park and Preserve, PO Box 29, Glennallen, AK 99588
Arizona
  Canyon de Chelly Nat. Monument, PO Box 588, Chinle, AZ 86503
  Casa Grande Nat. Monument, PO Box 518, Coolidge, AZ 85228
  Chiricahua Nat. Monument, Dos Cabezas Route, Box 6500, Willcox, AZ 85643
  Grand Canyon Nat. Park, PO Box 129, Grand Canyon, AZ 86023

Montezuma Castle Nat. Monument, PO Box 219, Camp Verde, AZ 86322

Navajo Nat. Monument, HC 71, Box 3, Tonalea, AZ 86044-9704

Organ Pipe Cactus Nat. Monument, Rte 1, Box 100, Ajo, AZ 85321

Petrified Forest Nat. Park, Petrified Forest Nat. Park, AZ 86028

Saguaro Nat. Monument, 36933 Old Spanish Trail, Tucson, AZ 85730-5699

Tonto Nat. Monument, PO Box 707, Roosevelt, AZ 85545

Tuzigoot Nat. Monument, PO Box 68, Clarkdale, AZ 86324

Walnut Canyon Nat. Monument, Walnut Canyon Rd., Flagstaff, AZ 86004-9705

Arkansas

Hot Springs Nat. Park, PO Box 1860, Hot Springs, AR 71902

California

Cabrillo Nat. Monument, PO Box 6670, San Diego, CA 92106

Channel Islands Nat. Park, 1901 Spinnaker Dr., Ventura, CA 93001

Death Valley Nat. Monument (Calif., Nev.), Death Valley, CA 92328

Devils Postpile Nat. Monument, c/o Sequoia and Kings Canyon Nat. Parks, Three Rivers CA 93271

Golden Gate Nat. Rec. Area, Fort Mason, Bldg 201, San Francisco, CA 94123

Joshua Tree Nat. Mon., 74485 National Monument Drive, Twentynine Palms, CA 92277

Kings Canyon Nat. Park, Three Rivers, CA 93271

Lasen Volcanic Nat. Park, Mineral, CA 96063

Lava Beds Nat. Monument, PO Box 867, Tulelake, CA 96134

Muir Woods Nat. Monument, Mill Valley, CA 94941

Pinnacles Nat. Monument, Paicines, CA 95043

Redwood Nat. Park, 1111 2nd St., Crescent City, CA 95531

Santa Monica Mts. Nat. Rec. Area, 22900 Ventura Blvd., Woodland Hills, CA 91364

Sequoia Nat. Park, Three Rivers, CA 93271

Yosemite Nat. Park, PO Box 577, Yosemite Nat. Park, CA 95389

Colorado

Black Canyon of the Gunnison Nat. Mon., PO Box 1648, Montrose, CO 81402

Colorado Nat. Monument, Fruita, CO 81521

Dinosaur Nat. Monument (Colo, Utah), PO Box 210, Dinosaur, CO 81610

Florissant Fossil Beds Nat. Monument, PO Box 185, Florissant, CO 80816

Great Sand Dunes Nat. Mon., Mosca, CA 81146

Mesa Verde Nat. Park, Mesa Verde Nat. Park, CO 81330

Rocky Mountain Nat. Park, Estes Park, CO 80517

Florida

Biscayne Nat. Park, PO Box 1369, Homestead, FL 33030

Canaveral Nat. Seashore, 2532 Garden St., Titusville, FL 32782

Castillo de San Marcos Nat. Mon., 1 Castillo Dr., St Augustine, FL 32084

Everglades Nat. Park, PO Box 279, Homestead, FL 33030

Fort Jefferson Nat. Mon., c/o Everglades Nat. Park, PO Box 279, Homestead, FL 33030

Gulf Islands Nat. Seashore, 1801 Gulf Breeze Pkwy., Gulf Breeze, FL 32561

Georgia

Cumberland Island Nat. Seashore, PO Box 806, St Marys, GA 31558

Fort Frederica Nat. Mon., Rte 9, Box 286 C, St Simons Island, GA 31522

Ocmulgee Nat. Monument, 1207 Emery Hwy., Macon, GA 31201

Hawaii

Haleakala Nat. Park, PO Box 369, Makawao, Maui, HI 96768

Hawaii Volcanoes Nat. Park, Hawaii Nat. Park, HI 96718

Idaho

Craters of the Moon Nat. Monument, PO Box 29, Arco, ID 83213

Indiana

Indiana Dunes Nat. Lakeshore, 1100 N. Mineral Springs Rd., Porter, IN 46304

Iowa

Effigy Mounds Nat. Monument, R.R. 1, Box 25A, Harpers Ferry, IA 52146

Kentucky

Mammoth Cave Nat. Park, Mammoth Cave, KY 42259

Maine

Acadia Nat. Park, PO Box 177, Bar Harbor, ME 04609

Maryland

Assateague Island Nat. Seashore (Md., Va.), Rte 2, Box 294, Berlin, MD 21811

Massachusetts

Cape Cod Nat. Seashore, South Wellfleet, MA 02663

Michigan

Isle Royale Nat. Park, 87 N. Ripley St., Houghton, MI 49931

Pictured Rocks Nat. Lakeshore, PO Box 40, Munising, MI 49862

Sleeping Bear Dunes Nat. Lakeshore, 9922 Front St., PO Box 277, Empire, MI 49630

Minnesota

Pipestone Nat. Monument, PO Box 727, Pipestone, MN 56164

Voyageurs Nat. Park, HCR 9, Box 600, International Falls, MN 56649

Mississippi
Natchez Trace Parkway (Miss., Ala., Tenn.), RR 1, NT-143, Tupelo, MS 38801

Montana
Bighorn Canyon Nat. Rec. Area (Mont., Wyo.), PO Box 458, Fort Smith, MT 59035
Glacier Nat. Park, West Glacier, MT 59936

Nebraska
Agate Fossil Beds Nat. Monument, PO Box 27, Gering, NE 69341

Nevada
Great Basin Nat. Park, Baker, NR 89311
Lake Mead Nat. Rec. Area, 601 Nevada Hwy, Boulder City, NV 89005-2426

New Mexico
Bandelier Nat. Monument, HCR 1, Box 1, Suite 15, Los Alamos, NM 87544
Carlsbad Caverns Nat. Park, 3225 Nat. Parks Hwy, Carlsbad, NM 88220
Gila Cliff Dwellings Nat. Mon., Rte 11, Box 100, Silver City, NM 88061
Salinas Pueblo Missions Nat. Mon., PO Box 496, Mountainair, NM 87036
White Sands Nat. Monument, PO Box 458, Alamogordo, NM 88310

New York
Fire Island Nat. Seashore, 120 Laurel St., Patchogue, NY 11772
Gateway Nat. Rec. Area, Floyd Bennett Field, Bldg 69, Brooklyn, NY 11234

N. Carolina
Blue Ridge Pkwy, 200 BB&T Bldg., One Pack Square, Ashville, NC 2881
Cape Hatteras Nat. Seashore, Rte 1, Box 675, Manteo, NC 27954

N. Dakota
Theodore Roosevelt Nat. Park, PO Box 7, Medora, ND 58645

Ohio
Mound City Group Nat. Mon., 16062 State Rte 104, Chillicothe, OH 45601

Oklahoma
Chickasaw Nat. Rec. Area, PO Box 201, Sulphur, OK 73086

Oregon
Crater Lake Nat. Park, PO Box 7, Crater Lake, OR 97604

Oregon Caves Nat. Mon., 19000 Caves Hwy, Cave Junction, OR 97523

Pennsylvania
Delaware Water Gap Nat. Recreation Area, Bushkill, PA 18324

S. Carolina
Congaree Swamp Nat. Mon., 200 Caroline Sims Rd., Hopkins, SC 29201

S. Dakota
Badlands Nat. Park, PO Box 6, Interior, SD 57730

Jewel Cave Nat. Mon., R-R. 1, Box 60AA, Custer, SD 57730

Wind Cave Nat. Park, Hot Springs, SD 57747

Tennessee
Great Smokey Mts. Nat. Park, Gatlinburg, TN 37738

Texas
Big Bend Nat. Park, Big Bend Nat. Park, TX 79834

Guadalupe Mts. Nat. Park, H.C. 60, Box 400, Salt Flat, TX 79847-9400

Padre Island Nat. Seashore, 9405 S. Padre Island, Dr Corpus Christi, TX 78418-5597

Utah
Arches Nat. Park, PO Box 907, Moab, UT 84532

Bryce Canyon Nat. Park, Bryce Canyon, UT 84717

Canyonlands Nat. Park, 125 West 200 South, Moab, UT 84532

Capitol Reef Nat. Park, Torrey, UT 84775

Glen Canyon Nat. Rec. Area, PO Box 1507, Page, AZ 86040

Natural Bridges Nat. Mon., Box 1, Lake Powell, UT 84533

Timpanogos Cave Nat. Mon. RR 3, Box 200, American Fork, UT 84003

Zion Nat. Park, Springdale, UT 84767-1099

Virginia

Shenandoah Nat. Park, Tre. 4, Box 348, Luray, VA 22835

Washington

Lake Chelan Nat. Rec. Area, 2105 WA 20, Sedro Woolley, WA 98284

Mt. Rainier Nat. Park, Tahoma Woods, Star Route, Ashford, WA 98304

North Cascades Nat. Park, 2105 WA 20, Sedro Woolley, WA 98284

Olympic Nat. Park, 600 E. Park Ave., Port Angeles, WA 98362

Wisconsin

Apostle Island Nat. Lakeshore, Rte 1, Box 4, Bayfield, WI 54814

St Croix & Lower St Croix Nat. Scenic Riverways, PO Box 708, St Croix Falls, WI 54024

Wyoming

Devils Tower Nat. Monument, Devils Tower, WY 82714

Fossil Butte Nat. Monument, PO Box 527, Kemmerer, WY 83101

Grand Teton Nat. Park, PO Drawer 170, Moose, WY 83012

Yellowstone Nat. Park, PO Box 168, Yellowstone Nat. Park, WY 82190

Bicycle Organisations

Bikecentennial
  PO Box 8303-AH, Missoula, MT 59807
  (for Hospitality Home List, Bicyclist's Yellow Pages,
    General Information)

The Int'l Human Powered Vehicle Association
  PO Box 2068, Seal Beach, CA 90740
  (for information regarding recumbent bicycles)

APPENDIX IV

Kite Aerial Photography

The aerial photography system we took along consisted of the following equipment:

Minolta 5000 with a program back and 24 mm lens
Peter Lynn Box Kite for medium–strong winds
A Genki Kite for light winds
Kite line (750 feet polyester, breaking strength 200 lbs)
Aluminium frame for the camera
An aluminium suspension rod
An aluminium rod for the kite line
100 and 200 ASA Ektachrome slide film

First the kite is put up (usually quite high, 300-450 feet, so that it catches steady winds). Then the aluminium rod with the suspension rod and camera frame is attached to the line. The camera is attached to the frame and placed at the required angle (straight down for topographical shots, at a slight angle for horizon shots) and programmed according to the number of photographs one wants to take and the desired interval time between shots.

The camera system is then lifted by feeding the kite with line – so that the kite pulls the system up – until the camera is at the first desired height. Before the first picture is taken, the kite is steadied by holding on to the line, and once the camera clicks more line is fed until the camera reaches the next desired height.

We usually took about five photographs during each session.

The above system is light but not very efficient; once the camera is airborne, one no longer has control over the angle of the camera nor the moments when the pictures are taken. The camera simply clicks at the pre-programmed time. A better method is the remote control system where you can determine the angle of the camera once it is airborne as well as determine when the camera should take a photograph. The disadvantage of this system is that it is much heavier.

INDEX

288

289